THE ARMORIAL BEARINGS
OF THE
GUILDS OF LONDON

The Armorial Bearings of the
GUILDS OF LONDON

A RECORD OF THE HERALDRY OF THE SURVIVING
COMPANIES WITH HISTORICAL NOTES BY

JOHN BROMLEY

WITH FORTY PLATES IN FULL COLOUR
AND NUMEROUS LINE DRAWINGS BY

HEATHER CHILD

Foreword by Anthony R. Wagner, C.V.O., D.Litt., F.S.A.
Richmond Herald

London: FREDERICK WARNE & CO. LTD
FREDERICK WARNE & CO. INC.: *New York*

© FREDERICK WARNE AND CO. LTD
LONDON ENGLAND
1960

PRINTED IN GREAT BRITAIN

FOREWORD

By Anthony R. Wagner, Richmond Herald

THE publishers and writers who have tried to satisfy the new popular interest in heraldry since the second world war have encountered a difficulty. Before a good popular account of a subject can be written, specialists and scholars must grapple with its raw material and produce from it detailed and documented learned works, for other specialists to criticize. And this process of analysis and argument must go far enough for a sound general picture of the subject to be built up before the popularizer can usefully set to work, using the work of scholarship as his quarry. So little of the raw material of heraldry, however, has yet been edited by scholars that an accurate popular work must either be very brief and general or must be confined to those limited and capriciously chosen aspects of the subject which have received critical study.

It is all too easy to fill the gap thus left with romanticism, jocularity, baseless speculation or a free expression of personal prejudice, but Mr. Bromley and his publisher have shown how these traps may be avoided. They have chosen a subject limited enough in scope to be both documented and interpreted between the covers of a single book, yet of deep and wide enough intrinsic interest to appeal to all students of heraldry and to many students of other subjects; and they have understood that heraldic history without its documentation is not only less useful but also much less interesting.

It is well known that heraldry, which began in the twelfth century on the shields of knights, today provides devices for many corporate bodies—local authorities, schools, colleges, professional societies and other institutions. What is less widely realized is the early date at which the non-martial application of heraldry began. Its use on the seals of noble ladies goes back to the twelfth century and on those of ecclesiastics to the thirteenth. In the fourteenth century arms for dioceses, abbeys, cities and boroughs began to appear in England, as they had done in the previous century on the continent.

The use of seals by these corporate bodies to authenticate documents was a practical necessity, but it was by no means necessary that the devices on the seals should be armorial. Many of them at first displayed the figures of patron saints or non-heraldic combinations of emblems. The later replacements of some of these by armorial devices was probably due both to the intrinsic elegance and satisfactoriness of heraldry as a system and to the prestige of its association with kings, lords and knights.

This is not the place for an essay on armorial bearings as ensigns of nobility. The development of this side of heraldry shows interesting differences in different countries. In England it is linked with the broad and adaptable concept of gentility, of which arms were held to be a mark. It may well be that the fifteenth-century Kings of Arms regarded bodies incorporated by royal charter as thereby ennobled and so proper to be granted arms.

The use of armorial devices by trade or craft guilds is found on the continent at least as early as the fourteenth century. In some cases one can watch the transformation of non-armorial devices into heraldry. The Cordwainers of Siena, for instance, displayed on a non-armorial seal of 1300 the sole of a shoe and a shoemaker's knife. But on their seal of 1338 these, together with an awl, were embodied in a shield of arms. In Bruges and Bâle and other free cities arms were used by guilds both on banners and on seals in the fourteenth century, but in England I have seen no good evidence of it before the Drapers' patent of 1438/9. It is clear, however, that craft devices were in use before this, for at the great pageant with which the City welcomed Henry VI on his return from his coronation in Paris, as king of France in 1431

> The Citizens each one of the City
> In their intent that they were pure and clean
> Chose them of white a full fair livery
> In every craft as it was well seen
> To show the truth that they did mean
> Toward the king had made him faithfully
> In sundry devices embroidered richly.[1]

The marginal note further explains the reference to " White Garmentes Brawderid wyth Conysaunces of every Crafft ". Many of these devices would no doubt be the tools of the several trades and others, perhaps,

---

[1] *The Great Chronicle of London*, ed. A. H. Thomas and I. D. Thornley (1938), p. 157. The spelling has here been modernized.

the emblems of their patron saints, both these elements being afterwards found in their arms.

The importance of the London guilds in the social and religious
sphere did not necessarily carry with it the power to regulate craft
activity as such and this power had at times been subject to challenge.
The charter of incorporation which Henry VI gave the Drapers in 1438
was regarded, however, as a turning point in the establishment of this
right. The chief men of the Company thereupon, wishing to do all
that might redound to its honour, came to Sir William Bruges, the
first holder of the office of Garter King of Arms, and requested him
to devise them an ensign " en forme de blason ", which they alone
might bear, on their common seal and otherwise. This is set out in
the splendidly illuminated letters patent which Bruges gave them on
the 10th of March 1438/9, the oldest which survive and still in the
possession of the Drapers' Company.

Between this date and the end of the fifteenth century twenty-eight
more patents of arms were issued to London companies; three by
John Smert, Garter 1450–1478[1]; one by William Tyndale, Lancaster
King of Arms[2]; one by John Moore, Norroy 1478–1491[3]; one by John
Wrexworth, Guienne[4]; one by Walter Bellengier, Ireland[5]; but the
great majority by successive holders of the office of Clarenceux, Roger
Legh 1435–60, who issued four,[6] William Hawkeslowe 1461–1476, who
issued six,[7] Sir Thomas Holme 1476–1493, who issued ten,[8] and Roger
Machado, Richmond alias Clarenceux 1493–1510, who issued one.[9]

The grants made by Guienne in 1461 and Ireland in 1469 or 1470
were regarded by Clarenceux as invalid (being made by them in his
province) and replaced by grants of his own in 1467 and 1482 respectively. The grant made by Norroy to the Leathersellers in 1479 was

[1] Girdlers 1454, Tallow Chandlers 1456, Glovers 1464.
[2] Ironmongers 1455.   [3] Leathersellers 1479.
[4] Cooks 1461.   [5] Parish Clerks 1469 or 1470.
[6] Haberdashers 1446, Vintners 1447, Barbers 1451, Pewterers 1451.
[7] Upholders 1465, Carpenters 1466, Cooks 1467, Fletchers 1467, Brewers 1468,
Masons 1472–3.
[8] Cutlers 1476, Grey Tawyers (now defunct) 1476, Merchant Taylors 1481, Parish
Clerks 1482, Wax Chandlers 1484/5, Painters 1486, Fletchers (crest) 1486, Bowyers
1488, Blacksmiths 1490, Weavers, 1490.
[9] Stockfishmongers (now Fishmongers) 1494. He further issued patents after
1500 to the Merchant Haberdashers 1503, the Leathersellers (confirmation 1505)
and the Coopers 1509.

made by Clarenceux's leave on the ground that Norroy had married a
wife of the Company. The grants by Garter are early and may have
been made by arrangement with Clarenceux or before the question of
their respective rights had become acute.

The grants of arms known to have been made by the Kings of
Arms to private persons during the same period (1439–1500) number
about ninety, so that those to the companies form a large proportion
of the whole output in this formative period of heraldry. If surviving
original patents of the period (as opposed to copies, dockets or other
records) are counted up, their pre-eminence is still more striking for
out of some eighteen known originals of before 1500 those of the
companies number thirteen.

The responsibility of the Kings of Arms for recording and controlling
the use of arms in their respective provinces was given new scope
and formality by the letters patent issued by Henry VIII in 1530 for
the assistance of the then Clarenceux, Thomas Benolt. In his ensuing
visitation Benolt included the City Companies, and a special section of
one of his visitation books (now labelled 1st H.7) is devoted to their
arms. The next visitation which dealt with them was made by Robert
Cooke, Clarenceux, in 1590, and a special section of his London visitation book (G.10) is assigned to them.

Between these two visitations not only had new companies been
formed and many arms granted to companies both new and old, but
the doctrinal changes of the Reformation had been reflected in the
removal from certain companies' arms of charges which had come to
be thought superstitious or otherwise objectionable. The Bakers' grant
of 1536 substituted an arm holding a balance for the papal tiara alluding
to their patron St. Clement. The Brewers' patent of 1544 no longer
showed the arms of their patron Becket, which had appeared in 1468,
though the subtle reference to him in the crest was allowed to remain.
The Innholders had similarly impaled the arms of St. Julian and ceased
to do so in the sixteenth century but, unlike the Brewers, had them
restored—on a chief—in their grant of 1634. The Drapers' patent of
1439 explains the reference of their shield to the Blessed Virgin, but their
confirmation of 1561, without changing the shield, changes the blazon
to omit the explanation. The Parish Clerks' new grant of 1582 says
in so many words that the older arms were " over much charged
with certain superstition ". Prick song books were accordingly sub-

stituted for holy water sprinklers. The Scriveners' confirmation of 1634 left out the glory which the eagle had had in the arms they had previously used. The City Corporation had in 1539 adopted a new seal from which the figure of Becket was omitted and it seems that the guilds themselves were able to survive only because their trading aspect had already largely superseded their older religious character.

By 1634 the companies' arms were so many that they were given a visitation book to themselves (2nd C.24) by Sir Richard St. George, Clarenceux. In 1677 their importance received the tribute of a handsome illustrated monograph, " The Arms, Crests, Supporters, Mantles and Mottos of every distinct Company and Corporate Societie in the Honourable City of London, Collected from their several Patents, approved and confirmed by divers Kings at Arms, engraved by Richard Wallis ". It would be interesting to know whether one particular feature of his treatment had the approval of the Kings of Arms of the day, namely his attribution to the twelve great companies of the open, barred helmet, which the Kings of Arms since the reign of James I have customarily reserved to the peerage and denied to those of lower rank and to corporate bodies.

However irregular it may be, Wallis's system is at least intelligible. This is more than can be said for the actual practice of some of the companies. The use of a peer's helm in the patent of 1575 granting the Fishmongers' supporters may be discounted because it antedates the official adoption of the system of helmets of rank. But this can hardly be said of its use in the Apothecaries' patent of 1617 and certainly not of that in the Clockmakers' patent of 1672. It must further be noted that these patents are official documents and that neither the Apothecaries nor the Clockmakers are numbered among the great companies. A painting of 1634 at Leathersellers' Hall, which shows the Glovers' and the Leathersellers' own arms with peers' helms, has indeed no official character but helps to confuse the evidence still further. It seems that before 1600 there was no rule governing the type of helmet, but soon after that date the matter was regulated, so that the above instances must be regarded as evidence of a period of uncertainty and transition and not as governing present practice.

Many other matters of especial interest to heralds are treated in the following pages, but only one more can here be mentioned—the evidence here afforded for the early use of heraldic badges by corporate bodies. Possibly the most characteristic use of lords' badges in the fifteenth century was on their retainers' liveries. It would therefore be most natural to find bodies which are to this day called Livery Companies, because membership entitles their members to wear a livery, using badges in the same way. Indeed we have seen that in 1431 the members of the crafts wore liveries " in sundry devices embroidered richly ". The specific evidence, though scanty, points the same way. The Girdlers' grant of arms of 1454 gives them a mantling azure doubled ermine " powdered with celestiaulx that is, to wit, of clouds with suns coming out or issuing ". Fifteenth-century Garter Stall Plates, such as those of Sir John Bourchier (K.G. 1459), with its mantling powdered with billets, knots and water bougets, show that badges were sometimes displayed in this way, and the *celestiaulx* may therefore be interpreted as the Girdlers' badge.

A fifteenth-century manuscript belonging to the Skinners refers to gifts of silver marked with a powder of ermine in 1461, marked with a powder of ermine tail in 1475, and marked with powdering in 1481. This may indicate that the Skinners used ermine tails for their badge and livery. The Pewterers' patent of 1533 gives " in their streamer our Lady's Assumption powdered with lilypots and strikes with their word accustomed ". This looks like the description of a standard of the normal Tudor pattern, powdered with the badges and traversed by the motto.

After the reign of Henry VIII the use of badges became much less frequent, but it has been revived in the present century by the grant of a number by letters patent. The greater number of these grants have been made to families, but the above examples show that historically corporate bodies are not less suitable grantees, while it is likely that in these days they will be able to use them more extensively and more nearly in the old way. The grants of badges to the Plumbers' Company in 1925, to the Farmers' Company in 1948 and to the Master Mariners' Company in 1951 show that this view has proved acceptable in the City of London.

CONTENTS

COLOURED PLATES

Illustrating the Armorial Bearings of the Companies

xiii

BLACK AND WHITE PLATES

ACKNOWLEDGEMENTS

THE author and the artist wish to express their thanks to the many people who have helped them during the compilation of this book. Their greatest obligations are to Dr. Anthony Wagner, C.V.O., F.S.A., Richmond Herald, Citizen and Vintner, and to Mr. A. Colin Cole, F.S.A., Portcullis Pursuivant of Arms, Citizen and Scrivener. Throughout the long process of gathering material, Dr. Wagner has given help and advice much beyond the requirements of his office, and his contribution of a Foreword is a final example of his interest which has been an encouragement from the outset. Apart from research at the College of Arms under the auspices of Richmond Herald, Mr. Colin Cole has been generous both with his knowledge of heraldry and in making available notes on the arms of the City guilds which he had himself collected over a number of years. In reading the typescript before publication he has made numerous suggestions for its improvement, and he has also contributed a number of line drawings which appear in the text. Much of the value that may be in this work is due to Dr. Anthony Wagner and Mr. Colin Cole, and while errors that survive are the author's responsibility, more would have been committed but for their help.

Others to whom thanks are due include the Librarian of the Guildhall Library for facilities in consulting the archives in his custody ; Clerks of the companies for permission to inspect documents in their care ; Mr. Donovan Dawe, F.R.Hist.S., for much help with the text ; Mr. P. E. Jones, F.S.A., Deputy Keeper of the Records of the Corporation of London, for advice on guild history ; Mr. Howard Blackmore ; Mr. G. A. Campbell ; Mr. Roland Champness, F.S.A. ; Miss Dorothy Colles ; Miss K. Garrett ; Mr. John Goodall ; Dr. A. E. Hollaender, F.S.A., F.R.Hist.S. ; Mr. C. W. Kellaway ; Mrs. Dorothy Thomas ; and the writer's wife who not only undertook much of the typing but also released him from domestic tasks which he should have shared.

INTRODUCTION

THE purpose of this book is to provide a series of coloured illustrations of the armorial bearings of the surviving London guilds, together with descriptive blazons, their history and symbolism. Hitherto there has been no single source of authentic information on this subject and nowhere could be found clear and accurate coloured representations of the arms. The innumerable illustrations found scattered among the many books on London and the guilds are mostly unreliable, and the use of such out-of-date or careless copies as models has in many instances resulted in distortion of the arms and the consequent obscuring of their significance. One serious attempt to fill this gap in London literature was made by Charles Welch in his *Coat Armour of the London Livery Companies*, 1914. His book is, however, primarily a collection of facsimile plates of the engravings in Richard Wallis's *London's Armory*, published in 1677. Apart from the fact that Wallis's plates contain inaccuracies, they are too old to be an acceptable guide to current usage and lack the advantage of reproduction in colour. The limitations of Welch's book must not, however, be stressed without a tribute to the thoroughness with which he sought out historical sources. To his industry the author owes a great deal for relieving him of much spade-work.

The blazons from which the coloured plates in the present volume have been prepared are based upon the original letters patent where they have survived, or upon the appropriate records in the College of Arms. For the thirteen companies using arms without the authority of a grant, the devices at present adopted by them have been followed as far as they could be determined. To amplify the smaller detail in the paintings of the arms, enlarged line drawings taken from contemporary models or other reliable sources have been included in the text. Many of the unfamiliar objects so depicted represent tools of former crafts and these have tended to become corrupted in later renderings of the arms.

When embarking upon this project the author was reminded of the strictures of Sir William St. John Hope. In discussing English municipal heraldry St. John Hope observed that he had had occasion to enquire what had been written on its history and origin, and he concluded that " with the exception of such catalogues as those of Guillim, Edmondson, and Berry, and a recent pretentious work called *The Book of Public Arms*,[1] I am unable to find anything on the subject, for none of these attempts to explain either the origin or meaning of the numerous arms ".[2] The present work cannot escape the slightly derogatory description of catalogue but it is hoped that the attempt to trace the development of the arms and to explain their meanings has removed some of the bleakness of a catalogue and added to the usefulness of the work.

With the completion of the material on the heraldry of the companies, the purpose of the work was achieved, but the addition of an account of each company seemed desirable in order that the significance of the arms might be more readily understood. Brief notes have therefore been included to serve as " dictionary definitions " intended to convey an impression of each company's antiquity and former functions. It must be emphasized that in writing these notes, reliance has been placed for the most part on printed sources, and not upon original documents.

The group of arms dealt with is of considerable importance to the study of the growth of modern heraldry. Twenty-four of the guilds were granted arms in the fifteenth century, and of these no fewer than thirteen patents still survive, including the earliest of all the English patents, namely that of the Drapers' Company granted in 1438/9. This record of survival is all the more remarkable when it is recalled that only six other English fifteenth-century patents are believed to be extant. Before 1439 there is no evidence of arms having been granted to the English guilds, but distinguishing devices had been adopted in the fourteenth century by their counterparts elsewhere in Europe, and it seems probable that the London guilds had followed a similar practice.

Some evidence of the established use of arms by the London companies at an early date may be found in the Pewterers' patent of 1451, the fourth oldest of the known grants to City guilds. The preamble to this document states that it was " custumed and used every crafte to have clothing by hem self to know oon crafte from another. And

---

[1] By A. C. Fox-Davies, 1st ed. (1894). It is quite unreliable on the companies' arms, even in the 2nd ed.

[2] *Archaeological Journal*, vol. 52 (1895), p. 173.

also signes of armes for every crafte in banner wyse to be borne con-
veniently in the worship of the Cyte. And so . . . the master and the
wardeyns . . . prayeng me Clarensew kyng of armes to conferme theyre
armes . . . I Clarensew . . . fully conferme the same . . .'' This assertion
that the use of some form of arms was a general practice among the
guilds is scarcely consistent with the fact that only three companies
are known to have had arms before this date, and it seems probable
that records of other instances, which may well precede the Drapers'
arms of 1439, are either lost or remain to be found. It is to be noted
that Clarenceux, in the passage quoted above, does not grant new arms
to the Pewterers, but confirms arms already in use ; no evidence of
these early arms has been traced. A further reference to the general
use of insignia by the guilds occurs in the Tallow Chandlers' patent
of 1456, the eighth patent in order of date. In this patent, which is
in French, Garter King of Arms recalls that notable cities and also
companies and fraternities of tradesmen, craftsmen and misteries have
insignia in tokens of arms and of blazon (" les compaignies et fraternitez
des marchans artificiers et mestiers . . . ont enseignes en signe de nobles
armes et de blazon separees les unes des autres . . .") to place upon
their seals used for their common business, and likewise on banners,
standards and pennons which they carry and place before them at
festivals and gatherings both in holy church and in their halls and
places where they hold their assemblies. Garter continues that worthy
men of the Company of Tallow Chandlers represented to him that
they desired arms, of which they hitherto had none (" dont jusques a
present nont eu aucune provision "), in the manner of the other companies and misteries of the City (" ainsi que ont les autres compaignes
et mestiers de la dite Cite leur armes enseignes et blason distingueement
apareulx et separez des autres "). Such phrases as the above seem to
indicate the use of arms by the guilds at a period earlier than is generally
supposed. It is improbable that at this early date they are merely
conventional formulas without relation to facts.

Many of the eighty-three existing guilds are survivals from a medieval
economy ; others were formed in later times for craft and trade purposes
in emulation of their forerunners ; and a few came into existence
during the present century. One new company, the Guild of Air
Pilots and Navigators, became a City company in July 1955 but at the
time of writing has not been granted armorial bearings although arms

are being negotiated. Two other companies, the Company of Tobacco Pipe Makers and Tobacco Blenders (a revival of an earlier guild) and the Company of Scientific Instrument Makers, have also been formed on the model of the ancient guild, but neither is as yet recognized as a City company by the Court of Aldermen.

It might here be mentioned that the term " worshipful ", now applied to the London guilds, is strictly a courtesy title and does not form part of the name of a company as formally constituted. Examples of its use exist as early as the fifteenth century.[1] The appellation is paralleled in City custom by the prefix " lord " in Lord Mayor of London which first appears in English, with antecedent Latin equivalents, soon after 1400 ; neither this title nor the slightly later " right honourable " have ever been conferred upon the office of mayor of London. The only instance among the companies of a conferred title of this nature is that of " honourable ", which was granted to the Company of Master Mariners by George V in 1928.

The precise origin and purpose of the early guilds or fraternities are uncertain. Signs of their emergence in London occur in the twelfth century. Contemporary with them were parish guilds composed of men and women united for religious worship. The craft guilds also had a fundamental religious element and the view has been advanced that parish guilds and craft or trade guilds had originally similar functions. As in all ancient towns, the several trades in London tended for convenience to become localized, each in its particular quarter of the City. It would therefore be natural for many of the parish guilds to be largely identified with local crafts or trades. Such a combination of religious and trade interests centred around a local church is strikingly exemplified in the early history of the Carpenters' and the Saddlers' Companies, while surviving ordinances of other guilds make it clear that worship at church, the care of members in sickness and poverty, a decent burial, and masses for the soul were the essence of guild life. Thus it is probable that the practical pursuit of religion by neighbourhood associations, rather than the seeking of trade advantage, was at first the motive of the guilds. Evidence of this religious

[1] e.g. in the 1485 patent of arms to the Wax Chandlers the Company is designated " the gode, sadde, worshipful and well-disposed ". Two entries in the Common Council Journal relating to the funeral ceremonies of Henry VII read : " ordered that the most worshipful companies shall stand next unto Pauls " and " the lowest crafts to begin at Pauls and the most worshipful crafts to be next to Temple Bar ".

devotion will be found in the symbolism in many of the companies' arms. Of the twenty-four fifteenth-century coats of arms of the London guilds, five are composed solely of religious symbols, five more combine religious and trade allusions, and the remainder refer only to the respective trades. The predominantly pious note of the mottoes and direct references in the letters patent of arms to religious allegiance are further testimony to this powerful force in guild organization.

With the development of trade the guilds grew in importance and wealth. Trade control, which had been in the hands of the civic authority, was assumed by them. Increased status and powers were achieved by the acquisition of charters of incorporation, and by the end of the fifteenth century many of the guilds had become incorporated bodies. By this time the religious aspect, although still important, was no longer dominant, and the emphasis shifted to trade. With the doctrinal changes of the Reformation the survival of such organizations depended upon their secular activities, and the religious element became further obscured. Signs of this process also are to be noted in the arms of the guilds, for much of the religious symbolism contained in them was suppressed during the upheaval of the Reformation, although this would appear to have been a measure of prudence rather than of conviction.

The predominance of the companies' trade and craft activities under the Tudors coincided with the beginnings of the decline of the guilds as an economic force. The expansion of trade and improved communications imposed a severe strain on an inflexible system which in the main set out to restrain entry into the trades of London. Nevertheless the guilds for some time struggled to impose their regulations upon an expanding economy. By the end of the eighteenth century the guilds' original functions, although never legally rescinded in London, became with a few exceptions largely inoperative. Many, however, continue to administer considerable charitable funds, and have found new life in promoting general and technical education, and in the development of strong interests in their respective crafts. The progress of technology owes much to the practical encouragement given by the guilds in recent times, notably through the City and Guilds of London Institute. By no means least is the debt that the historian owes to the careful preservation of the companies' archives, and to their increasing accessibility as sources of economic and social history.

Without these records, the bulk of which are now deposited in
the Guildhall Library, and the ready co-operation of the companies
through the courtesy of their Clerks, this book could not have been
written.

JOHN BROMLEY

OPIFERQVE · DICOR

PER · ORBEM

MAKE · ALL · SURE

WE · ARE · ONE

Pl. 1

B.1

APOTHECARIES, p. 1
ARMOURERS AND BRASIERS, p. 5

THE WORSHIPFUL SOCIETY OF APOTHECARIES

The sale of drugs was originally under the control of the Grocers' Company, and apothecaries did not become an independent body until 6th December 1617. Their charter incorporated them as the Master, Wardens and Society of the Art or Mystery of Apothecaries, and had as its object the restraint of " presumptuous empirics and ignorant and unexpert men ". The company is one of the few which continue to fulfil the functions for which they were founded. The apothecary, who formerly concerned himself with the preparation and sale of drugs for medicinal purposes, later assumed the role of a physician, and today the Society of Apothecaries is one of the bodies responsible for the control of both callings. It is entitled to conduct examinations and issue diplomas which give holders the right to be registered under the Medical Acts as medical practitioners, or to serve as qualified dispensers.

Although the Apothecaries differ from the other guilds in being called a Society rather than a Company, there is no especial significance in the term, which is no more than an alternative to the more usual generic word of " commonalty " to denote the whole body of freemen of the company. Similar usage is to be found in the charters of other companies, for example, in those of the Bowyers (Master, Wardens and Society of the Mystery of Bowyers), the Framework Knitters (Master, Wardens, Assistants and Society of the Company of Framework Knitters), and the Fanmakers (Master, Wardens, Assistants and Society of the Art or Mystery of Fanmakers).

THE ARMORIAL BEARINGS (Pl. 1)

Azure, Apollo, the inventor of physic, proper with his head radiant holding in his left hand a bow and in his right hand an arrow or, supplanting a serpent argent.

Crest : Upon a wreath of the colours a rhinoceros proper.
Supporters : Two unicorns or armed and unguled argent.
Mantling : Gules doubled argent.
Motto : Opiferque per orbem dicor.   Grant [1] by William Camden, Clarenceux
12th December 1617

[1] Original in the possession of the Society.

I

The Apothecaries' grant was made but six days after the Society's incorporation by James I. Discharge of the debt to the Heralds' College for the grant does not appear to have been as speedy as the seeking of it, for on 6th April 1620 occurs an entry in the Society's Court Minute Book :[1] " It was then likewise ordered to the Mr. and Wardens to give wt. ffees they shall think fitt to the Harrolds for the Armes of the Companie and to provide a Comon Seale . . ." This entry has been interpreted as an instruction to negotiate for an achievement.[2] It would seem, however, to be an authorization for belated payment of what was due.

The source of the designer's inspiration is clearly Ovid's *Metamorphoses*. The motto, which is a quotation from the first book, reads in its context :

Inventum medicina meum est, opiferque per orbem dicor, et herbarum subiecta potentia nobis.

The medical art is my discovery and I am called throughout the world the bringer of aid. The potency of herbs is at my will.

The passage follows the episode of Apollo's slaughter of Python, a formidable dragon which guarded Delphi. In the original grant the artist has depicted Apollo overcoming a wyvern, a species of heraldic dragon emblematic of pestilence, thus symbolizing the struggle of medicine against disease.

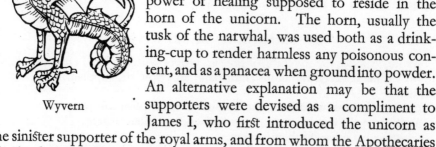

Wyvern

The supporters are probably intended to recall the ancient belief in the miraculous power of healing supposed to reside in the horn of the unicorn. The horn, usually the tusk of the narwhal, was used both as a drinking-cup to render harmless any poisonous content, and as a panacea when ground into powder. An alternative explanation may be that the supporters were devised as a compliment to James I, who first introduced the unicorn as the sinister supporter of the royal arms, and from whom the Apothecaries obtained their charter. But the symbolic use is the more likely.

[1] Guild. Lib. MS. 8200/1.
[2] Barrett, *Hist. of the Society of Apothecaries* (1905), pp. 6, 276.

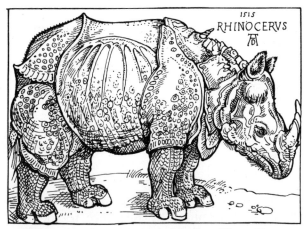

Rhinoceros, from the woodcut by Albert Dürer

In the adoption of the rhinoceros as the crest can be seen the typical punning association used in heraldic art. The rhinoceros is an obvious parallel with the unicorn, and the fact that its horn also was reputed to have been a medical prophylactic gave it additional relevance.[1] The design of the rhinoceros as it appears in the original letters patent of arms is a version of Dürer's famous woodcut which he executed in 1515. For many years Dürer's drawing of the gomda, or rhinoceros, was the model for all representations of this beast whose appearance was otherwise almost unknown in Europe. Dürer himself had never seen the animal and made his drawing from another's sketch and brief description.[2]

The painting of the arms in the margin of the patent shows a form of helm now used only in the crests of peers. There is no obvious explanation of this exceptional usage for the Society of Apothecaries, and it may be no more than artistic caprice. If it were intended as a mark of especial honour to the Company, reference to the helm would be expected in the patent, but there is no such mention. As, however, this form of helm does appear in the official grant, it has been also retained in the illustration of the arms which accompanies this text.[3]

[1] Thompson (C. J. S.), *Mystery and Art of the Apothecary* (1929), p. 219.
[2] Underwood (E. A.), editor, *Science, Medicine and History*, vol. 1 (1953), p. 347, in which Dürer's gomda as the prototype for subsequent artists is fully discussed.
[3] Other arms incorporating peers' helms are Clockmakers, Fishmongers and Goldsmiths.

Peer's helm   Esquire's helm

Whether the Kings of Arms would now uphold the right to this distinction can only be determined by reference to them.

The blazon of the original grant runs as follows :

In a Shield azure, Apollo, the inventor of phisique, proper, with his heade Radiant, holding in his left hand a bowe and in his right hande an Arow dor, supplanting a serpent argent, above the Shield an Helme theruppon a mantle gules, doubled Argent, and for their Creaſt upon a Wreath of their Colours, a Rhynoceros proper, supported by too Unicorns or, armed and ungulated argent, uppon a Compartiment to make the Atchievement compleat the motto, Opiferque per orbem dicor.

PRAISE GOD FOR ALL

DE PRÆSCIENTIA DEI

Pl. 2   B.4

BAKERS, p. 9
BARBERS, p. 14

THE WORSHIPFUL COMPANY OF ARMOURERS AND BRASIERS

THE Armourers' and Brasiers' Company represents the union of a number of allied crafts which have over the years been absorbed by the Armourers' Company. Among these were the heaumers (makers of helms) furbishers (garnishers and repairers of arms and armour) and bladesmiths; only the brasiers have the distinction of survival in the formal title. The Armourers existed as a separate entity at least as early as the beginning of the fourteenth century, but were not incorporated by charter until 8th May 1453. The Brasiers, whose existence as a fellowship can also be traced back to the fourteenth century, at no time had a charter. Thus they were less able to resist the encroachment by the Armourers' Company upon their trade in brass and copper wares. Formal acknowledgement of the new activity of the Armourers, whose proper trade was then a dying one, was made in a charter of 1685, and the union of the two companies took place on 17th June 1708 by the issue of new letters patent.

THE ARMORIAL BEARINGS (Pl. 1)

The united Company uses arms by custom; there is no formal grant. The device adopted comprises the arms of the Armourers' Company, granted in 1556, together with a shield representing the Brasiers, and supporters which have no official recognition. Although usually displayed on two separate escutcheons, these arms are sometimes found impaled. Their description is as follows:

Dexter, the Armourers: argent on a chevron sable an "attõney" (*sc.* tournament) gauntlet between two pairs of swords in saltire argent the swords porfled pommelled and hilted or, on a chief sable a plate between two helmets argent garnished or a cross gules.

Sinister, the Brasiers: azure on a chevron between two ewers in chief and a three-legged pot with two handles in base all or, three roses gules seeded or barbed vert.

Crest: On a wreath argent and sable a demi-man of arms armed argent open-faced porfled or holding in his hand a mace of war.

Supporters: Two men in complete armour proper, the dexter argent

5

garnished or, the sinister all or; on their heads plumes of feathers, and each holding in his exterior hand a sword proper.

Mantling: Gules doubled argent.

Mottoes: Make all sure. We are one.

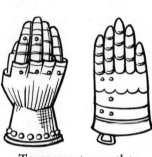

Tournament gauntlets

Heraldic rose

Negotiations for a grant of arms were begun soon after the union of the two companies in 1708, but contemporary records show them to have been abortive. In the minute books of the Company, under the date 28th February 1708/9, appears the following entry: " The Master and Wardens are desired to treat and agree with the King at Arms for a new Coat of Arms for the Brasiers upon their being united to this Company of Armourers, and that a Common Seal be made thereupon at as reasonable a price as they can procure the same." A later entry records the cost of the seal to have been £19. 6s. 9d., but no further reference is made to armorial bearings. Light is cast upon the problem, however, by records in the College of Arms. On 31st March 1715 it is recorded that the Deputy Earl Marshal revoked an outstanding warrant for a new grant, dated 18th April 1709, which had been issued by him at the solicitation of Robert Dale, Suffolk Herald Extraordinary. On 13th October 1709 a re-entry of the 1556 patent to the Armourers was made.

When the device, as at present used, was first adopted is uncertain. Numerous representations of guild heraldry in literature of the eighteenth century depict only the arms of the Armourers, and the earliest example of the combined arms that has been found from this source appears in John Noorthouck's *History of London*, 1773. Illustrations of companies' arms immediately prior to this are shown in the margin of an

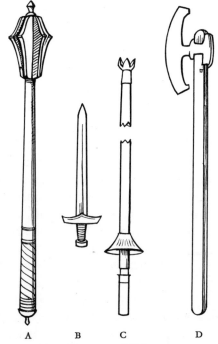

A. Mace of war.   B. Sword.   C. Tilting spear.   D. Battle-axe

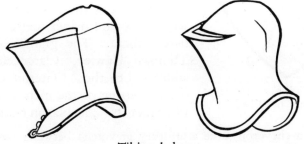

Tilting helms

engraved map of Middlesex by R. W. Seale, *c.* 1750, wherein the coat of arms of the Armourers and Brasiers is shown as that of the 1556 patent.[1]

The earliest device known to have been used by the Armourers is

[1] *Some account of the Armourers and Brasiers* (*Anon.*) by Timothy Morley (1878), p. 10, gives a transcript; cf. also *Proc. Soc. Ant.* 2nd series, vol. 1, p. 197.

on a silver seal of the reign of Henry VI.   It is still in the possession
of the Company and represents St. George, the patron saint of the
Armourers, on foot piercing a dragon with a spear.   On the dexter
is a shield charged with two swords in saltire, and on the sinister
another shield bears the cross of St. George.   Above each escutcheon
is a helm.   The legend reads *in extenso : Sigillum commune artis armur-
ariorum Londonearum*.   This would appear to be the seal struck for the
Company soon after its incorporation in 1453.

On 7th October 1556 the court minute book of the Company enters
an agreement to pay the King of Arms for renewing letters patent of
the arms of the Company.[1]   It is possible that the arms attributed to
the Armourers in a manuscript of about 1530 in the College of Arms[2]
may represent their arms before this renewal, although no trace of
an actual grant has been found.   This manuscript gives : Sable a

Early Arms (Coll. Arms; Vincent,
" Two Ears of Wheat ")

battle-axe and a tilting spear both or
headed argent in saltire debruised by a
cross couped gules all between three
helms argent.   Similar armorial bearings
are shown in a fragment of Glover's
Ordinary in the British Museum.[3]   The
reason cited in the ensuing grant of 15th
October 1556 for the Company's seeking
new arms was their uncertainty " under
what sorte and maner theire predecessors
bare " them.   The grant was made by
Thomas Hawley, Clarenceux, and is
addressed to the " Fraternitye or Guylde
of St. George of the men of the mystery
of Armerors " ; its blazon reads as follows:

Silver on a cheveron sable a attorney gawntelet betwene Fower Swordes
in sawltre silver porfled pomeled and hilted gold on a chef sable in a plate
betwene two hellmettes silver garnyshed golde a playne crosse geules.
Upon the healme on a Torse silver and sable a demy Man of Armes armed
silver open faced porfled golde holdyng in his hande a mace of warre
manteled geules dobled silver.

[1] Morley, loc. cit.   [2] Vincent, " Two Ears of Wheat ".
[3] Cotton MS. Tib. DX. fo. 360-2.

THE WORSHIPFUL COMPANY OF BAKERS

THE Bakers were an organized body by the middle of the twelfth century. Their corporate life was confirmed to them by royal charter dated 2nd June 1486.

Bread was originally made in two main categories, white and brown, the latter being the staple diet of the poor. Bakers were similarly divided into White and Brown Bakers, and an article of their craft confined the making of each category of bread to its respective class of baker. The increasing standard of life in London much reduced the sale of brown bread, and in 1645 the union of the bakers was effected by joint agreement and confirmed by royal charter of 2nd March 1685/6.

Apart from the normal welfare and trading activities of a guild, the Bakers were entrusted with the control of the weight and price of bread through the Assize of Bread which had originated in an act of the thirteenth century. The Assize was abandoned in London in 1815, and in 1822 the alteration of the laws affecting the weight of bread relieved the Company of these legal functions.

THE ARMORIAL BEARINGS (Pl. 2)

Gules three garbs or on a chief barry wavy of six argent and azure two anchors or cabled gules over all issuant from a cloud proper radiated in chief or a cubit arm descending therefrom vested argent cuffed sable the hand proper holding a balance or.

Grant not extant; probable date 1536

Crest : On a wreath gules and or two arms embowed issuing out of a cloud proper holding in their hands a chaplet of wheat or.

Mantling : Gules doubled argent.

Supporters : On either side a buck proper attired or, gorged with a chaplet of wheat also or.

Motto : Praise God for all.

Grant [1] of crest and supporters by Robert Cooke,
Clarenceux
8th November 1590

Although the Bakers did not acquire a coat of arms by letters patent

[1] Coll. Arms. 2nd C.24/3.

9

until 1536, there is evidence that the Company was using a device at an earlier date. According to their accounts[1] for the year 1529/30, six metal escutcheons of arms were purchased, apparently in connection with the Lord Mayor's annual pageant. No details of the arms are given, but from the fine window, fortunately surviving, in the church of St. Andrew Undershaft, it is probable that they closely resembled those in use today. This window, which is considered to date from about 1525, was installed by a benefactor at the rebuilding of the church in the second decade of the sixteenth century. The arms depicted are : argent a balance gules between three garbs or, on a chief azure a papal tiara between two anchors or. Apart from the variation of the tinctures, it differs from its later, and current version, by the use of the papal tiara in the place of the arm descending from a cloud. That the present arms were granted in 1536 cannot be proved from any record in the College of Arms, although the 1590 grant of crest and supporters does in fact assert that the arms had been granted long before. Nevertheless the evidence from the Company's account books [2] leaves little doubt that such was the case. The precise date is not given, but from internal evidence the four following entries relate to the year 1536, and indicate clearly the Company's negotiations for its armorial bearings

Arms of the White Bakers (ancient), St. Andrew Undershaft, N. aisle, 4th window from E. 4th light. 16th cent. (*c.* 1525)

Paide and spent upon Master Norrey for solycytyng of Master Clarenceux to be good for one Armes . . . . 14*d.*

Paide in expences on Masters Clarenceux and Norrey Kynges at Armes . . . . 2*s.* 8*d.*

Paide to Master Clarenceux Kyng at Armes for the letteres patentes of the Armes of the Bakers . . . . £4. 10*s.*

Paide the same tyme in expences upon Master Clarenceux at the delyverie of the saide patent . . . . . 2*s.*

---

[1] Guild. Lib. MS. 5174/1 fo. 135.   [2] ibid., fo. 196b.

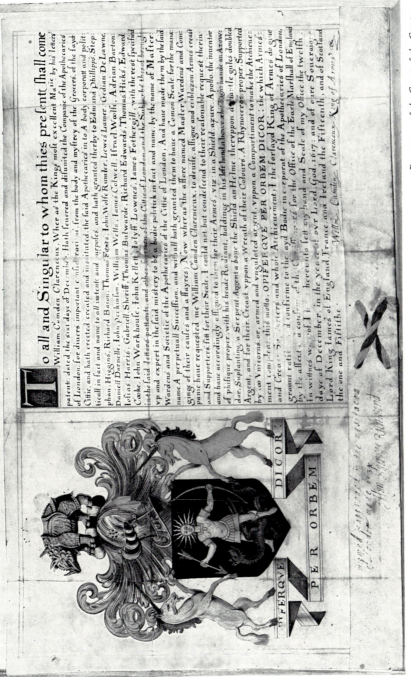

Pl. 3

By courtesy of the Court of the Company

B.10

LETTERS PATENT OF ARMS TO THE WORSHIPFUL COMPANY OF APOTHECARIES,
12TH DECEMBER 1617, SHOWING A PEER'S HELM IN THE EXEMPLIFICATION

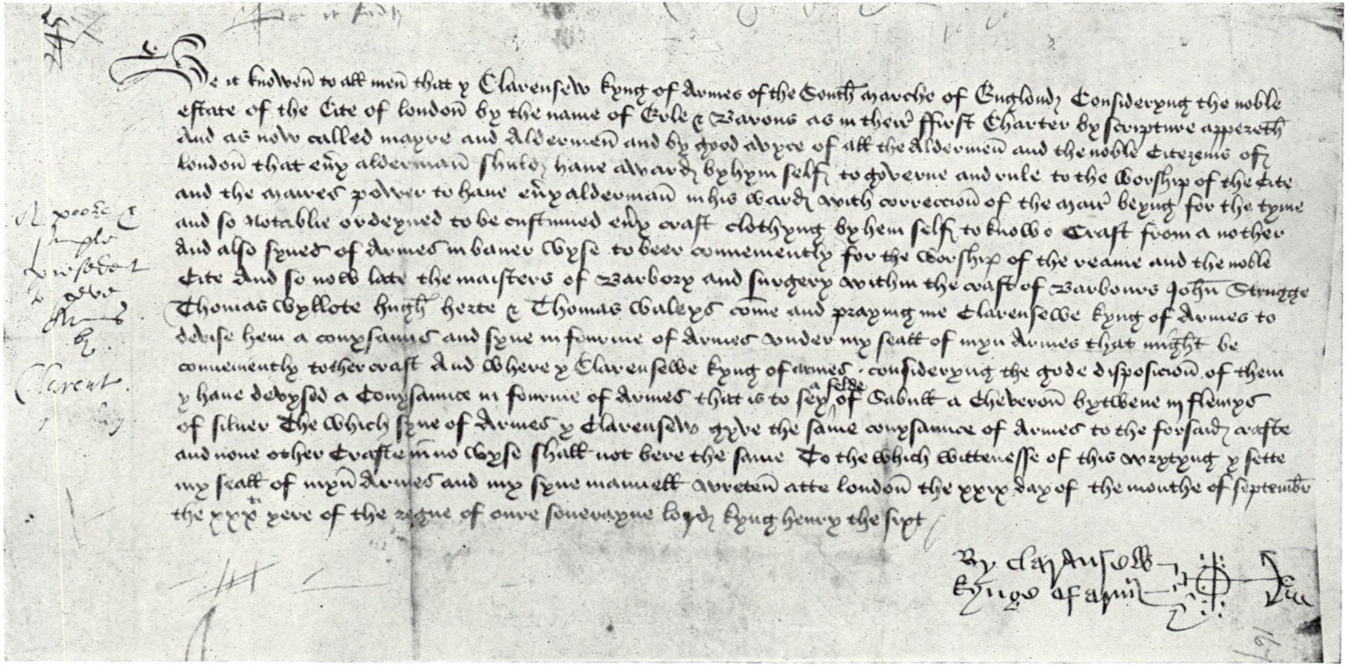

Be it knowen to all men that I Clarencell kyng of Armes of the South marche of England Consideryng the noble estate of the Cite of london by the name of Erle & Barons as in their ffirst Charter by scripture apperith And as now called mayre and Aldermen and by good advyce of all the Aldermen and the noble Citezeins of london that eny alderman shuld have award by hym self to governe and rule to the Worship of the Cite and the mairs power to have eny alderman in his Ward with correccion of the mair beyng for the tyme and so notablie ordeyned to be enformed eny craft clothyng by hem self to knowe o Craft from a nother And also signes of Armes in baner Wyse to beer comenently for the Worship of the reame and the noble Cite And so nowe late the maisters of Barbory and surgery within the craft of Barbours John Strugge Thomas Wyllote hugh herte & Thomas Waleys come and prayng me Clarencelle kyng of Armes to devise hem a conysaunce and signe in fourme of Armes under my seall of myn Armes that might be comenently to ther craft And Where I Clarencelle kyng of armes considering the gode disposicion of them I have devysed a conysaunce in fourme of Armes that is to sey a felde of Sable a cheveron betwene iii flemys of silver The Which signe of Armes I Clarencell gyve the same conysaunce of Armes to the forsaid crafte and none other Crafte in no Wyse shall not bere the same To the Which Wittenesse of this wrytyng I sette my seall of myn Armes and my signe manuell Wreten atte london the xxix day of the monthe of Septembr the xxxti yere of the regne of oure soveraygne lord kyng henry the sixt

By Clarencell kyng of armes

By courtesy of the Court of the Company

Pl. 4 C.11

LETTERS PATENT GRANTING ARMS TO THE WORSHIPFUL COMPANY OF BARBERS, 29TH SEPTEMBER 1451

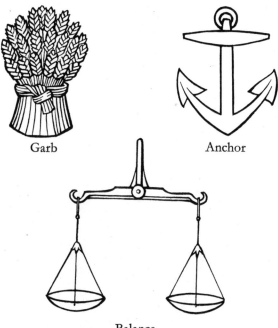

Garb   Anchor

Balance

There is no doubt significance in the Company's seeking, two years after the Act of Supremacy, a new coat of arms which discarded the triple tiara of Clement, the third holder of the papal throne and patron saint of the Bakers. The retention of the anchors, which also symbolize St. Clement, is not easy to explain; it may be they did not so obviously represent the " errors and abuses " which Henry was determined to suppress. The omission of the anchors in the 1633 edition of Stow's *Survey of London* would appear to be an error.

An early example of the new arms may be seen in the manuscript *Breffe description of the royall Citie of London*,[1] 1575, written by William Smith who subsequently, in 1597, was created Rouge Dragon Pursuivant of Arms.

The Company's arms were completed in 1590 by the grant of crest and supporters referred to above.

In the official history of the Bakers' Company[2] the arms are described as barry wavy of four; all the evidence at the College of Arms establishes

[1] Guild. Lib. MS. 2463.

[2] Thrupp (S.), *Short History of the Bakers' Company* (1933), p. 11.

C

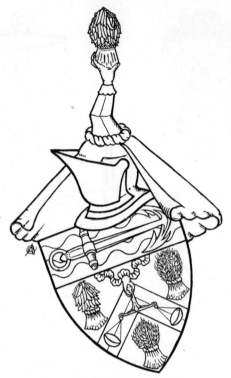

Arms of the Brown Bakers

that they should be barry wavy of six.[1]   Moreover, the supporters
are given as ſtags whereas they would appear from official records to
be bucks, a subtle heraldic diſtinction indicated by a broadening of the
antlers in the buck.   The illuſtration of the arms that appears in the
official hiſtory is not consiſtent with the correct blazon nor does it
conform to the rendering of it as given in the text.

The Brown Bakers, who had for long ſtruggled to maintain their
separate identity as a craft in the face of continued attempts by their
fellow miſtery to absorb them, emphasized their independence by the
acquisition of their own coat of arms on 28th June 1572.[2]   These
were very similar to the White Bakers' arms and consisted of : vert on
a chevron quarterly or and gules between three sheaves of beans, rye

[1] Coll. Arms MSS. 1ſt H.7/62 ; F.13/40b ; 2nd C.24/3.
[2] Granted by Sir Gilbert Dethick, Garter.   Coll. Arms references : 2nd C.24/11 ;
N. G./28 ; Dethick's gifts 29b ; Vincent 162/138 ; Vincent 183/86. Cf. also
Accounts of the Brown Bakers, Guild. Lib. MS. 5203.

and wheat proper a balance azure supported by a hand proper issuing from clouds proper attached to a chief barry wavy of four argent and azure charged with an anchor fessewise or, the stock to the dexter; the crest an arm embowed, vested quarterly or and gules, cuffed argent, holding in the hand proper a sheaf of beans proper.

The symbolism in both coats is obvious : the garbs or sheaves are the source of the bakers' products, and the balance in divine hands represents fair dealing through the immediate agency of the Assize of Bread. The anchors, as stated above, are in honour of St. Clement, the patron saint of the Company, and recall the religious origin of the Company as a guild of Our Lady and Saint Clement. The anchor is universally the emblem of St. Clement who, as legend asserts, was martyred by drowning with an anchor around his neck.

The bucks as supporters, with their chaplets of wheat, form a perfect rebus for buckwheat. This interpretation of the designer's allusion reinforces the opinion that the supporters are bucks and not stags as commonly regarded, for buckwheat was an additional coarse grain used in cheaper breads as well as for cake for horse-feed.

THE WORSHIPFUL COMPANY OF BARBERS

UNTIL 1745 the Barbers had controlled also the craft of surgery. This curious combination of occupations arose from the customary employment of the barber in medieval monasteries for the purpose of blood-letting as well as for the preservation of the tonsure. The Company was incorporated by charter dated 24th February 1461/2. This charter, while confirming all the Company's rights and privileges in the control of barbery and surgery, did not extinguish an unincorporated Fellowship of Surgeons which continued to practise surgery in the City of London with the approval of the civic authorities. In 1540 an Act of Parliament united the fellowship with the Barbers as the Company of Barbers and Surgeons, and enacted that none who pursued the trade of barber could practise surgery, and that no surgeon could cut hair or shave another; the only common activity was the extraction of teeth. The rising status of the surgeon made the association increasingly uneasy, and in 1745 an act constituted the surgeons as a separate body, the forerunner of the Royal College of Surgeons of today.

THE ARMORIAL BEARINGS (Pl. 2)

Quarterly, the first sable a chevron between three fleams argent, the second quarter per pale argent and vert on a spatter of the first a double rose gules and argent crowned or, the third quarter as the second and the fourth as the first, over all on a cross gules a lion passant guardant or.

Crest : On a wreath argent and sable an opinicus or.

Mantling : Gules doubled argent.

Supporters : On either side a lynx proper about the neck a crown with a chain argent pendent thereat.

Motto : De praescientia Dei.

Granted [1] by Sir Gilbert Dethick,
Garter
Robert Cooke,
Clarenceux
William Flower,
Norroy
2nd June 1569

[1] Original deposited in Guildhall Library, MS. 5254.

14

Pl. 5

C.15

BASKETMAKERS, p. 20   BLACKSMITHS, p. 22
BOWYERS, p. 25   BREWERS, p. 28

The above arms incorporate the devices used respectively by the Company of Barbers and the Fellowship of Surgeons before the union of those two bodies in 1540. The origin of the coat is fully recited, albeit incorrectly in some particulars, in the 1569 patent.

The Barbers were first granted armorial bearings by Roger Legh, Clarenceux, on 29th September 1451. These were " sabull a cheveron bytwene iii flemys of silver ".[1]

The unincorporated Fellowship of Surgeons had no coat. They had, however, been granted a cognizance, or badge, by Henry VII in 1492. A contemporary record of this appears in an ordinance book (temp. 1492-7) of the Fellowship of Surgeons where beneath a painting of the device, flanked by the patron saints of the surgeons— St. Cosmos and St. Damian—is a statement that these " armys " were granted in the year 1492 to the Craft of Surgeons of London " at the goyng ovyr the see of oure sovēyn Lord Kyng Harry the VIIth in to fraunsse ".[2] The 1569 patent refers to this cognizance of the Surgeons, describing it as " a spatter thereon a rose gules, crowned golde ". It further states that it was given by Henry VIII [sic] to the Surgeons " for their warrant in the fielde, but no authorite by warrant for the bearinge of the same in shilde as armes ". The assertion that the grantor was Henry VIII is clearly an error. Henry VII had, in fact, crossed to France in 1492, landing at Calais on 6th October to go to the assistance of Brittany, then threatened by the French king.

On 10th July 1561, at the request of the now united Company of Barbers and Surgeons, an augmentation was made to the 1451 arms of the Barbers by William Hervey, Clarenceux, namely " a chefe payley argent and vert on a pale gewles a lyon passant regardant gold betwene two spattors argent and sable on ech a roze gewles crowned golde ".[3] A crest was also added at this time : " an opinagus golde standinge upon a wreathe argent and sables manteled gules dubled argent ".[4]

Supporters to the arms are said to have been given also by William Hervey, by inference in the year 1565. The patent of these supporters has not survived, nor is there any contemporary record of such a grant in the College of Arms. The only authority for them that exists is

[1] Brit. Mus. Harl. MS. 1470 fo. 167. This appears to be the original patent. Transcript in Young (S.), *Annals of the Barber-Surgeons* (1890), p. 432, and in *Misc. Gen. et Heraldica*, vol. I, p. 11.

[2] Guild. Lib. MS. 5248.

[3] Coll. Arms ICB.101/19.   [4] ibid.

Surgeons' cognisance, from 15th cent.   Ordinance book of Fellowship of Surgeons
(Guild. Lib. MS. 5248)

Barbers' arms, ancient, after Coll. Arms; Vincent, "Two Ears of Wheat"

the current patent of 1569, which recites that Hervey granted supporters in the time of Robert Balthrop, Master of the Barbers and Surgeons, George Vaughan, Richard Hughes, and George Corron, Governors of the same corporation, all of whom held office during the year 1565.

Hervey's grant of arms of 1561 was superseded in 1569 by another, which is the operative one today. According to the new patent, the grant of 1561 was found to be " in some respectes . . . not onely contrary to the wordes of the Corporation of the sayd Barbours and Chirurgeons " but also contained " sondrey other thinges contrary, and not agreinge with the auncient lawes and rules of armes ". That the patent was " contrary to the wordes of the Corporation " suggests an incorrect use therein of the title of the incorporated body, but owing to the loss of the 1561 patent this cannot be established. The other objection raised by the Kings of Arms seems to refer to the excessively complicated chief of Hervey's augmentation, which is certainly much too crowded for so small a compass.[1]

The blazon of the 1569 patent reads as follows :

Quarterly the first sables a Cheveron betweene three flewmes argent : the second quarter per pale argent and Vert on a Spatter of the first a double-Rose gules and argent crowned golde the third quarter as the second and the fourth as the first : over all on a Cross gules a lyon passant gardant golde : and to their Creast upon the heaulme on a Torce argent and sable an Opimacus golde : Mantelled gules doubled argent : Supported with two Linxe in their proper coulor about their neckes a crowne with a chayne argent pendent therat.

It is of interest to note that in this grant the term " gardant " is used to describe the lion, whereas " regardant " occurs in the 1561 grant. In both cases the lion is depicted full-face, that is to say gardant in the modern sense. " Regardant " had, in fact, always been used for full-face, until the latter part of the sixteenth century, and only subsequently have the terms " gardant " and " regardant " acquired their separate significance.[2]

The Company's motto is noted for the first time beneath the painting of the arms which appears in the margin of the 1569 patent. There seems no obvious reason for its choice unless it be that the uncertain outcome of the surgeon's attentions were, good or bad, attributed to

[1] Cp. Cooke's objection to the former arms of the Merchant Taylors.
[2] For full discussion of this point see H. S. London on " Lion guardant and regardant " in *The Coat of Arms*, Jan. 1953.

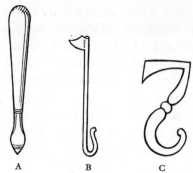

A. Spatter. B. Fleam, 15th cent. (Wellcome Historical Museum). C. Fleam as a charge in the arms

Opinicus

Double rose and crown

the wisdom of God. Of the charges, the " spatter ", which is barely visible beneath the rose, is a spatula, a symbol of the surgeon's craft ; the fleam is a form of lancet representing the blood-letting activities of the early barber. The lynx of the supporters presumably suggests the keenness of vision necessary for the surgeon, while the opinicus, a fictitious beast, part lion and part eagle, is without apparent symbolism in this connection.

Since 1569 no modification of the arms has occurred and, despite the dissolution of the two constituent bodies in 1745, they still incorporate the original device given to the Surgeons in 1492.

It should perhaps be mentioned that a grant of 1568 is referred to in the Company's official history,[1] whereby it is alleged that the crest and supporters were confirmed, but a considerable variation of the charges was introduced, with a resulting coat identical with that of the 1569 grant. No evidence for this assertion can be traced in the College of Arms, and it is probable that a confusion of dates has occurred, and these arms are those of the 1569 patent.

[1] Young (S.), *Annals of the Barber-Surgeons* (1890), p. 436.

THE WORSHIPFUL COMPANY OF BASKETMAKERS

THE Basketmakers appeared comparatively late as an organized body, achieving a constitution from the Court of Aldermen in 1569. It is probable that, in its beginnings, the trade, although of great antiquity, was a humble one subservient to the wealthier callings which employed these wares; in early times basketmakers are to be found as freemen of other companies, notably of the Butchers who would no doubt have been among the most frequent users of baskets. Attempts to acquire a charter of incorporation were made in the latter half of the seventeenth century but without success, and it was not until 27th April 1937 that this dignity was conferred upon the Company.

THE ARMORIAL BEARINGS (Pl. 5)

Azure three cross baskets in pale argent between a prime and an iron on the dexter and a cutting-knife and an outsticker on the sinister of the second.

Crest: On a wreath of the colours a cradle therein a child rocked at the head by a girl and at the feet by a boy both vested proper.

Mantling: Azure doubled argent.

Motto: Let us love one another.

Granted [1] by Gerald Woods Wollaston,
Garter
Arthur William Steuart Cochrane,
Clarenceux
Algar Henry Stafford Howard,
Norroy
12th October 1931

There is no record of any grant of arms prior to 1931, but arms have been used by the Company at least from the seventeenth century. The earliest known reference to armorial bearings occurs in the Company's account books [2] where, on 26th August 1672, an entry appears recording a payment of £1. 5s. 0d. " for the coate of armes ". The earliest exemplification that has been discovered is found on an engraved almanac, *c.* 1680, a copy of which is in the Pepysian Library at

---

[1] Original patent in the possession of the Company.
[2] Guild. Lib. MS. 2873.

Cambridge;[1] apart from the omission of the crest, the arms there shown are identical with those of today.

The arms over the years have exhibited the vagaries that are apt to afflict those that have no authoritative grant to control their design.

So far as examples are available, it is clear that the helm has always been absent until an heraldically correct blazon was authorized in 1931.

Other misconceptions of the laws of heraldry were exhibited from time to time by the use of decorative devices taking the place of supporters. These seem to be branches of willow, while in the nineteenth

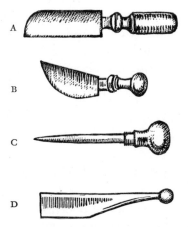

A. Shop knife or cutting knife. B. Picking-knife or outsticker.
C. Bodkin or prime. D. Iron

century two griffins also appear, flanked by a willow tree on the dexter and a bundle of withes on the sinister. The Company has in fact no supporters.

The tools of the trade, as shown in the arms, represent the prime or bodkin for raising the woven cane during the process of basket-making; the iron which is a flat piece of metal used for inserting between two upright canes in order to press down the horizontal bands; the outsticker or picking-knife for trimming protruding ends; and the general purpose knife for cutting the canes to size.

[1] *London Almanack for XXX years* by R. Morden and P. Lee.

THE WORSHIPFUL COMPANY OF BLACKSMITHS

THE Blacksmiths were first incorporated by charter dated 20th April 1571, and are referred to in the letters patent as the Art and Mistery of Blacksmiths-spurriers. The germ from which the Blacksmiths grew is to be found in the year 1299 when a number of citizens were brought before the Mayor to answer a charge of unlawful assembly. On the plea that the assembly was for the purpose of regulating the trade of smiths and to maintain a wax taper in honour of the Blessed Mary and St. Laudus, the defendants were acquitted. The dedication of this fellowship to St. Laudus, or St. Eloi, an eminent metal worker of the seventh century who subsequently became a bishop, reveals the patron saint of the Company.

Among the ranks of the Blacksmiths were originally to be found gunsmiths and clockmakers until each of these crafts later formed independent associations.

THE ARMORIAL BEARINGS (Pl. 5)

Sable a chevron or between three hammers argent handled and crowned or.
Crest : On a wreath of the colours a phoenix proper standing upon a hill vert firing herself with the sun's beams.
Mantling : Sable doubled or.

Granted[1] by Sir William Segar,
Garter
24th June 1610

Motto : By hammer and hand all arts do stand.

The first grant of arms to the Blacksmiths was dated 12th April 1490 and was made by Sir Thomas Holme, Clarenceux. Unfortunately the original 1490 patent is no longer in existence, but the College of Arms cites Glover's Ordinary,[2] *c.* 1613, where the arms are given as " sable a cheveron silver betwene thre hamorys crouned gold. The crest upon a healme a fenyx in his proper colours, a croune of gold about his necke with a chayne, stondinge upon a Tarege within a wreathe gold and sable." The Blacksmiths' first charter,[3] dated 20th

---

[1] The original is not extant. The authority for the blazon is Coll. Arms MS. Misc. Gts. II/267. [2] Brit. Mus. Cotton MS. Tib. DX./360b.
[3] Deposited in Guildhall Library, MS. 2962.

OMNIA DESUPER

SUB PEDIBUS
OMNIA SUBJECISTI OVES ET BOVES

Pl. 6   C.23

BRODERERS, p. 31
BUTCHERS, p. 34

Hammers and sledge-hammer (after the woodcut of a blacksmith's shop from *Flores Musicae*, Strassburg, A.D. 1488)

April 1571, includes in its elaborate illuminated border a painting of the Company's arms which agrees with the above, except that the hammers are shown with the heads argent and the handles and crowns or. The latter rendering is supported by the illumination which decorates the second charter[1] of 21st March 1605. It is thus clear that the only changes effected in the charges by the patent of arms of 1610 were the substitution of a chevron or for a chevron argent, and the omission of the chained crown from the phoenix of the crest which is made to stand in the rays of the sun.

The "tarege"[2] mentioned in Glover's blazoning is probably a terrace and is shown in both the charters as a green mound.

The grant of 1610 is recorded in the College of Arms in the following terms:

Sable a cheveron or, between three Crouned Hamers as in the margin herein depicted & for the Creast forth of a Wreath of their Cullors on a hill vert a Phenix proper Fireing her selfe with the sonne beames & by the agitation & working of her winges (according to the Description of Wryters) shee kyndleth certeyne Sticks of Cinamon & other Spices, & therein consumeth her selfe to Ashes, out of which there arriseth another.

[1] Guild. Lib. MS. 2964.
[2] The context seems to exclude the obvious meaning of targe, or shield.

A. Phoenix crest (from Blacksmiths' Charter of 1571, Guild. Lib. MS. 2962)
B. Phoenix (Modern)

Although the tinctures of the hammers are not given in this blazon, the drawing accompanying it shows that they have silver heads with handles and crowns of gold as in the earlier arms.

The Motto anciently in use by the Company was " As God will so be it ".

An entry in the Company's accounts for the year 1609/10 [1] records the sum paid for the 1610 grant:

Paied to ye herold att Armes for the renewing of the Armes of
this Companye and to his man and for a dynner thereabouts £7. 12s.

[1] Guild. Lib. MS. 2883/3.

THE WORSHIPFUL COMPANY OF BOWYERS

IN the motto of its coat of arms the Bowyers' Company celebrates the major triumphs of the English archer whose prowess established the predominance of the infantryman over the knight-at-arms. Yet in the same year as the battle of Crecy, the use of gunpowder at the siege of Calais heralded the decline of the bowman. The Bowyers' Company accordingly suffered eclipse as a trade guild earlier than most.

In London the provision of archers' equipment depended on three separate crafts : the bowyers, the fletchers or arrowmakers, and the stringers or longbow-string makers. The first two were originally a single trade, but in 1371 the bowyers and the fletchers are found enforcing an ordinance of mutual exclusion for the two crafts.

It is apparent from the City records that archery was only maintained by constant pressure from the Crown. Various measures to enforce its practice culminated in an Act of 1541 which in the interests of the declining art proscribed " sondrie newe and crafty games and plays as logatinge in the feilds, slydethrifte otherwise called shovegrote ". The Lord Mayor championed the cause of the companies concerned, declaring that their adversity was due to the holding of such " spectacles as bear-baiting, unchaste interludes, and bargains of incontinence ". In a final endeavour to restore the Bowyers' craft, James I, on 25th May 1621, granted the Company its first charter of incorporation, but neither this nor legislation was able to prolong the life of an outmoded weapon, and archery entered upon its less heroic role of a sport and recreation.

THE ARMORIAL BEARINGS (Pl. 5)

Sable on a chevron or three mullets pierced sable between three floats argent.

Crest : Upon a helm three bows bent gules stringed or, set within a wreath or and azure.

Mantling : Sable furred with ermine.

Motto : Crecy, Poitiers, Agincourt.

Granted by Sir Thomas Holme,
Clarenceux
10th November 1488

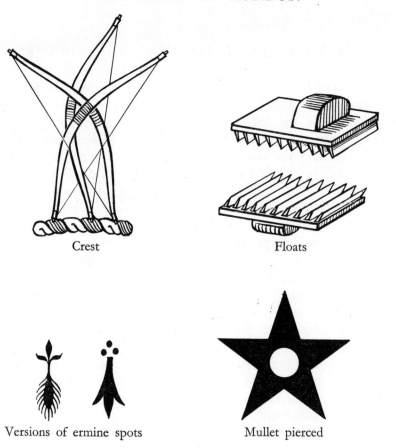

Crest

Floats

Versions of ermine spots

Mullet pierced

This is the only grant made to the Company and there are no supporters.

The original has not survived, but a record of the patent at the College of Arms [1] describes the arms as " Sable uppon a cheveron gold thre mollets [sable] persyd betwene thre flotys silver, the Crest uppon the helme thre bowes bent goulys strynkyd gold sette withyne a wreyth golde and asure the mantell sable forred with ermyn."   No colour is given for the mullets, but the coloured representation in the margin shows them clearly as sable.

[1] Gts. II/440b.   A transcript of this document, in which the date of the grant is wrongly given as 20 Nov. 1488, appears in *The Charter and some other Records of the Bowyers Co.* (1901).

C.26

Pl. 7

LETTERS PATENT GRANTING ARMS TO THE WORSHIPFUL COMPANY OF BREWERS,
23RD JULY 1468

Pl. 8

D.27

LETTERS PATENT GRANTING ARMS TO THE WORSHIPFUL COMPANY OF CARPENTERS,
24TH NOVEMBER 1466

Holme in the *Academy of Armory* (1688), bk. III, ch. 8, pl. 2, shows a " flote " which he describes (p. 351) thus : " it is an iron instrument all teeth on the lower side, streight cross the same . . . with an iron crooked handle on the top : its operation is for working off the timber to make it in the shape of a bow ".

Archers using bows and cross bows at the battle of Creçy,
from Froissart's Chronicle

THE WORSHIPFUL COMPANY OF BREWERS

BEER and bread were the staple diet of the common man in the Middle Ages, and both were rigidly controlled in price and quality. Brewing in London appears at first to have been regulated by the aldermen of the wards. Signs of the emergence of an organization of brewers are seen in 1292 when a number sought the favour of the king to redress their grievances. By 1376 the Mistery of Brewers was sending four members to represent the trade in Common Council. In 1406 detailed ordinances submitted by the mistery for self-government and the governance of the trade were agreed by the mayor and aldermen, and on 22nd February 1437/8 the status of incorporation by royal charter was achieved.

Although national licensing laws have long since rendered powers under its charter inoperative, the Brewers' Company still preserves an intimate association with the trade, and only persons employed therein are admitted.

THE ARMORIAL BEARINGS (Pl. 5)

Gules on a chevron engrailed argent, between six barley sheaves in saltire or, three kilderkins sable hooped or.

Crest : On a torse argent and azure a demi-Moorish woman proper vested azure fretty argent, crined or, holding in either hand three barley ears of the same.

Mantling : Sable doubled argent.

Motto : In God is all our trust.

Grant[1] by Thomas Hawley,
Clarenceux
29th February 1543/4

The above achievement replaced a grant by William Hawkeslowe, Clarenceux, dated 23rd July 1468.[2] The original arms were : azure on a chevron gules, between three barley sheaves or, three barrels argent garnished sable. In the margin of the grant they are depicted impaled with the arms of the see of Canterbury and those attributed to St. Thomas a Becket, the Company's patron saint.

---

[1] Deposited in the Guildhall Library, MS. 5437.　　[2] Guild. Lib. MS. 5436.

No reason is given for the Company's requiring new arms; the grant merely states that the Wardens desired to have " the armes of their said occupacion and corporacion set forthe trew and lefull to be borne ". There is, however, a strong presumption that the explanation

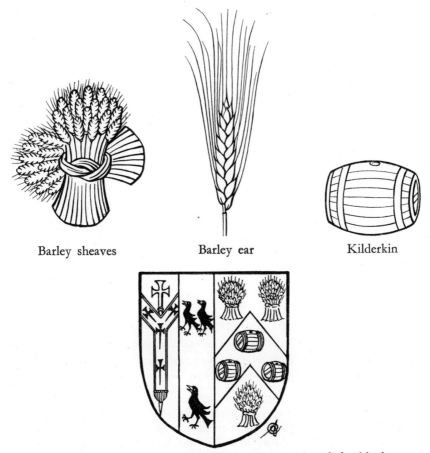

Barley sheaves   Barley ear   Kilderkin

Arms of the Brewers from the margin of the 1468 grant impaled with the arms of the see of Canterbury and those attributed to St. Thomas a Becket

lies in the religious convulsion of the period. The city of London itself had in 1539, the year following the destruction of the shrine of St. Thomas at Canterbury and the erasure of his name from the service-books, ordered a new seal on which its arms were substituted for the effigy of the saint. Other City companies at this time had eliminated from their arms such devices as might have compromised their survival, and it seems certain that the Brewers similarly decided to cloak their religious origins. But, although prepared to accept a new grant which abandoned the obvious pictorial reference to their patron saint as represented by the impalement of his arms, they appear to have been unwilling entirely to forgo a perpetual reminder of his patronage. For the introduction of the Moorish woman as their crest seems only to be explained as referring to the Saracen princess who, according to a popular legend was the mother of Thomas Becket.[1] This legend, which dates from the thirteenth century, asserts that Becket's father, Gilbert, while on a pilgrimage to Jerusalem, was captured by the Saracens and enslaved in the household of a certain prince. The daughter of the house fell in love with Gilbert and having contrived his escape, set out after him to England. Although knowing no English word but " London ", her search was rewarded and her marriage to Gilbert followed upon her conversion to the Christian faith. The story has no basis in fact, and is merely a romantic embellishment of the origin of a popular saint. But if it be the explanation of the Company's crest—and no other connection between brewing and a blackamoor can be suggested—then it would seem that the Brewers, with the connivance of the King of Arms, had changed their arms for reasons of prudence rather than conviction, and their loyalty to St. Thomas remained.

An alternative, though less probable, cause of the change may be that the placing of a colour (a chevron gules) upon another colour (the azure field) in the earlier arms was not pleasing to the later heralds.

A transcript of the blazon from Hawley's grant reads as follows :

Geules on a cheveron engrailed silver thre kilderkyns sable hoped golde betwene syx barly Sheves in saultre of the same Upon the Helme on a torse silver and asur a demy Morien in her proper couler vestid asur fretid silver the here golde holding in either hande Thre barley eres of the same manteled sable dobled silver.

---

[1] See *Life and Martyrdom of Thomas Becket*; ed. by W. H. Black. Percy Society no. 59 (1845).

Pl. 9

CARMEN, p. 37
CLOCKMAKERS, p. 43

THE WORSHIPFUL COMPANY OF BRODERERS

LITTLE is known of the part played by the Company of Broderers in the development of English embroidery in the Middle Ages when that art was most famed. The few references that exist in the City records to the craft in the fourteenth century do little more than establish the existence of the guild at that time.

Unlike most of the other companies, the Broderers were faced with competition from private domestic production and from a considerable output by nuns before the Reformation. These skilful amateurs, being outside the reach of guild regulation, no doubt limited the demand upon the professional. It is probable that workshop pieces were confined for the most part to the larger and more complicated works such as throne and bed canopies, heraldic work, and funeral palls of which examples still survive in the possession of some City companies.

The Company received its first charter on 25th October 1561. By 1634 the craft had so decayed that a petition to the king represented that for want of employment a great part of the Company were constrained to become " porters, waterbearers and the like ".

THE ARMORIAL BEARINGS (Pl. 6)

Paly of six argent and azure on a fesse gules between three lions passant guardant or langued and armed gules two broaches in saltire between as many quills or.

Crest: On a wreath argent and gules the holy dove argent displayed membered and beaked gules upon a roundel azure radiated or.

Supporters: Two lions rampant or gutté de sang armed and langued gules.

Motto: *Omnia desuper.*

Grant[1] by William Harvey,
Clarenceux
17th August 1558

Appended to this grant, which is still in the possession of the Company, is an undated inscription signed by William Camden, Clarenceux, authorizing the Broderers to omit at their will and pleasure the charges on the fesse. No explanation can be offered for this unusual concession

---

[1] For a literal transcript see *Misc. Gen. et Heraldica*, vol. 1 (1865), pp. 183–4.

and the loss of the Company's records for this period diminishes the possibility of finding one. The Broderers do not appear to have made use of the privilege so far as can be ascertained.

It may be noted that the original phraseology of the grant describes the lions as " passant regardant ". " Regardant " at this period was synonymous with the present term " gardant ". The latter word for full-face was only introduced into heraldry late in the sixteenth century and the restriction of "regardant" to mean looking backwards was a similarly late innovation.[1] The drawing in the margin of the grant makes it clear that full-face is intended here.

The charges upon the fesse represent two of the implements of the craft. The broach, or broche, was a combined bodkin and spindle on which was wound the gold thread used by the broderer. It is

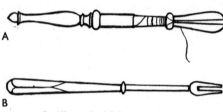

A

B

A. Quill or bobbin.   B. Broach

clearly illustrated by Holme and described by him as " a piece of turned wood .... having a nick or notch at one end, and 3 square at the other, which is to keep it from turning about; on this they use [*sic*] to roll or wind their gold thread or silk twist ".[2] It bears a strong resemblance to the spindle still used for gold and silver embroidery. One authority[3] describes the latter as " made of hard wood about nine inches long for winding metal threads upon, and directing them as you work, so that they should not suffer from contact with the hand ". The quill is a bobbin or spool, and seems to differ in function from the broach in that the latter was an actual tool.

The crest is described in its original phraseology as " the holy ghoost . . . upon a hurt leamed golde ". The " holy ghoost " is symbolized in heraldry by a dove. Hurt is a term used for an azure roundel ; its origin is obscure but it has been suggested that it is derived from the blue hurtleberry otherwise whortleberry.[4] Leam is an obsolete word meaning to glow or shine.

[1] This point is further discussed in the chapter on the Barbers' arms.
[2] Holme, *Academy of Armory*, (1688), bk. III, ch. 7, p. 310.
[3] de Dillmont, *Ency. of Needlework* (c. 1905), p. 179. Cf. also Christie, *Embroidery and Tapestry weaving* (1906), p. 44.
[4] On the origin and meaning of the complex of terms for the roundel see Stanford London in *Notes and Queries*, vol. 195, p. 288 et seq.

There is no certain record of any earlier grant to the Broderers' Company but it is possible that one noted in a roll of grants of arms,[1] now in the possession of the Society of Antiquaries, may refer to the Broderers. This roll was prepared by Sir Thomas Wriothesley, Garter King of Arms, about 1530, and records a grant made in the reign of Henry VII to " Broders ". A corresponding record occurs in the College of Arms[2] but this equally leaves the identity of the grantee uncertain. The arms there given are : " Party per pale gules and sable on a fesse or between three griffins' heads erased gutty azure three lozenges sable ermined argent."

The wording in the letters patent of 1558 is as follows :

Pale of six peces argent and azure a fece gules betwene iii lyonceiux passant regardant golde langed and armed gulz, on the fece ii broches in saulter betwene ii quilles of the third, the creste uppon the heaulme the holy ghoost argent displayde membred and becked gules on a hurt leamed golde on a wreth argent and gules manteled of the same, and for to supporte the sayde armes ii lyons rampant golde gouted gules armed and langued gulles.

Arms from the painting in the margin of the 1558 grant

---

[1] Printed in *Archaeologia*, vol. 69. [2] Coll. Arms MS. E.D.N.56 fo. 34.

THE WORSHIPFUL COMPANY OF BUTCHERS

BEING a victualling guild, the Butchers' Company is among the oldest of the trade fraternities of the City; it is one of the four named trade or craft guilds which the pipe roll of 1179/80 records as being fined for operating without a licence. Frequent references occur in the City records to the control of the trade, the price of meat, slaughtering and the disposal of offal. In 1423 the earliest ordinances for the self-government and control of the butcher's trade were approved by the Court of Aldermen, and on 16th September 1605 the Company obtained its first royal charter.

In addition to the usual functions of a trade guild, the Company acquired certain powers of a public health character and of market control. Although these passed to the civic authority in the nineteenth century, and its chartered functions have lapsed with the decay of the guild system, the Company is still associated with the meat trade from which it largely recruits its members.

THE ARMORIAL BEARINGS (Pl. 6)

Azure two poleaxes in saltire or, blades inwards, between two bulls' heads couped in fesse argent, on a chief argent a boar's head couped gules, tusked or, langued azure, between two bunches of holly vert, banded or.

Crest: On a wreath of the colours a bull statant with wings addorsed or lined with argent, the head, forequarters, hoofs, and tuft of the tail or, the hindquarters argent, armed gules, about the head a nimbus or.

Mantling: Gules doubled argent.

Granted[1] by Thomas Hawley,
Clarenceux
7th February 1540/1

Supporters: On either side a bull with wings addorsed, the head, forequarters, wings, hoofs, and tuft of the tail or, the hindquarters argent, armed gules, about the head a nimbus or.

Granted[2] by Sir Henry Farnham Burke,
Garter
28th June 1922

Motto: *Omnia subiecisti sub pedibus, oves et boves.*

---

[1] Coll. Arms Grants 90, p. 19.
[2] Grant of supporters deposited in Guildhall Library, MS. 6471.

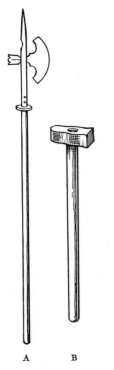

Common Butcher's-broom or
Knee-holly

A B

A. Pole-axe (War).
B. Pole-axe (Butcher)

The original patent of arms has not survived, and the achievement as blazoned above is based upon an interpretation of early records in the College of Arms. As a result a minor modification has been introduced into the crest, as at present used by the Company, by rendering the wings of the bull or lined with argent instead of wholly or. Although the exemplification of the arms, crest and supporters appearing in the margin of the 1922 grant of supporters shows these wings as or, it is likely that this decision was influenced by a sixteenth-century entry[1] which, in the opinion of Richmond Herald, has less authority than two other entries[2] of the same period. These latter give " or lined with argent " and this has accordingly been accepted as the blazoning more likely to be correct.

It is also possible that the tail of " argent tufted or " may be a misunderstanding of the early records. The word " or ", which is attached

[1] Coll. Arms G.10/122b.   [2] Coll. Arms 1st H.7/62, and 2nd C.24/329.

to the end of the tail in the early tricks, may indicate that the whole of the tail is or rather than tufted or.   But in the absence of the original patent, or of a contemporary authoritative coloured drawing, this can be no more than speculation.

The winged bull of the crest and supporters alludes to St. Luke, the patron saint of the Company, who is represented in ecclesiastical symbolism by a winged calf or ox.   This emblem is derived from the description of the heavenly liturgy in Revelation (chap. iv, v. 7) and was probably suggested by the vision of Ezekiel (chap. i, v. 10).

The bunches of holly are not true holly but " knee-holly " or " butcher's broom " (*Ruscus aculeatus*), the shoots of which were wont to be bound into bundles and sold to butchers who used them for sweeping their blocks.[1]

Arms of the " Bochers " (Coll. Arms ; Vincent, " Two Ears of Wheat " *c.* 1530)

The Company's motto is taken from Psalms viii. 6–7 : " Thou hast put all things under his feet, all sheep and oxen . . ." The pole-axe and the Psalmist's praise associate rather oddly as allusions to the butcher's trade.

The supporters, although for long adopted by the Company, received no formal grant until 28th June 1922.

A possible earlier grant of the Butchers is given in an interesting entry, of the time of Henry VIII, in an unofficial volume in the College of Arms.   This is Vincent's Collection in which, under the reference " Two Ears of Wheat " and folio reference K, appears arms for " The Bochers ".   The arms there shown are : Azure two poleaxes in saltire, blades outwards, or, between four roses argent.

[1] John (C. A.), *British Trees* (n. d.), p. 119.

THE WORSHIPFUL COMPANY OF CARMEN

CARMEN plied for hire for the transport of goods both within the City and to distant towns. Less acceptable tasks were the compulsory cartage at low rates for the Court whenever required and the disposal of refuse. Regulation of these duties was effected by the City authorities until the founding in 1517 of a Fraternity of St. Katherine. This body entered into an agreement with the mayor and aldermen to govern the carmen's trade, and in 1528 ordinances were granted which extended its authority over the owners of wood wharves and carriers of timber. The woodmongers, whose major occupation was the supply of fuel, were far more numerous than the carmen and soon dominated the fraternity. Undue subordination was avoided by the transference of the licensing of carts for hire to the Governors of Christ's Hospital to whom the proceeds were a welcome income for the relief of the poor children in their care. On 29th August 1605 the Woodmongers, by a royal charter, once again secured control over the Carmen. A bitter dispute between the two bodies persisted throughout the Stuart period until in 1665 car licensing was again placed under the rule of Christ's Hospital, whose Governors remained responsible for licences until 1838. In that year the Company of Carmen became answerable directly to the civic authority, and the Keeper of Guildhall still conducts an annual scaling of carts plying for hire within the City.

On 15th July 1946 the Company was granted its first charter.

THE ARMORIAL BEARINGS (Pl. 9)

Or a sword erect point upwards in pale proper Pomel [*sic*] and Hilt Gules between two Cart Wheels in fesse of the last.

Crest : On a Wreath of the Colours a demi Cart Horse Argent collared Sable resting the sinister hoof on a wheel as in the Arms.

Mantling : Gules doubled or.

Motto : Scite, cito, certe.

> Granted[1] by Sir Henry Farnham Burke,
> Garter
> Arthur William Steuart Cochrane,
> Clarenceux
> Gerald Woods Wollaston,
> Norroy
> 28th February 1929

[1] Original deposited in Guildhall Library, MS. 4924.

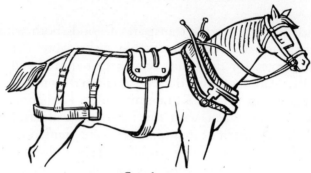

Cart harness

Supporters : On either side a Dray Horse Argent harnessed and bridled proper gorged with a wreath of Roses Gules barbed seeded and leaved also proper.

Granted[1] by Sir Gerald Woods Wollaston, Garter
7th April 1938

The above blazon has been transcribed from the original grants of 1929 and 1938. Before 1929 the arms of the City of London are frequently found upon publications of the Company, but no arms peculiar to the Carmen appear ever to have been adopted.

During the period of 1605 to 1668, when the Company was united with the Woodmongers, the joint Company had borne the following coat which was granted by William Camden, Clarenceux, on 1st October 1605 : [2]

Gules a sword erect argent, hilt and pommel or, enfiled with a ducal coronet of the last, between two flanches argent charged with a faggot proper.
  Crest : A mount vert, thereon a grove of trees all proper, a lion issuing from the grove or.
  Supporters : Two human figures, the dexter representing St. John the Baptist, vested with a short coat of camel's hair belted round the waist, holding in his dexter hand an open book on which are the following words : *The axe is laid to the roote of ye tree,* all proper, his arms and legs naked, round his head a circle of glory; the sinister a female figure representing St. Katherine, vested and habited all proper, on her head an eastern crown or, resting her sinister hand on a wheel of her martyrdom of the last.

In these arms the sword and the figure of St. Katherine represent the

[1] Original in Guildhall Library, MS. 4925.
[2] Welch (C.), *Coat-armour of the London Livery Companies* (1914), p. 32.

MY TRUST IS IN GOD ALONE

Pl. 10   D.38

CLOTHWORKERS, p. 45

Carmen whose corporate life began in 1517 as a Fraternity of St. Katherine. Her martyrdom on the wheel and final death by the sword explain Camden's use of these emblems. It may well be that the symbol of the wheel as alluding to the carman's activities was responsible in the first place for the adoption of St. Katherine as the Company's patron saint. It is clear from the current patent that the wheel, which is therein described as a cart wheel, has now no religious significance attached to it. Whether the present sword is intended as an allusion to St. Katherine is not so clear, for the former use by the Company of the City's arms upon its official publications may equally well account for its introduction into the arms.

THE WORSHIPFUL COMPANY OF CARPENTERS

THE religious and charitable preoccupation of the ancient City guilds is well illustrated by a surviving book of ordinances of the Carpenters' Company. Bearing the date 1st September 1333, these ordinances are solely concerned with the mutual assistance of members of the brotherhood in poverty, sickness and death, and with their moral and spiritual welfare. No mention occurs therein of the trade.

Ordinances for the conduct of the trade were indeed made, but by the civic authority, for in 1339 a number of carpenters were brought before the Mayor and Aldermen accused of forming a confederacy among men of the trade to prevent non-freemen from accepting work at less than 6*d.* a day.

The carpenter's trade was vital to the medieval City with its predominantly timber and plaster dwellings, and the importance of the brotherhood grew. Ordinances of 1456 gave direct powers to the Carpenters, who had also acquired a hall of their own, and on 7th July 1477 the first of their charters was granted to the Mistery of Freemen of the Carpentry of the City of London.

The demand for fireproof buildings after 1666 no doubt accelerated the decline of the guild's powers, which other economic factors had already affected in common with the guild system as a whole. The Company nevertheless maintained its association with the craft. Through the Building Crafts Training School, which it founded in 1893, and by specific grants and scholarships, it provides instruction in all branches of the building trade.

THE ARMORIAL BEARINGS (Pl. 13)

Argent a chevron engrailed between three pairs of compasses sable.
Motto : Honour God.

Granted by William Hawkeslowe,
Clarenceux
24th November 1466

After the engraving on the Company's seal

The blazon given in the original patent[1] reads as follows: "A felde Silver a Cheveron sable grayled iii Compas of the same."

The arms have no crest or supporters, although both on the Company's common seal, which the accounts record as being paid for in 1478, and in a sixteenth century manuscript in the British Museum,[2] two naked boys are depicted in the form of supporters. These have, however, no authority and have not been otherwise in use. They were possibly intended as cherubs which were common decorative features of carpenters' work in church art. Similar supporters, also unofficial, were adopted by the Company of Joiners.

Compasses are included in the arms as instruments of the carpenter's craft, and the chevron may also be an allusion to his trade. Normally

---

[1] Deposited in the Guildhall Library, MS. 8353. There is a coloured facsimile in the *Catalogue of the antiquities and works of art exhibited at Ironmongers' Hall*, (1869), facing p. 264.
[2] Harl. MS. 472.

in heraldry the chevron is merely a decorative device without significance, but since *chevron* is the French term for rafter, or roof support, one of the products of the carpenter, it was probably in this instance introduced with intent. A similar, though more remote, allusive use of the chevron is to be seen in the arms of the Cordwainers' Company.

A version of the Carpenters' Arms (Coll. Arms Vincent, " Two Ears of Wheat," *c.* 1530)

Vulnerati · non · victi

SURGIT · POST · NUBILA · PHOEBUS

Pl. 11

COOKS, p. 52
COACHMAKERS, p. 50

THE WORSHIPFUL COMPANY OF CLOCKMAKERS

THE Clockmakers' Company as an independent body is of recent origin, but the clockmaker's art is of greater antiquity and was formerly carried on under the supervision of the Company of Blacksmiths. While simple iron clocks were confined to those for public edifices, the craft was a minor one, but when portable clocks and watches became of common use, the increasing number of those who made them acquired a sense of their corporate identity. Discontent with their subordinate position within the Blacksmiths' Company led those freemen who practised clockmaking to seek a charter. This was granted on 22nd August 1631 and gave the Company full control of the trade in the City and within ten miles therefrom. These powers are now no longer exercised.

THE ARMORIAL BEARINGS (Pl. 9)

Sable, a clock, each of the four pillars of the case based on a lion couchant and capped with a globe surmounted by a cross, and on the dome of the case an imperial crown, all or.

Crest : On a wreath of the colours a sphere or.

Mantling : Gules doubled argent.

Supporters : Dexter, a naked old man representing Time, holding a scythe and an hour glass, sinister, the figure of an emperor robed and crowned holding a sceptre, all proper.

Motto : Tempus rerum imperator.

Granted[1] by Sir Edward Walker,
Garter
31st January 1671/2

The painting of the arms in the margin of the original patent shows the crest borne upon a peer's helm. As the practice of differentiating rank by variant forms of helm was systematized in the reign of James I, it might be supposed that such a helm was given as a signal honour to the Company. But no obvious explanation for this distinction has been found and the patent itself is significantly silent on the subject. As in the case of the other three companies having this type of helm,[2]

[1] The original patent is deposited in the Guildhall Library, MS. 3970.
[2] See the Apothecaries, Fishmongers and Goldsmiths.

Armillary sphere according to Ptolemy   Scythe

that of the Clockmakers may also be solely the result of the artist's whim. Nevertheless its appearance in so authoritative a document as the patent of arms is thought to justify its use also in the illustration of the arms that accompanies this text. Only a ruling of the Kings of Arms can settle the Company's claim to this distinction.

The following is a transcript of the original blazon:

Sable, a Clock ye 4 Pillars thereof erected on four Lyons, and on each Capitall a Globe with a Crosse, and in the Middest an Imperiall Crowne all or, and for their Crest upon an Helmet Proper Mantled Gules Doubled Argent and Wreath of their colours a Spheare Or, The Armes Supported by the Figures of a Naked Old Man holding a Scithe and an Hour Glass representing Time, and of an Emperour in Roabes Crowned, holding a Scepter Their motto Tempus rerum Imperator.

THE WORSHIPFUL COMPANY OF CLOTHWORKERS

ON a joint petition of the misteries of Fullers and Shearmen, Henry VIII granted a charter, dated 18th January 1527/8, incorporating the two fraternities in one body as the Master, Wardens and Commonalty of Clothworkers in the City of London. Fullers and shearmen were two specialist crafts of the highly organized and complex industry of clothmaking. After the weaver had produced the raw cloth it was subjected to a process of cleansing and thickening, or fulling. This was effected by trampling the cloth in water, cleansing with grease-absorbent fuller's earth, and scouring with teasel, or thistle heads to remove loose particles and raise a nap. The material then was passed to the shearman who cut the raised fibres to produce a fine, even finish to its surface.

The fullers were organized as a craft as early as 1298, when, in association with the dyers, they promoted an ordinance for the regulation of the trade. On 28th April 1480 the Fullers were incorporated by royal charter.

Records of an association of shearmen are later than those of the fullers, and from ordinances of 1350 it appears that, although the shearmen had existed as a craft, they had not until then achieved any formal organization. After a period of rule by ordinances sanctioned by the mayor and aldermen, they acquired the status of a corporate body by royal charter dated 24th January 1507/8.

The united Company exercised the powers granted by its charter of 1528 until the middle of the eighteenth century, by which time the national economy had outgrown the guild system. The subsequent removal of the London cloth industry did not terminate the Company's interest in the trade, for the Clothworkers have fostered the northern cloth industry by substantial educational endowments and grants for technical research.

THE ARMORIAL BEARINGS (Pl. 10)

Sable a chevron ermine between in chief two havettes argent and in base a teasel cob or.

> Granted[1] by Thomas Benolt,
> Clarenceux
> 1530 (22 Hen. VIII)

Crest : On a wreath argent and sable a mount vert, thereon a ram statant or.
Mantling : Sable doubled argent.
Supporters : On either side a griffin or pellety.

> Granted[2] by Robert Cooke,
> Clarenceux
> 25th March 1587

Motto : My trust is in God alone.

Thomas Benolt states in his patent of arms :

Be it knowen that I the said Clarencieux Kyng at armes aforesaid consideryng that where as the occupacion, as well Sheremen as fullers of this honorable Citie of London, be now . . . united adjoyned and corporated in one holle compeny, now named and called the occupacion crafte and mystery of Clotheworkers do assign unto that Company Sable a cheveron ermynee, between two havettes i' the fece silver and a tasell cob in the poynt golde.

Teasing cloth

[1, 2] Original grants in the possession of the Company. Full transcripts are given in *Misc. Gen. et Heraldica*, vol. II (1876), pp. 173–5. The contemporary record of the 1530 grant in the College of Arms (Coll. Arms MS. L.6/17) is reproduced in colour in the *Heralds' Commemorative Catalogue* (1936), pl. 32.

LOVE AS BRETHREN

SPES NOSTRA DEUS

Pl. 12   E.47

COOPERS, p. 55
CURRIERS, p. 62

The Fullers and the Shearmen were incorporated as the Company of Clothworkers in 1528, and in devising their joint arms, Benolt has used features from the arms of both the older companies. They bore respectively " azure a fesse ermine between six teasel cobs or ",[1] and

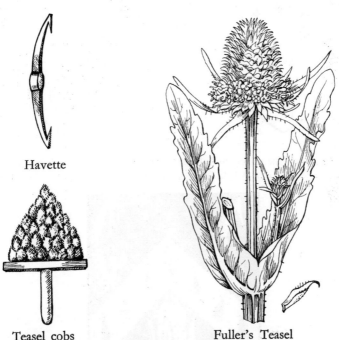

Havette

Teasel cobs   Fuller's Teasel

" azure a chevron ermine between three havettes argent ",[2] the teasels and the havettes indicating the different activities of each craft. The fuller occupied himself in cleansing, scouring and thickening, or fulling, the cloth, using in the process the heads of the teasel plant to comb out and remove all loose particles of wool ; the shearman's task was to finish the cloth, levelling or shearing the nap with shears. The shearing process involved stretching and securing the material upon a padded bench with the aid of the havette which was a form of double-ended hook.[3] Since the end of the seventeenth century the word *havette* appears in blazons of the Company's arms as *habick*, and its

---

[1] Coll. Arms MS. Vincent, " Two Ears of Wheat ", p. K (*temp.* 1530).
[2] ibid.
[3] An excellent engraving of this tool is found in Diderot : *Encyclopédie—planches* (1763), s. v. *Draperie*, pl. VIII, no. 33–4.

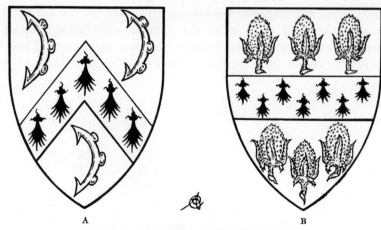

A. and B. Arms of Shearmen and Fullers respectively before their union in 1510 as the Clothworkers (Coll. Arms; Vincent, " Two Ears of Wheat ")

Arms from the 1530 grant

meaning and etymology have been a puzzle to the lexicographer.[1] Its original form, however, shows it to be derived from the French word *havet* which still has in some trades the technical meaning of hook, but formerly was equivalent to *crochet*,[2] the French clothworker's name for his English counterpart's *havette* or *habick*.[3] Since the form *habick* is an obscurity and may well be a phonetic corruption or a textual

[1] Cp. *N.E.D.* s.v. *Habick*.
[2] See the dictionaries of Littré and Hatzfeld and Darmesteter.
[3] Diderot: *Encyclopédie*, vol. 9 (1765), art. *Laine*, p. 193.

misreading, it seems desirable to abandon it in the blazon and restore the original spelling.

The blazon of the crest and supporters in the original patent reads as follows :

> Upon the healme on a wreathe Silver and Sables on a mounte vert a Rame gold the supporters two Griffens gold pelletye, mantled Sables doubled Silver.

In the margin of the patent is a full exemplification of the arms which introduces a minor modification in the tinctures of the teasel by colouring the stalk and leaves vert ; in the 1530 patent the teasel is wholly or. There is no other record of this change and it is probably no more than the whim of the artist.

In using a ram for the crest there is possibly more significance than the relationship to the source of wool. *Rame* is in French the technical name for the clothworker's stretching-frame, or tenter, and the word has been, in the past, adopted in English[1] to mean a frame, or as a verb, to stretch. Thus, the herald in choosing a ram, or as it is spelled in the patent, rame, may well have been consciously employing allusive heraldry.

[1] Halliwell (J. O.), *Dictionary of Archaic and Provincial Words*, 2 vols. (1872).

THE WORSHIPFUL COMPANY OF COACHMAKERS AND COACH HARNESS-MAKERS

By the nature of its craft the Coachmakers' Company is of comparatively recent origin. Its beginnings are found in 1631 when the coachmakers and wheelwrights of the City addressed a joint petition to the Court of Aldermen emphasizing the advantages to the trade of incorporation. It appears that the intention was to incorporate a company of coachmakers and wheelwrights. Although general approval was given by the aldermen, subject to conditions that would prevent interference with the existing rights of members of other companies, the scheme bore no immediate fruit. The Wheelwrights, however, pressed their own case, achieving a charter in 1670, while the coachmakers were compelled to wait until 31st May 1677 before acquiring the desired status of a chartered company.

THE ARMORIAL BEARINGS (Pl. 11)

Azure a chevron between three coaches or.

Crest : Upon a wreath of the colours Phoebus in his glory sitting in a chariot or, drawn through a cloud proper by four horses argent, housed, reined and bridled or.

Mantling : Gules doubled argent.

Supporters : On either side a horse argent, bridled and harnessed sable, the harness studded or, garnished gules and housed azure with fringe and porfling or, adorned with a plume of feathers or, azure, argent and gules.

Motto : Surgit post nubila Phoebus.

Granted[1] by Sir William Dugdale,
Garter
Sir Henry St. George,
Norroy
17th July 1677

The original wording of the grant gives the blazon as follows :

Azure a Cheveron betwixt three Coaches Or : For their Crest, upon a wreath of their colours, A Phoebus in his glory sitting in a Chariot Or, drawn through a cloud proper by four horses Argent, housed, reined and

---

[1] The original patent of arms is deposited in Guildhall Library : MS. 6237.

Coach harness

brideled Or: and for the Supporters Two horses Argent, brideled and
harnessed sable, the harness studded Or, garnished Gules, and housed
Azure, with fringe and purfling Or, adorned with plumes of feathers Or,
Azure, Argent and Gules, And this motto at the bottom of the Shield
Surgit post nubila Phoebus.

In spite of the obvious classical allusion in the blazon, the motto
itself appears to have no earlier traceable origin than a medieval Latin
proverb dating from about the twelfth century.[1]

The Lord Mayor's State Coach, A.D. 1757

---

[1] See Stevenson's *Book of Proverbs* (1949), p. 2244, no. 7.

THE WORSHIPFUL COMPANY OF COOKS

SOME confusion exists as to the early functions of the Cooks, the Pastelers, and the Pie-Bakers, each of which appears to have existed formerly as a separate mistery with its own master and ordinances. Regulations of 1379 and again of 1388, forbidding pastelers to buy " garbage " (probably offal) from cooks for the purpose of making pasties, indicates that the pastelers' trade was concerned with the manufacture of meat pies ; the name of pasteler suggests that it was in fact confined to this activity, an assumption which is supported by numerous other references to pie baking in the City records. The Cook's trade was presumably of a wider nature. By the end of the fifteenth century the terms of Cook and Pasteler seem to have been used indiscriminately. As no formal act of union is known, it may be that the pastelers and piebakers, neither of which emerged as a separate body much beyond the fifteenth century, were absorbed by natural process by the Cooks who survived to acquire their first charter on 11th July 1482. This was succeeded by later charters, culminating in an *inspeximus* of 1817, which, although legally operative, now no longer functions with regard to the trade, being inapplicable to a modern economy.

THE ARMORIAL BEARINGS (Pl. 11)

Argent a chevron engrailed sable between three columbine flowers azure.
Granted by William Hawkeslowe,
Clarenceux
13th October 1467[1]

Crest : On a wreath of the colours a mount vert thereon a cock pheasant proper.

Mantling : Gules doubled argent.

Supporters : Dexter a buck, sinister a doe, both proper.
Granted by William Camden,
Clarenceux
1st August 1614[2]

Motto : Vulnerati non victi.

---

[1] *Visitation of London, 1687* : Coll. Arms MS. K.9/442.   [2] ibid.

The first grant of arms was made by John Wrexworth, Guyenne King of Arms, on 31st May 1461. The patent is not now in the Company's archives but was extant in 1687 when it was produced at the visitation of that year. According to the record of this visitation the arms then were " Argt. 3 Cullambines flowers azure ".[1] In a full copy of the text of Wrexworth's grant the blazon appears as " Silver iii columbynes floures asure ".[2]

A grant by Guyenne King of Arms in Clarenceux's province was presumably regarded by Hawkeslowe as *ultra vires* since it is not even mentioned in the latter's own patent of 1467. This patent also was exhibited at the 1687 visitation and its blazon is quoted therein as " Silver a cheveroun sable engrayled, 3 Columbynes aseer ".

Common Columbine
(*Aquilegia vulgaris*)

The engrailed chevron sable of Hawkeslowe's grant became in later years corrupted to gules. The reason for this unauthorized change has not been discovered but it appears that the alteration occurred between the years 1750 and 1780: up to and including the blazon shown in *The Citizen's Companion*, published *c.* 1750, the chevron is recorded as sable but Edmondson in his *Complete Body of Heraldry*, 1780, gives the tincture as gules, and thereafter the error is continued. At the time of writing the Company has decided to revert to the orthodox colour.

Camden's blazon of the crest and supporters, as quoted in the 1687 visitation, was " A phesant standing on a mount vert Manteled gules doubled Argent " and " A buck and a doe proper each transfixed with an arrow ". The supporters were however modified on the authority of the 1634 visitation by the omission of the arrows, and both the 1634 and 1687 visitations bear the note " the arrows left out of the supporters ".[3]

Columbine flowers as charges do not immediately suggest any connection with cooking, but it is probable that the flowers represent one of the three forms of ginger which were much used for culinary

[1] ibid.   [2] Coll. Arms MS. Philipot's *Stemmata Annulet* ff. 1–1b.
[3] Coll. Arms MSS. 2nd C.24/208–9 (1634); K.9/442 (1687).

and especially preservative purposes. This variety of ginger was known as colambyne, columbyne or other phonetic variant, deriving its name from Colombo, the country of its origin.[1] Whether the adoption of the *aquilegia* was a deliberate piece of canting heraldry or was due to ignorance of natural history can only be a matter for speculation.

An alternative theory has been advanced which is based on supposed herbal virtues of the columbine. Guillim[2] says of this plant that it is " holden to be very medicinable for dissolving of impostumations and swellings in the throat ". This has led to the suggestion that the flowers may have been put into the Cooks' arms as a kind of talisman against the consequences of members of the Company preparing food that might provoke such throatly impostumations. Gerard,[3] too, records this property of the columbine, though with reserve, and adds that it is also reported to be useful in restoring a disordered liver. It might, therefore, serve as a charm to avert this disaster as well. This is a pleasant conceit and may well be the true explanation ; such fanciful origins are not inconsistent with the playful spirit of early heraldry.[4]

[1] The derivation of this word is fully discussed in *Ginger ; a loan-word study* by Prof. A S. C. Ross (1952).
[2] Guillim (J.), *Display of Heraldry* (1610), p. 116.
[3] Gerard (J.), *Herbal* (1633), p. 1095.
[4] I have to thank Mr. A. Colin Cole, F.S.A., for making this suggestion.

Pl. 13   E.54

CORDWAINERS, p. 59

CARPENTERS, p. 40   FRUITERERS, p. 105

FANMAKERS, p. 82

THE WORSHIPFUL COMPANY OF COOPERS

COOPERS are makers of wooden casks and similar utensils such as wooden buckets, made from wooden staves held together by iron hoops. Until well into the nineteenth century barrels were commonly used for the storage of many commodities, especially of food and drink. Only ale and wine are now thus stored, and working coopers are mostly employed in breweries.

In London, Coopers first appear as an organized fraternity in 1396, when ordinances were approved for the prevention of oil and soap barrels being sold for the use of brewers with the consequent contamination of the ale. Overseers also were appointed at this time to regulate the craft. On 29th April 1501 the Company received its first royal charter of incorporation by which it was formed into a perpetual corporation as a fraternity in honour of the Blessed Virgin Mary, who is symbolized by the lilies in the Company's arms. In addition to the powers conferred by its charters, the Company operated under a number of Acts of Parliament, notably in the gauging and sealing, or marking, of casks. While at first a source of income, the duty of sealing became by the end of the eighteenth century a financial burden. The practice was therefore abandoned, and the Company's control of the trade ended. Its charitable and educational activities remain.

The governing charter of the Coopers' Company is that of 30th August 1601.

THE ARMORIAL BEARINGS (Pl. 12)

Gyronny of eight gules and sable, on a chevron between three annulets or a royne between two broad axes azure, a chief vert thereon three lilies argent.

Crest : On a wreath or and azure a demi-heathcock the body azure semee of annulets gold the wings argent semee of annulets sable holding in the beak a lily silver slipped and leaved vert, the mantling azure doubled argent.

Supporters : On either side a camel gules semee of annulets bridled or.

Motto : Love as brethren.

Re-exemplification[1] by Sir Alfred Scott Scott-Gatty,
Garter
20th February 1909

---

[1] Deposited in Guildhall Library, MS. 7550.

The warrant for the Coopers' Company to bear arms was made by a grant by Sir Thomas Wriothesley, Garter, and Roger Machado, Clarenceux, on 27th September 1509.[1] The arms then given were " Gowlys and geronney of eight peces. A cheveron betwene three Aneletts golde on the cheveron a Royne betwixt twoo brode axes azur. A chief vert on the chief three lylyes silver." The ancient motto of the Company—*Gaude Maria Virgo*—appears on a label beneath the arms as drawn in the margin of the grant, and the crest, although not referred to in the blazon itself, is illustrated in the opposite margin.

Supporters were added in 1574[2] by Robert Cooke, Clarenceux, which were " Two Camells gules, semy annelets the brydells gold."

In 1909, at the Company's request, Garter King of Arms re-exemplified the arms as shown above.

Two of the cooper's tools are represented in the arms, namely the royne and broad-axe, while it is possible that the annulets were introduced as symbolic of the hoops of a cask. From the drawing in the exemplification of 1509 and from a larger drawing of the royne which forms part of the decorative border, it is clear that this implement is a form of the present-day croze with which the cooper makes the grooves

Cooper using the croze or royne to cut the groove in the barrel

---

[1] Original deposited in Guildhall Library, MS. 5806. Full transcript in *Catalogue of antiquities exhibited at Ironmongers' Hall, 1861*, London (1869), vol. 1, p. 273.

[2] Grant not now extant.

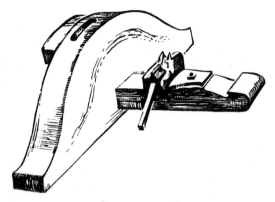

Croze or royne

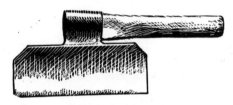

Broad axe used for chopping the staves

in the ends of the staves to receive the heads, or covers, for his casks. Holme calls it a " drawing board " and describes it as " a half round board near an inch in thickness with a square piece of timber fixed in the middle of it, which is to move up and down as occasion serveth ; in this square piece is the drawing iron fixed. This may be termed the cooper's grooping tool." [1] The term " royne " is derived from the French *rogner* : to cut.

When the original motto was changed to that in use today cannot be determined, but it is probable that so obvious a reference to the Company's patron saint was discreetly suppressed during the Reformation. The phrase appears to be taken from an antiphon to the Psalms in the third nocturne of matins of the office of Our Lady. It also occurs in the tract said (or sung) after the Epistle for Holy Saturday. When the full context—*Gaude, Maria Virgo : cunctas haeres sola interemisti*[2]

[1] *Academy of Armory* (1688), bk. III, p. 318.
[2] Rejoice, O Virgin Mary ; thou alone has brought all heresy to nought.

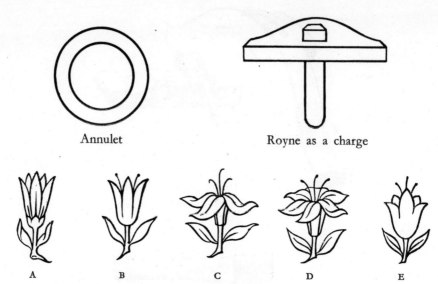

Annulet   Royne as a charge

A   B   C   D   E

Variety of lilies slipped and leaved from Coll. Arms records
A. (Vincent, " Two Ears of Wheat".)   B. 1590 charge in the arms.   C. 1590 crest.
D. 1634 arms and crest.   E. 1925 crest.

—is considered, it is not surprising that such a motto would be thought to be tactless at that time.

This ancient motto has been misread by some as *Laude Maria Virgo*[1] but the original grant clearly establishes that the first word is *Gaude*.

[1] e.g. Fox-Davies, *Public Arms* (1915).

POUR · PARVENIR

A · BONNE · FOY

DROP AS RAIN

DISTIL

AS DEW

Pl. 14

E.58

CUTLERS, p. 66
DISTILLERS, p. 69

THE WORSHIPFUL COMPANY OF CORDWAINERS

CORDWAINERS were makers of boots and shoes, the finest of which were produced from goatskin of Cordova thus giving to the craft the name of Cordovaners, or cordwainers.

The organization of the leather workers in London was highly complex, with numerous separate misteries dealing with particular aspects of the trade. From the thirteenth century onwards, ordinances and acts were made which attempted to define the limits of crafts such as curriers, tanners, cobblers and cordwainers. The earliest of these ordinances directly dealing with the Cordwainers are dated 1271/2. They appointed twelve men as wardens of the craft to ensure that the regulations for the conduct of the respective trades of curriers and tanners as well as those of the dominant craft of Cordwainers, were faithfully kept. Further ordinances and regulations were made from time to time to strengthen the power of the craft and to resolve conflicts which were especially persistent with the cobblers. Cobblers differed from cordwainers in that they sold old shoes which they had repaired. The extent to which new leather was used in the process of repairing was of great concern to the Cordwainers lest the old shoes might in effect become new shoes and so infringe the prerogative of their own craft.

On 26th April 1439, Henry VI granted a charter of incorporation to the freemen of the Mistery of Cordwainers which gave to the Company control over the trade in new shoes and tanned leather throughout the City and within two miles thereof. This was succeeded by additional charters, culminating in that of 1685.

The powers of the Cordwainers' Company were effective for longer than most of the other City guilds, being continued into the nineteenth century with special powers under Act of Parliament. The Company is now prominent in furthering technical education in the craft as a whole.

THE ARMORIAL BEARINGS (Pl. 13)

Azure a chevron or between three goats' heads erased argent horned and bearded or.

Crest : On a wreath or and azure a goat's head erased argent the erasures gules, the horns wreathed or and azure.

Mantling : Gules doubled argent.

Granted[1] by Robert Cooke,
Clarenceux
25th June 1579

Motto : Corio et arte.

The original blazon reads as follows :

asur a cheveron gold betwen thre Goates heads rased silver horned and bearded of the cheveron and to the creast uppon the healme on a wreathe golde and asure a Goates heade rased silver the rasures gules, the hornes wreathed golde and asur Manteled gules dobled silver.

Evidence of the use of these arms by the Cordwainers before their grant of 1579 is provided by a document among the Company's archives.

Crest

In a MS. volume[2] entitled *Booke of Charters and Grants made by the Prince* . . . , is an exemplification of coat armour finely executed in colour ; no crest is shown but the arms are otherwise similar to those of the grant. Below the arms are the names of the master and three wardens who together served office in the fourteenth year of Elizabeth I's reign (1571/2). The names are enclosed in a decorative label forming part of the ornamental border of the arms, and are written in a hand contemporary with the document. Another example of the pre-grant arms is given in the *Breffe description of the royall Citie of London*, written by William Smith in 1575.[3]

The goats as charges refer to the source of the original skins with which the cordwainer worked. These skins were brought from Cordova in Spain whence the term cordwainer is derived ; the Company is, in fact, designated " Cordovaners " in the grant.

---

[1] Deposited in the Guildhall Library, MS. 7527. For transcript see *Misc. Gen. et Heraldica*, vol. I, p. 242.

[2] Guild. Lib. MS. 8033.   [3] Guild. Lib. MS. 2463.

The use of the chevron is so common a feature in coats of arms that its presence may generally pass unremarked. In the case of the Cordwainers' arms, however, it is possible to see in the chevron a direct allusion to the goat, from whose Latin root, *caper*, comes the French word *chevron* with its primary meaning of " rafter ", the V-shaped roof support.

THE WORSHIPFUL COMPANY OF CURRIERS

THE term "currier" is derived from the medieval Latin *coriarius*, a worker in leather (*corium*, skin, hide). Currying leather was the process of rendering tanned skins suitable for making up into finished leather goods, and involved stretching and shaving to a smooth finish with the shaving knife which is featured in the Curriers' arms.

Originally the London curriers formed part of the Cordwainers' guild, but separation was foreshadowed by a civic ordinance of 1272, which ordained that cordwainers, tanners and curriers should in future have separate working regulations. Although the Curriers appear soon after as a separate mistery, general control of the trade seems to have remained in the hands of the Cordwainers. Full self-government was achieved with the approval of ordinances in 1415. Confirmation and extension of their powers was made by an Act of 1516, and a royal licence in the following year, and on 30th April 1606 the Company's first charter was received.

THE ARMORIAL BEARINGS (Pl. 12)

Azure a cross engrailed or between four pairs of shaves in saltire argent handled or.

Crest : On a wreath or and azure out of the clouds proper two arms embowed carnation, the shirt sleeves folded beneath the elbows argent, in the hands a shave argent handled or.

Mantling : Gules doubled argent.

Supporters : Dexter, an elk proper attired and unguled or; sinister, a goat argent flashed sable.

> Grant by Robert Cooke,
> Clarenceux
> 8th August 1583

Motto : Spes nostra Deus.

Although the original patent of arms was known to have been in the possession of the Company in 1914,[1] it appears now to be lost. Partial transcripts which exist[2] are in agreement with records in the

---

[1] Welch, *Coat Armour of the London Livery Companies* (1914), p. 8.
[2] Welch and Burkitt, *Short History of the Curriers*, 2nd. ed. (1923), p. 11.

UNTO GOD ONLY BE HONOR AND GLORY

Pl. 15

F.63

DRAPERS, p. 72

College of Arms except in one particular, namely, the colour of the shirt sleeves on which the transcripts are silent. An examination of the early records discloses that the colour is argent and an official blazon of the time of Elizabeth I reads as follows :

Azure a cross engrayled gold betwene eighte shaving knyves in saulter silver the handelles golde the Creaste on a wreath gold and azur out of the Clowdes proper tow Armes Carnat with the shirt sleves folden beneath the elbow silver, in the handes a shaving knyfe silver handell gold supported on the right side with a Elke proper the hornes and howfes gold and one the other side with a gote silver flashed sables.[1]

The currier's shaving knife shown on the shield is more often than not depicted, in representations of the arms, with a cross-piece attached to each of the handles. This can only be attributed to a desire for artistic symmetry which has on occasion further corrupted the handles by giving them trefoil-like endings or forming them into ornamental crosses. In fact, the true currier's knife, which is used as a form of plane or spokeshave to pare the skins after their initial treatment by the tanner or tawer, has a cross-piece only on one of the two handles and is so shown on the common seal of the Company, made in 1606 and now in Guildhall Museum.

To prepare his knife the currier, having ground the blade to a fine edge, places the cross-piece firmly between his knees and, while kneeling and with the straight handle resting upon the ground, turns the edges with a steel so that they are at right angles to the plane of the blade. With the edges so formed he is able to shave hides and skins, which rest upon a flat surface (his " beam-board "), to a uniform thickness.

Among the finer skins processed by the currier of old were buffe and cordwain, or cordovan, leather. These are represented in the supporters by the elk and the goat respectively.

In the course of the preamble to the grant of arms, it is stated that the Company is an incorporated body desiring to use a common seal bearing a properly assigned coat of arms. The actual words are as follows :

The Companie of Curriours of the Cittie of London are incorporated by the name of the Wardens and Commonaltie and that they shoulde have a perpetuall succession and one Comon Seale for the necessary busynes of the said Companie and they have requiered me the said Clarencioulx to

---

[1] Coll. Arms MS. R.21/39.

assigne unto them suche Armes Crest and Supporters as they may use in theire Comon Seale and otherwaies att their libertie and pleasure . . .

It would appear from this that a charter of incorporation had ante-dated the coat of arms. In fact, no charter is known before that of 30th April 1606, and no reference is made therein to any earlier charter. The explanation can only be that the Curriers' Company was regarded as a corporation by prescription, that is to say, a company that had

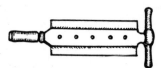

Currier's knife or shave

Leather shaver at work on a skin

Crest

existed so long that the law would presume that it had from the Crown a grant or charter of incorporation which had been lost.[1] The tradition of an earlier charter, before the first known one, which survives among some City companies, is explicable in this way.

Incorporation, however achieved, entitles a number of persons to hold land without the intermediary of trustees and otherwise to act as a legal *persona*, distinct from its members. The possession of a

[1] This legal presumption was recognized in 1615 by Chief Justice Coke, when he stated that a corporation must be created either by the common law, by Act of Parliament, by royal charter or by prescription (cf. 10 Coke Rept. f. 29b. and Holds-worth, *History of English Law*, IX, 46).

common seal is a vital incident of corporate existence and, although there is no necessity that this should be armorial, in the case of corporations of sufficient stature it is often their desire that a grant of arms should follow incorporation. The practice of the Kings of Arms is —and was, as the grant to the Curriers shows—to recite the fact of incorporation and, in modern phraseology, to grant arms to be borne and used " upon Seals, Shields or otherwise according to the laws of arms ".

THE WORSHIPFUL COMPANY OF CUTLERS

THE cutlery trade of the Middle Ages included the making of swords, daggers and knives of all kinds. Originally it was a highly specialized industry, comprising the separate trades of hafters who made handles or hafts, bladesmiths and sheathers, with the cutlers acting as assemblers and salesmen. Both hafters and sheathers were ultimately merged in the Cutlers' Company, while the bladesmiths were first united with the Company of Armourers, and then allowed by a decision of the Court of Aldermen of 1518 to " depart unto the fellowship of Cutlers " at will.

The first direct mention of an organized craft of Cutlers occurs in 1328 when seven cutlers were elected to govern the craft and search for false work. On 4th December 1416 the fellowship became an incorporated company by royal charter.

The Company's powers of control of the trade have long since fallen into disuse. An attempt to stem the increasing invasion of the craft by non-freemen was made in 1756 by the passing of an act of Common Council which forbade all but members of the Company to be employed as cutlers. Such restraint was later recognized as inapplicable in a changed economy, and the act was repealed in 1838 at the instance of the Company itself on the grounds that it had ceased to be of benefit to the trade.

THE ARMORIAL BEARINGS (Pl. 14)

Gules three pairs of swords in saltire argent hilts and pommels or.

Crest : On a wreath of the colours an elephant argent armed and harnessed or, bearing on its back a castle or thereon two pennons displayed, the dexter argent a cross gules, the sinister a pennon of the arms of the Cutlers' Company.

Supporters : Two elephants argent armed or.

Motto : *Pour parvenir a bonne foy.*

> Granted by Sir William Segar,
> Garter
> 10th May 1622

The former arms of the Company, granted by Thomas Holme, Clarenceux, on 7th May 1476, differed from their successors only in the

Crest, A.D. 1476 (Coll. Arms 1st H.7 fo. 59b)

absence of supporters and by the use of a variant crest which was an elephant's head couped gules armed or. These arms were confirmed by Thomas Benolt, Clarenceux, on 12th October 1530, and by Robert Cooke, Clarenceux, on 22nd October 1590. "Last of all, Sir Wm.

Crest, A.D. 1622 (Coll. Arms 2nd C.24 fo. 199)

Segar Kt., Garter, being a brother of that Company, doth not only confirme the said Coate and alter the Creaſt, but addeth thereunto Supporters . . ." [1]

The adoption of the elephant as the device of the Cutlers antedates their earlieſt grant for it is recorded that, at the City's welcome to Queen Margaret on her marriage to Henry VI in 1445, those of the Company at their " riding " wore elephants as decorations upon their coats or shields.[2] The elephant may have represented the ivory used by the craft for the hafts of products.

A fifteenth century seal, probably ſtruck soon after the 1476 grant of arms, is ſtill in the possession of the Company. It depiĉts the early arms and bears the inscription *"Pervenir a bonne foy "*.

Neither of the original patents of arms has survived.

[1] Coll. Arms 2nd C.24 (199).
[2] Welch (C.), *History of the Cutlers' Company*, (1916), vol. 1, p. 139.

THE WORSHIPFUL COMPANY OF DISTILLERS

BEFORE the grant of a charter to the Distillers' Company on 9th August 1638, members of the trade were not organized in a single mistery but pursued their craft in London through the freedom of other companies. Reference to this is made in a series of forceful letters from Charles I to the Lord Mayor. The letters were induced by the refusal of the Court of Aldermen to enrol the new charter on the grounds that it would weaken other companies of which distillers were then members. Even threats that failure to comply would be regarded as contempt of the royal command did not move the City, and the charter was not enrolled in the Chamber of London until 17th March 1658. Under its charter the Company was entrusted with the supervision of the trade within the City of London and an area twenty-one miles therefrom. As late as 1774 the Common Council of the City passed an act imposing penalties for trading as a distiller unless free of the Company. Although national laws have now eliminated the local control of the manufacture of spirituous liquors, the Distillers' Company still maintains a close association with the trade.

THE ARMORIAL BEARINGS (Pl. 14)

Azure a fesse wavy of water argent between in chief a sun or drawing up a cloud argent distilling drops of rain proper and in base a distillatory double-armed or with two worms and bolt receivers argent.

Crest : On a wreath argent and azure a garb of barley or wreathed about with a vine branch vert bearing grapes proper.

Mantling : Gules doubled argent.

Supporters : Dexter a Russian and sinister an Indian savage, each in his proper habit.

Motto : Drop as rain, distil as dew.

Granted by Sir John Borough,
Garter
18th March 1638/9

The above description is based upon the blazon given by Welch[1] who states that the " exemplification " was, at the time of his writing,

[1] Welch (C.), *Coat Armour of the London Livery Companies* (1914), p. 8.

69

in the possession of the Company. Whether or not this was the original patent, it appears that it is now lost and no information is available as to its fate. Welch adds to his transcript of the blazon a note on the supporters as he observed them in the " exemplification ". This describes the " Russe " as being habited in a red coat with facings of gold, a blue cloak and a fur cap, while the Indian has wreaths of feathers round his head and waist, a sheaf of arrows at his back and a bow in his left hand.

Records in the College of Arms[1] mainly confirm the accuracy of this blazon but show some variations in the tinctures of the supporters

Sun

Crest

which are given in considerable detail. Further, the garb of barley is tricked in one place as or and in another as proper, and the vine branch similarly appears as vert and proper. In the case of the supporters, the College of Arms records have been preferred in the preparation of the painting of the arms. For the garb of barley and the vine branch, the various tricking is a difference of terminology rather than effect and the terms or and vert have been adopted as being more precise.

It should be mentioned that the date of the grant is given in the records of the College of Arms as simply March 1639 ; the day of the month is not recorded.

A wood-engraving of the arms is included in *The Distiller of London* [anon.], printed in 1639, the year of the grant of arms, and bearing an

---

[1] Misc. Grants IV fo. 8 ; E.D.N.56 fo. 184 ; and Dethick's Gifts fo. 59.

DA GLORIAM DEO

GIVE US OUR DAILY BREAD

Pl. 16   F.70

DYERS, p. 79
FARMERS, p. 84

imprimatur dated 16th November 1639. The title states that the volume was " compiled and set forth by speciall licence . . . for the sole use of the Company of Distillers of London ", and the preface recalls that by its royal charter the Company was required to provide a " Book of rules and directions concerning distillation of strong-waters etc. and making vinegars etc." This book was accordingly issued with the approval of Sir Theodore de Mayerne and Dr. Thomas Cademan who, as founder and master of the Company respectively, subscribe their names. As would be expected from the date and authority of the volume, the engraving and description of the arms give an accurate rendering.

One of the charges illustrates a contemporary distillatory with two spiral condensers (the " worms "), the " bolt receivers " being the globular flasks designed to receive the distillate.

The significance of the supporters is obscure, and the motto has scarcely more obvious relevance to the Company's activities, being adapted from Deuteronomy xxxii, 2,[1] solely on the grounds of the occurrence therein of the word distil. Since the charges so obviously symbolize the distiller's trade, it is possible that the supporters have been also adopted for this purpose ; they are certainly not representative of the more conventional devices used in heraldry. The most likely explanation is that the figures signify those territories from which came some of the raw materials of the trade. The Russian might well have been considered an adequate symbol for the Baltic lands which supplied England at this period with a proportion of her grain, and the Indian possibly represents the spice trade of the Indies upon whose products much of the distilling trade depended. A very comprehensive list of such ingredients is included in the appendix to *The Distiller of London* (1639), referred to above.

[1] " My doctrine shall drop as the rain, my speech shall distil as the dew."

THE WORSHIPFUL COMPANY OF DRAPERS

As in the case of the victualling trades, the primary importance of the cloth trade caused it to develop early into separate crafts or misteries, and the monopoly of the retail sale of cloth was confirmed to the mistery of drapers by a charter of 1364. This was not a charter of incorporation but merely empowered the Mistery of Drapery to govern itself and ordained that none should sell cloth within the City and suburbs of London except drapers free of the said mistery. Functions of the mistery included ensuring the accurate measurement of cloth sold at cloth fairs in London, and the appointment of the keeper of Blackwell Hall which was founded in 1397 as a market for the sale of woollen cloth. On 30th November 1438 the mistery was incorporated as a perpetual community by the name of the Guild or Fraternity of the Blessed Mary of the Drapers of London. The grant of a common seal which was a necessary accompaniment to incorporation led the Company to seek its patent of arms in the following year. A succession of charters down to the reign of James I confirmed the Company's powers.

While retail sale of cloth was originally the predominant interest of members of the guild, the tendency grew, as it did in other leading companies, for the more wealthy members to become general merchants who traded in all kinds of commodities both at home and overseas. By the seventeenth century the company was composed of men of numerous callings, for even among the humbler members there were many who pursued activities other than drapery.

The company now has little direct connection with the drapery trade but devotes considerable sums towards technical and general education. It ranks third in precedence among the Great Twelve livery companies.

THE ARMORIAL BEARINGS (Pl. 15)

Azure three clouds with sunbeams issuing proper crowned with imperial crowns or.

Crest: On a wreath of the colours a mount vert thereon a ram jacent or armed and unguled sable.

Mantling: Gules doubled argent.

Supporters : On either side a lion or pellety.
Motto : Unto God only be honor and glory.

Granted[1] by Sir William Segar,
Garter
6th June 1613

The grant of 1613 supersedes two earlier patents dated 10th March 1438/9[2] and 10th July 1561.[3] The former is not only the earliest grant to a City Company but is moreover the oldest known English patent of arms to survive. This fine document still remains in the custody of the Company and, although the text is mutilated, is a notable example of illumination and heraldic painting. Its significance in the development of modern heraldry has been discussed by a leading authority who comments on the phrasing of this early patent.[4]

Sir William Bruges, first Garter King of Arms, in making the 1439 grant does so in the following terms :

Je lez ay devisez enseigne en forme de blason . . . Cestassavoir en lonneur du tres gloriouse vierge et meer Marie le quel est en oumbre de soleyll et replendisant en tout claritee et nestete leur ay devisez en lour blason troys Royes de soleille issantz hors de troys nues de flambe coronnez de troys corons imperialx dore assisez sus une escue dasure . . . et pour veritablement blasonier le dit armorie Il covient duc Il porte dasure troys soleilles issantz de troys nues de geullez coronnes de troys Imperials corons dore . . .

An exemplification of the arms appears in the upper margin, the shield being supported by two kneeling angels which do not, however, form part of the blazon of the grant.

The phrasing of this patent which has evoked comment is that Garter merely says that he devises an ensign " en forme de blason " ; it is noted that he does not specifically grant arms to the Company. In this wording has been seen the uncertainty of Garter's authority which was not defined by territorial limits as was the case of the jurisdiction of Clarenceux and Norroy.[5] There is the possibility, however,

---

[1] Original in the possession of the Company. The text, with a reduced monochrome facsimile of the patent, appears in Johnson (A. H.), *History of the Draper's Company,* vol. IV (1922), pp. 50–1.

[2] Original with the Company. Text in Johnson, op. cit., vol. I (1914), pp. 221–8. Frontis. of the *de luxe* ed. gives a coloured facsimile of a portion of the patent.

[3] Original with the Company. Text in Johnson, op. cit., vol. II (1915), pp. 421–2.

[4] Wagner (A. R.), *Heralds and Heraldry in the Middle Ages* (1956), p. 75.

[5] ibid. p. 77. John Smert similarly devised one blazon for the Girdlers in 1454, but two years later, in 1456, he devised ordained and assigned arms to the Tallow Chandlers.

that " devise " is here used in the legal connotation of " assign " rather than " invent " or " design ", in which case the patent would assume the normal pattern of grants of arms.[1]

On 10th July 1561 these arms were confirmed by William Hervey, Clarenceux, who added crest and supporters to them. The reason for the confirmation of the arms appears in the patent :

> Wheras the Wourshipfull Companye and Corporacion of the Fellowshipe and Mystery of Drapers . . . had assigned[2] unto them by one Wyllyam Bruges, alias garter kinge of armes one scochin of armes . . . the same beinge thought by somme undiscreat and ignorante persons not to be lawfull armoire. In consideracion wherof [the Master and Wardens] . . . not wyllynge to do anythinge prejudisiall to any decent order . . . requyred me . . . to shew myne opynyon . . . Wheruppon I . . . have perused the same, and further, consyderinge the antyquyte therof, and that the sayde armes cannot convenyentlye be altered nor changid, but to their greate diswourshipe and hinderaunce . . . so that I coulde not, without theyre greate prejudyse, alter or change the same, but accordinge to my calling in offyce, do ratefye and confyrme theyr sayde armes as followeth. That is to saye, azure, thre sunbeames yssuinge owt of thre clowdes gulz, corened with thre Imperiall crownes goulde, which is perfect and good blason. And for a testimonye and further increase of theyr Wourshippes, I have graunted and assigned unto them, for an augmentacion of theyr saide armes, healme, and creaste, with two supporters, as followeth ; that is to saye, uppon the healme, a mounte vert, theron a ramme couchant golde, horned and cleyed sable, on a wrathe argent and sable, mantelled gulz, dobled argent. And for theyr supporters, two lyons golde, spotted sable, armed and langed gulz . . .

Why " undiscreat and ignorante persons " considered the earlier grant not to be " lawfull armoire " is not disclosed. Clarenceux says that the arms are " perfect and good blason", with the possible implication that they had been called in question on technical grounds. But the only detail at which the armorist might cavil was the use of three sunbeams issuing out of three clouds gules on an azure field, i.e. a colour on a colour. It seems improbable that this would have disturbed the Company to the extent of seeking a confirmation ; unless it were, perhaps, that the seeking of crest and supporters was used as

---

[1] Since the above was written, the meaning of the term " devise " in early grants of arms has been exhaustively treated by A. Colin Cole in *The Coat of Arms*, April, July and October, 1957.

[2] It is to be noted that Hervey clearly regarded Smert's patent as a true grant in that he uses the term " assign ".

Pl. 17

LETTERS PATENT OF ARMS TO THE WORSHIPFUL COMPANY OF CLOCKMAKERS, 31ST JANUARY 1671–2, SHOWING A PEER'S HELM IN THE EXEMPLIFICATION

F.74

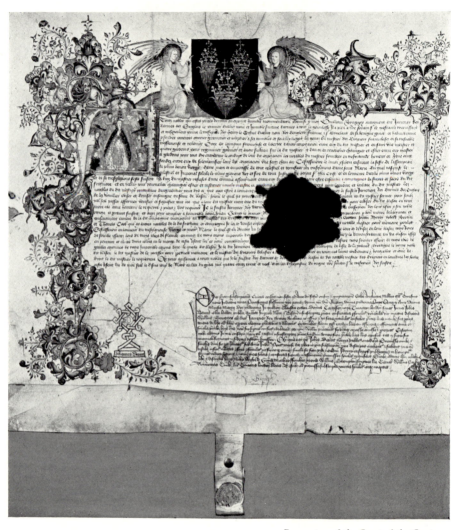

Pl. 18   G.75

LETTERS PATENT GRANTING ARMS TO THE WORSHIPFUL
COMPANY OF DRAPERS, 10TH MARCH 1438–9

Imperial crowns from the painting in the margin of the 1439 grant

an opportunity to settle a point of detail that might well have been an issue of some moment to the formularist devotees of heraldry at this period.

Might the Company's unwillingness to do " anythinge prejudisiall to any decent order " point to an alternative explanation ? During the prolonged period of the English Reformation a number of guilds had discreetly eliminated from their arms any features that could have implicated them as amenable to the papal rule. Among these prudent guilds was the Bakers' Company, whose arms bore the triple crown of the pope ; in 1536 this tiara had been replaced by symbolism less suspect. It is therefore conceivable that exception had been taken on religious grounds to the triple crowns in the Drapers' arms, either in the mistaken assumption that they were papal tiaras, or because they were too symbolic of the worship of the Virgin. Rebellion against Rome's supremacy in things spiritual had had a brief respite under Mary, but the resurgence under Elizabeth was less than three years old when the 1561 confirmation was sought. The City of London in particular suffered from an excess of zeal on the part of Protestant reformers.[1] In this atmosphere the Drapers might with reason have felt sensitive to accusations of retaining symbols in their arms which were interpreted as " prejudisiall to any decent order " at a time when emblems of a like nature were being destroyed. If this were so, it is

[1] On 19th Sept. 1560 a royal proclamation was issued to restrain the destruction of " monumentes of antiquitie " in London.

G

unlikely that William Hervey, whose position was dependent on the patronage of the monarch, would have resisted the criticism solely on the grounds of antiquity and convenience to the Company : " consyderinge the antiquyte therof, and that the sayde armes cannot convenyentlye be altered nor changid, but to their greate diswourshipe and hinderaunce ".   His apology in the patent might, however, be an acknowledgement that a change would be desirable to avoid confusion and misconstruction, but only at the greater inconvenience to the Company.

Bishop kneeling before the Pope (after the woodcut in Turrecremata's
Meditationes, A.D. 1481)

That the crowns are not papal tiaras[1] is established by the illuminated initial with which the 1439 patent begins.   This depicts God the Father and God the Son, each crowned with a triple crown, together similarly crowning the Virgin at her Assumption.   It is evident that the illuminated initial and the crowns of the arms have a common inspiration. The crowned clouds of the arms refer, in fact, to the illuminator's rendering of the Assumption of the Virgin Mary, Queen of Heaven,

[1] Such a mistake is not improbable. A near-contemporary representation of the papal tiara bearing a very close resemblance to the crowns in the Drapers' arms appears in a metal-cut in Turrecremata (J. de), *Meditationes* (1481). Furthermore, about 1530 Thomas Wall described the imperial crown of the Fishmongers' crest as a papal tiara and Wall was Windsor Herald—see chapter on the Fishmongers' Company.

whose triple crown, thrice repeated in the manner conventional to a single charge, is the true motif of the arms.

With such obvious implications, together wth the specific reference in the grant to the founding of the Company " en lonneur du tres gloriouse vierge ", Clarenceux would have had no difficulty in disposing of a charge that the crowns were papal tiaras. But it would have been impossible to deny their allusion to the Virgin Mary. Clarenceux seems to have resolved the conflict between his obvious sympathy with the Drapers' Company and the criticism of " undiscreat and ignorante persons " by eliminating from his new patent to the Company all reference to the latter's being a guild of the Blessed Virgin.

It has been suggested that the crowned clouds of the arms were a mistaken rendering of pyx-canopies in the form of veils, such as were sold by drapers, hanging from triple crowned pyxes ;[1] these, it is assumed, were used as charges in an earlier form of arms adopted by the Company before its grant of arms. But this theory is no more than a speculative attempt to link the arms with the drapers' trade.

The arms of the Company were not finally determined by the confirmation of Clarenceux Hervey, for on the 6th June 1613 another grant was made by William Segar, Garter. The terms of this are interesting and a model of modesty :

> whereas . . . the Guild or fraternity of the blessed Mary the Virgin of the mistery of Drapers of the Citty of London have aunciently had assigned to them by Sir Thomas [sc. William] Burges . . . one escuchion of Armes . . . by the Patent thereof bearing date the Tenth day of Marche . . . 1438 [i.e. 1439 in new style chronology] . . . The which armes also were sithens confirmed and ratified by William Hervey Clarencieulx . . . Anno Dni 1561 with affirmacon of the saide Armory to be lawfull and good . . . Nevertheles, withoute ympeachment to their judgemente, or arrogating to myselfe more knowledge than I can avowe, I . . . have perused, examyned, and corrected the same, and doe fynde that the Blason of the said Armory ought to be as followeth . . . Asure uppon three clowdes proper the sonne beames yssuing three Imperiall crownes gould tripled ; And for their crest upon a Healme forthe of a wreath of their coullers a Mount vert thereon a Ram jacent fleeced gould unarmed[2] and unguled sable . . . Supported by two Leons or, pellated . . .

---

[1] Hope (W. H. St. J.), *Grammar of Heraldry*, 2nd ed. (1953), p. 68. Johnson in his *History of the Drapers* (vol. I, p. 226) also advances this theory.

[2] " Unarmed " is clearly a scribe's error by analogy with the succeeding word " unguled ". It should, of course, be " armed ".

It will be noted that the Drapers' allegiance to the Blessed Virgin is once more admitted, and that the only effect of the new blazon, apart from a change in terminology, is to alter the colour of the clouds from gules to proper, in deference to the convention that a colour may not be placed upon a colour, a rule which Clarenceux had not conceded in 1561.[1]

This blazon of 1613 is that which guides the present arms of the Company.

[1] Since the above was written, a full discussion of the symbolism and iconography of the crowns in the 1439 grant has appeared in *The Coat of Arms* (Jan. 1957), pp. 171–183 ("Heraldry and Iconography", by John A. Goodall).

VI · ET · VIRTUTE

SPEED · STRENGTH · AND · TRUTH · UNITED

Pl. 19   G.79

FARRIERS, p. 86
FRAMEWORK KNITTERS, p. 101

THE WORSHIPFUL COMPANY OF DYERS

DYERS were concerned with the dyeing of leather and cloth for apparel and furnishing hangings.   The craft is mentioned in 1298 in association with the fullers who processed cloth and who later united with the shearmen to form the Clothworkers' Company.   A prominent dye much used by the Dyers was woad.   It was for long a monopoly of the craft and in 1343 the mistery is recorded as being responsible for appointing brokers of this product.   Incorporation of the Dyers as a perpetual guild was effected by royal charter on 16th February 1470/1. The charter constituted the Company as a fraternity to the glory of God and the Blessed Virgin Mary and gave to its members control of the trade within twenty miles of the City.   In 1482 ordinances for the governance of the craft were submitted for the approval of " the right honourable lord the mayor and the right worshipful sovereigns the aldermen of the City ".   Regulation of the trade was continued by the Company, although with diminishing effect, until late in the eighteenth century.   In common with most other guilds it has now ceased to exercise its chartered powers but its interest in the craft persists through its encouragement of research in the dyeing industry.   The Dyers' Company shares with the Vintners' Company and the sovereign custodianship of swans on the Thames, and its officers assist in the annual ceremony of swan-upping when cygnets are marked to indicate ownership.

THE ARMORIAL BEARINGS (Pl. 16)

Sable a chevron engrailed argent between three bags of madder argent corded or.

No recorded grant ; arms anterior
to 1530

Crest : On a wreath of the colours a grain-tree proper.
Mantling : Sable doubled argent.
Supporters : On either side a panther rampant proper incensed gules, crowned or and semée with roundels gules, azure, vert, purpure and sable.
Motto : Da gloriam Deo.

Crest and supporters granted[1] by Robert Cooke,
Clarenceux
14th November 1577

---

[1] Coll. Arms Misc. Gts. I, 55 ; Vincent, 169/73.

Robert Cooke in his grant of crest and supporters refers to the "Auncient Armes of the . . . Mistery of Dyers" but no record of any formal grant of arms has been traced. A trick of the arms is shown in a series of the arms of the City companies at the end of the visitation of Surrey and the Isle of Wight by Thomas Benolt, Clarenceux, made about 1530;[1] these arms may have been entered at any time between 1530 and Benolt's death in 1534. The shield is here tricked with the chevron plain, and it so occurs in Cooke's visitation of London of

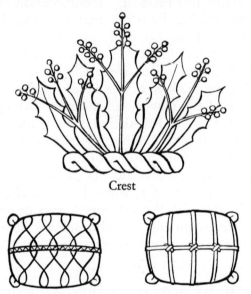

Crest

Variety of madder bags (Coll. Arms; Vincent, "Two Ears of Wheat" and Vincent 169)

1590.[2] But the 1634 visitation[3] agrees with the record of the 1577 grant of crest and supporters in making the chevron engrailed.

The bags of madder and the grain-tree represent two of the staple materials of the former dyer's trade.

Madder, a product from the roots of a plant, formed the basis of a pigment for dyeing wool, cotton and linen. The colour so produced was a dull red or terra-cotta shade, and lacked the brilliance of the scarlet dye which is symbolized by the Company's crest.

[1] Coll. Arms 1st H.7/62b.   [2] Coll. Arms G.10 fo. 121b.
[3] Coll. Arms 2nd C.24/385.

The grain-tree was once supposed to be the direct source of the "berries" from which scarlet dyes were produced before the later use of the cochineal insect, which in turn was replaced from about 1880 by the discovery of aniline dyes. The berries or grains are in fact the females of a species of shield-louse or kermes which attach themselves mainly to the holly and the oak in various parts of Europe and the Near East. The insects were harvested and their dried bodies constituted the material from which the scarlet dye was made.

Although known to the ancient peoples of the East to be of animal origin, as the word kermes—meaning worm—indicates, the "grain" was believed by the Greeks and Romans to be vegetable, and it was not until the eighteenth century that it was generally accepted in Europe as belonging to entomology rather than to botany.[1]

The panther was a badge of the House of Lancaster, and as Henry VI granted to the Dyers their first charter, it may be that panthers were introduced as supporters in reference to this notable event in the Company's corporate life. The coloured spots or roundels which appear on the supporters can no doubt be regarded as tokens of the various colours which the dyer could produce. There is a parallel here with the panther supporters of the Painter-Stainers which are for a similar reason spotted with many colours.

[1] See article by W. Born in *CIBA Review*, March 1938.

THE WORSHIPFUL COMPANY OF FANMAKERS

The stimulus for the formation of a guild of fanmakers in the City of London is said to have been due to the influx of large numbers of Protestant fanmakers from the Continent after the revocation of the Edict of Nantes in 1685. To prevent the dilution of their trade by aliens, the native craftsmen formed themselves into an organized body. On 19th April 1709 the guild was incorporated by royal charter in the name of the Master, Wardens, Assistants, and Society of the Art or Mystery of Fanmakers in the Cities of London and Westminster and twenty miles round. Increasing pressure from non-freemen and foreign imports finally broke down the Company's control of the trade, and after a petition of 1806 against the " extinction by foreigners of British fan craft" had failed, the Company's powers were gradually abandoned. Following a period of almost complete cessation, the Company was revived in 1877 and has since continued as a traditional City guild, at the same time evincing a benevolent interest in the development of the mechanical fan, in all its forms, as the successor to the product of its ancient craft.

THE ARMORIAL BEARINGS (Pl. 13)

Or a fan displayed with a mount of various devices and colours, the sticks gules; on a chief per pale gules and azure on the dexter a shaving iron over a bundle of fan-sticks tied together or ; on the sinister a framed saw in pale or.

Crest : On a wreath or and gules a hand couped proper holding a fan displayed or.

Mantling : Gules doubled or.

Motto : Arts and trade united.

The above blazon describes the arms as used by the Company since the early part of the eighteenth century ; they are without authority.

Inserted in the Company's earliest minute book, commencing 1775, is a description of the arms, but this is of no antiquity, being written in a nineteenth-century hand, and bears no evidence of its source. It does, however, agree, apart from the omission of the crest, with the earliest record of the arms that has been found, namely that shown in Maitland's *History of London*, 1739, and does not deviate from sub-

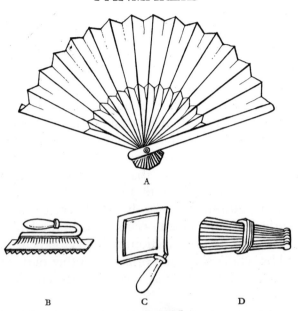

A

B   C   D

A. Fan displayed.   B. Shaving iron.   C. Framed saw, as in the arms.
D. Bundle of fan sticks

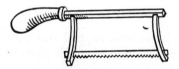

Framed saw

sequent examples.   The crest would appear to be a later addition since
it does not occur in literature until 1780 when it is given by Edmondson
in his *Complete Body of Heraldry.*

A slight variation is found in renderings of the motto which is now
accepted by the Company as given above although in all early versions
" trade " is invariably shown in the plural.

THE WORSHIPFUL COMPANY OF FARMERS

THE Farmers' Company is one of the few London guilds founded in this century. During the late war a number of representatives of the farming industry were associated in raising money for the Red Cross Agriculture Fund. When their immediate purpose was served it was felt that the association should continue in the interests of farming but with wider aims. Accordingly in 1946 a voluntary body was founded as the Farmers' Company. On 10th June 1952 the Court of Aldermen agreed to the constitution of this body as a livery company. Its aims are to foster agriculture and allied occupations in the United Kingdom, to improve marketing, the production and development of mechanical appliances, and by scholarships and prizes and other means to encourage research into soil fertility and pest control and generally to promote good husbandry.

The Company is now seeking a charter of incorporation from H.M. the Queen.

THE ARMORIAL BEARINGS (Pl. 16)

Azure three ears of wheat in fesse slipped and leaved or, a chief of the last.

Crest : On a wreath of the colours a bull passant gules semée of mullets or armed and unguled or.

Mantling : Azure doubled or.

Supporters : On either side a farm labourer proper holding in the exterior hand a sickle also proper.

Motto : Give us our daily bread.

Granted[1] by Sir Algar Henry Stafford Howard,
Garter
Sir Arthur William Steuart Cochrane,
Clarenceux
Sir Gerald Woods Wollaston,
Norroy
6th May 1948

In these arms the wheat and the bull, as symbols of arable and livestock farming, are too obvious for further comment. The mullets with which the bull is powdered recall the origin of this word from

---

[1] Original grant in the possession of the Company.

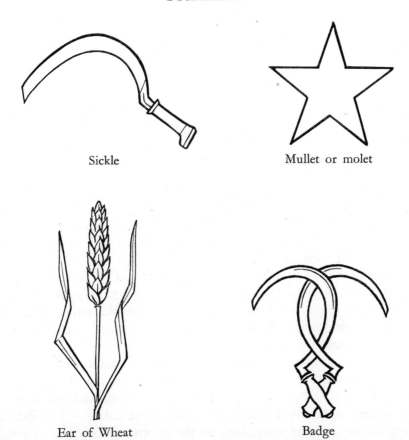

Sickle

Mullet or molet

Ear of Wheat

Badge

the Latin *mola*, a mill, and so symbolize the flour needed to satisfy the injunction in the motto.

The letters patent include an interesting addition of a grant of a badge to the Company " to be borne and used upon standards or otherwise ", namely, two sickles interlaced or. The Plumbers and Master Mariners have also acquired badges by grant in recent times.

THE WORSHIPFUL COMPANY OF FARRIERS

THE fact that the contemporary farrier is frequently called a black-smith tends to obscure the original functions of the separate Companies of Farriers and Blacksmiths. The blacksmith was a worker in iron and the scope of his former activities is indicated by the inclusion of gun-makers and clockmakers in the ranks of the early guild. The farrier, on the other hand, was a shoe-smith, as the horse-shoes of the Company's arms testify. He practised also as a horse-leech, or primitive veterinary surgeon, and ordinances for the regulation of the craft, which were approved in 1356, required all members to "loyally advise all those who shall ask counsel of them as well in the purchase of horses as in their cure".

In spite of a very flourishing trade in an age of horse-transport, the Farriers did not achieve incorporation until 17th January 1673/4. Their charter gave them control of the trade in the cities of London and Westminster and within seven miles therefrom, with power to search for "defective workes and medicines".

Attempts to compel all practising farriers in London to become free of the Company became increasingly difficult during the eighteenth century and the Company reported to the Commissioners of 1837 that their powers were "not exercised to any great extent. The increase of population and the alterations in the habits of society . . . render . . . such exercise inexpedient." The Company has since instituted examinations to raise the standards and proficiency of the modern shoe-smith.

THE ARMORIAL BEARINGS (Pl. 19)

Argent three horse-shoes sable pierced argent.

Crest : On a wreath of the colours an arm embowed issuing from clouds on the sinister side all proper, holding in the hand a hammer azure handled and crowned or.

Mantling : Sable doubled argent.

Supporters : Two horses argent.

Motto : Vi et virtute.

Pl. 20

G.86

FELTMAKERS, p. 88
FOUNDERS, p. 98

FLETCHERS, p. 96
GIRDLERS, p. 109

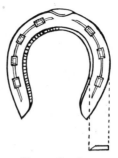

Horse-shoe (Diderot)   Hunter's shoe

The Company has no formal grant of arms but it has used arms at least from the sixteenth century. The earliest established use of these occurs in a manuscript dated 1591 in the British Museum;[1] no crest or supporters are given. The arms are also shown in the *Breffe description of the royall Citie of London*, 1575,[2] but since they have been sketched in after the compilation of the volume, and the Farriers is not included in the list of companies given elsewhere in the manuscript, the work is valueless as evidence for the existence of the arms at this date. It may be significant that in the 1588 copy[3] of this volume, of which the 1575 manuscript appears to be a rough draft, the Farriers' arms are absent.

[1] Harl. MS. 2220.   [2] Guild. Lib. MS. 2463.   [3] Harl. MS. 6363.

THE WORSHIPFUL COMPANY OF FELTMAKERS

FELT is produced by a process of matting hair, fur or wool by a combination of moisture and heat under pressure. In the Middle Ages this process in London was shared by the fullers and the hatters or cappers. Fullers produced cloth by treading the material in water-mills; their craft or mistery merged in 1528 with the shearmen to form the Clothworkers' Company. The early feltmakers were known as the hatters, cappers or hurers, and were at one time subordinate to the Haberdashers' Company. Their trade was confined to the manufacture of hats and caps, in the course of which there was frequent conflict with the fullers. In 1376 ordinances of both crafts included complaints of mutual interference, notably in the use of the fullers' mills by some of the hatters. The hatters themselves represented to the mayor and aldermen that the " chief duty of their trade was the fulling of caps and they know not how to do any other thing ". They asserted that some of the craft fulled caps by treading at water-mills " whereby such caps were not so good " and therefore they sought the agreement of the mayor and aldermen that caps be not fulled at any mills " but only by hand ". Emphasis on hand fulling of caps is frequent in the City records, and further ordinances of 1404 asked the civic authorities to ordain " that no work of the said trade shall be fulled in mills or by the feet but only by the hands of men ". This use of the hand as essential to the proper fulling of felt hats and caps explains the presence of the hand in the Company's armorial bearings.

The union of the hatters with the Company of Haberdashers, which was effected on 7th April 1501, was severed by a charter of 2nd August 1604 constituting a separate company of the Art or Mistery of Felt-makers of London. This charter was not at once recognized by the City but it received confirmation by Charles II on 27th June 1667 and by subsequent charters.

In spite of an act of Common Council in 1759 restraining under penalty all non-freemen from trading as feltmakers in the City or its liberties, the Company's control of the craft had ceased by the end of the eighteenth century.

THE ARMORIAL BEARINGS (Pl. 20)

Argent a dexter hand appaumé couped at the wrist gules between two hat-bands nowed azure, in chief a hat sable banded azure.

Crest : On a wreath of the colours a dexter arm embowed proper holding in the hand a hat sable banded azure.

Mantling : Gules doubled argent.

Granted by Sir Algar Henry Stafford Howard,
Garter
Sir Arthur William Steuart Cochrane,
Clarenceux
Sir Gerald Woods Wollaston,
Norroy
31st May 1946

Motto : Decus et tutamen.

The patent of arms, from which the above transcript is taken, is in the possession of the Company. Its preamble states that the Master

Dexter hand appaumé

Hat-band nowed

in seeking a formal grant, represented that " upon examination of the records of the College of Arms it appears that the Armorial Ensigns long used by the said Company are not duly registered therein ". The arms have been unquestionably " long used ",[1] and may well have been adopted in emulation of other City guilds soon after the granting of the Company's charter of 1604.

The term " nowed " derives from the French *nouer :* to knot.

[1] The earliest example that has been found occurs in the border of *The London Almanack for XXX years*, by Morden and Lee (*c.* 1680), the only known copy of which is in the Pepysian Library at Cambridge.

THE WORSHIPFUL COMPANY OF FISHMONGERS

THE earliest document relating to the Fishmongers of London recognizes two separate misteries dealing in fish, namely the Pessoners (Fishmongers) and the " Stokfysshemongers ". This document, a charter of 10th July 1363, regulates the internal government of the guild as well as the fish trade in London. It acknowledges the sole right of the Stockfishmongers to trade in dried fish, of which large quantities mainly of the cod family were imported during the Middle Ages, notably from Iceland. Control of the trade in fresh and salt fish was the prerogative of the Fishmongers.

By mutual agreement the two misteries became one body in 1512 and this union, although it is said not to have been confirmed by royal charter until 1536, was marked by a grant of arms to the joint company in the same year.

The present operative charter of 30th August 1604 assigns to the company powers for the " full and entire survey " of all persons selling fish in the City of London, its liberties and suburbs. Under this charter and certain statutory provisions, the Fishmongers' Company still has the duty of preventing offences in the sale of shellfish, undersized fish or of fish during the close seasons. It appoints, and pays for this purpose, inspectors and " fishmeters " whose duty it is to examine fish offered for sale in the City.

The Company ranks as the fourth among the Great Twelve. Apart from the exercise of its statutory duties, it maintains a close association with representative organizations connected with the fishing industry, and administers considerable funds which are devoted to a wide variety of charitable purposes including school, university and technical education.

THE ARMORIAL BEARINGS (Pl. 23)

Azure three dolphins naiant embowed in pale argent, finned, toothed and crowned or, between two pairs of stockfishes in saltire argent, over the mouth of each fish a crown or; on a chief gules three pairs of keys of St. Peter in saltire or.

Crest : Out of a wreath argent and sable two cubit arms, the dexter vested

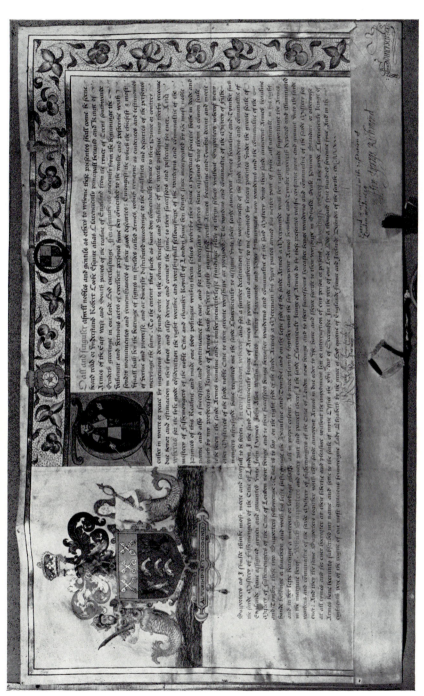

By courtesy of the Court of the Company

G.90

Pl. 21

LETTERS PATENT OF ARMS TO THE WORSHIPFUL COMPANY OF FISHMONGERS,
17TH DECEMBER 1575, SHOWING A PEER'S HELM IN THE EXEMPLIFICATION

H.91

Pl. 22

LETTERS PATENT GRANTING ARMS TO THE WORSHIPFUL COMPANY OF FLETCHERS

or cuffed azure, the sinister vested azure cuffed or, the hands argent holding an imperial crown proper.

Mantling : Gules doubled argent.[1]

Granted[2] by Sir Thomas Wriothesley,
Garter
and Thomas Benolt,
Clarenceux
19th October 1512

Supporters : Dexter a merman armed holding in his right hand a falchion[3] and sustaining with his left hand the helm and timbre, sinister a mermaid holding in her left hand a mirror and supporting the arms with her right hand all proper.

Motto : Al [*sic*] worship be to God only.

Granted[4] by Robert Cooke,
Clarenceux
17th December 1575

These arms commemorate the union in 1512 of the Fishmongers with the Stockfishmongers, a body formerly operating under a charter of 1508 and whose trade was confined to the sale of dried fish. Before the union, the Fishmongers used as their arms : azure three pairs of keys in saltire or, on a chief gules three dolphins naiant embowed argent ; the position of the dolphins and the keys are sometimes found reversed. The Stockfishmongers' arms were : azure two lucies, otherwise stockfish, in saltire argent crowned or. These latter were granted in 1494 by Roger Machado, Richmond *alias* Clarenceux King of Arms.[5]

On 12th October 1512 " the said Fishmongers and Stockfisshmongers before the maire and aldermen aggreed to be made oon mistery or craft that ys to say Fishmongers ".[6] The issue of letters patent for their joint arms within one week of this agreement suggests that negotiations for union and for a grant of arms had been pursued concurrently.

---

[1] The mantling shown in the exemplification in the 1575 patent is : dexter, gules doubled or and sinister, azure doubled argent. This has been preferred for the illustration in this book, but either is admissible.

[2] The original patent has not survived, but the grant is recorded in *Coll. Arms Old Grants* ✠, pp. 7–10

[3] A short broad sword with curved blade.

[4] The patent is at Fishmongers' Hall. A transcript appears in Munday (A.), *Chrysanaleia* ; ed. J. G. Nichols, 2nd ed. (1859), p. 3.

[5] Coll. Arms 1st H.7/60b.

[6] Guild. Rec. Off. Rep. 2/142b.

H

Dolphin naiant

Pair of stockfish

Pair of keys of St. Peter

Imperial crown

Although the original grant has been lost, an abstract by Elias Ashmole is preserved in the Bodleian Library;[1] it reads as follows:

> A grant of Armes made to the Company of Fishmongers by Tho: Wriothisley Garter & Thom: Benolt Clarenciaulx: Cestasavoyr d'azure, 3 Daulphins en pale enter quater Stockfishes, deux a deux per saltier d'argt: les Finnes, les dentes & sur le test d'chescun pisce un corone d'or, un chief gules, sur le chief 6 Cleifs d'St. Pierre, deux a deux per saltier des Corones. A leur timbre, deux brasse et deux mains argent, les Manches l'un d'or laut d'azure & les bordures d'ycells enterchangee, sortizantes hors dun torse d'argt: & sab: sustenantes un Corone impiall, Mantelle d'gules doblee d'arg: Dated 19 Oct: 1512.

On 31st March 1536 further terms[2] for the conduct of the Company provide that " such armes as Garter and Clarenceux Kinges at Armes have appoynted and granted joyntly to the said craftes shall contynue and alwayes be kepte and maynteyned without alteracion or change . . .

[1] Bodleian Lib. MS. Ashm. 858/17 *recto*.
[2] Guild. Rec. Off. Lib. P.95.

as yn the saide letters patentes . . . wherin and by the said letters patentes the Armes of bothe the saide misteries be joyned and knytt together in one Skutchyn ".

These arms are those in use today and are the arms referred to by Robert Cooke, Clarenceux, when making his grant of supporters in 1575. The appropriate passage of Cooke's grant reads as follows:

> Unto their sayde auncient Armes heaulme and Tymbre these two Supporters followenge: That is to say on the right syde of the sayde Armes a Mereman his upper partes armed his nether part of fyshe, all naturall, in his right hande holdinge a faucheon and with his lefte susteyninge the Heaulme and Tymbre: and on the left syde of the sayde Armes a Mermayde with her right hande supportinge the Armes and in her lefte bearinge a mirrour or lookinge glasse all in proper colour. As more playnly together with the sayde auncyent Armes heaulme and Tymbre appeereth depicted and illuminated in the margine herof.

The painting of the arms and crest in the margin of the grant of supporters deviates from the original blazon as recorded by Elias Ashmole in the tinctures of the mantling which are depicted as gules doubled or on the dexter side, and azure doubled argent on the sinister; and in the tincture of the hands in the crest which appear as proper. An unusual feature of this painting is the artist's inclusion of a form of helm now reserved for use in the arms of peers. The system of distinguishing degrees of rank by types of helm was not settled until the reign of James I, and the use of this helm may well be no more than the arbitrary choice of the artist. Certainly there is no reference to such exceptional usage either in the record of the 1512 grant of arms and crest in the College of Arms, or in the patent of supporters of 1575. Nevertheless, as the helm is given in an

Falchion

official document, it has bee˜ retained also in the illustration of the arms that appears in the present work.[1] The Company's title to this distinction can only be finally settled by a ruling of the Kings of Arms.

In heraldic symbolism the dolphin is regarded as pre-eminent among

---

[1] Other arms incorporating peers' helms are Apothecaries, Clockmakers and Goldsmiths.

Early arms of the Fishmongers, *ante* 1512

fish as the lion is among beasts. It was no doubt for this reason that the Fishmongers adopted it. The stockfish, on the other hand, is of occupational significance, representing the trade in dried fish, mainly of the cod family, carried on by the Stockfishmongers. In Denmark the word *stokfisk* is still current for dried cod, and in the royal arms of that country a crowned stockfish, split open in the manner of the familiar haddock, symbolized Iceland before it became an independent republic in 1944.

Stockfish are sometimes found blazoned as lucies. The luce or lucy was in the Middle Ages the freshwater pike (Lat. *lucius*) but the term here signifies the sea pike or cod (Lat. *merlucius*). Stow, in describing an early Fishmongers' pageant, refers to " armed knights riding on horses, made like luces of the sea ".[1]

The keys on the chief, as symbols of St. Peter, allude to the Company's patron saint. There is no evidence of the Company's origin as a religious guild of St. Peter, but fishmongers in London were called " petermen " at least as early as the fourteenth century, and an ordinance of 1426 required members of the trade to attend each year on St. Peter's day a solemn mass in honour of God and St. Peter.[2]

St. Peter's traditional role as the first bishop of Rome and his custom-

---

[1] Stow (J.), *Survey of London*; ed. C. L. Kingsford, vol. 1 (1908), p. 96.
[2] Herbert (W.), *The Twelve Great Livery Companies* (1836), vol. 2, p. 44.

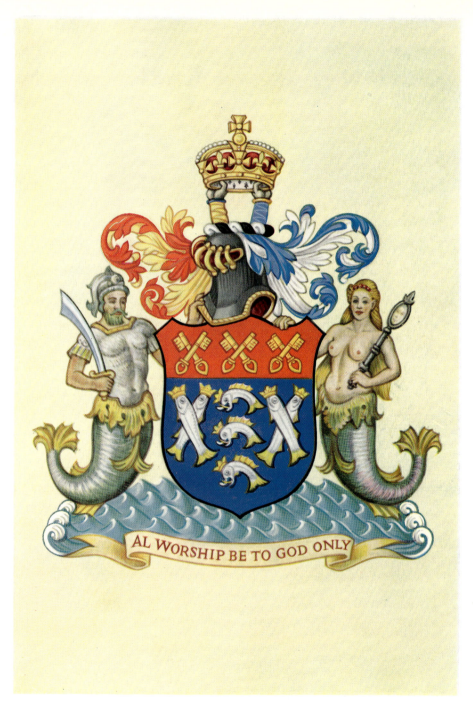

AL WORSHIP BE TO GOD ONLY

Pl. 23

H.95

FISHMONGERS, p. 90

Early arms of the Stockfishmongers, A.D. 1494

ary association with the Fishmongers' Company may have given rise to the interpretation of the imperial crown in the crest as a papal tiara. This occurs in a collection of crests formed by Thomas Wall about 1530.[1] Wall, who was at the time of his compilation Windsor Herald and later (1534–6) Garter King of Arms, renders the Fishmongers' crest as " two armes clothed with chasubles asur lynyd gold the hand sylver holdyng up a popes tyare purple the crownes gold wt. perry full [i.e. pierry, or set with stones] ". This is no doubt a rather free blazoning on the part of Wall, but it is interesting to note that he could regard the imperial crown as a papal tiara. Such an interpretation lends support to the suggestion that a similar recognition of the imperial crowns in the Drapers' arms was the cause of the latter's being challenged as unlawful in 1561.

[1] Original MS. in the library of the Society of Antiquaries. Published in *The Ancestor*, vols. 11 and 12, pp. 178–190, 63–98 ; see item 545 for the Fishmongers' crest.

THE WORSHIPFUL COMPANY OF FLETCHERS

THE fletcher was a maker of arrows and the Norman derivation of his name is a confirmation of the antiquity of the craft. It is likely that the fletchers and the bowyers, or makers of bows, were at one time a single craft, but increasing demand and the tendency to specialization which was a feature of medieval trade, effected a separation. In 1371 the men of the fletchers and bowyers agreed with the consent of the mayor and aldermen that no man of the one trade should meddle with the trade of the other; those whose stocks were at the time committed to the sale of both bows and arrows were allowed time to comply with this regulation. Ordinances for the election of wardens to survey the mistery and ensure its good conduct were proclaimed in 1403.

When the English bowman was the main arm in battle, the Fletchers were a flourishing community, but the use of gunpowder supplanted the bow, and by the end of the sixteenth century the archer was obsolete. In spite of royal and mayoral attempts to enforce the practice of archery, the fletcher's trade decayed and the mistery ceased to exercise any craft functions after the beginning of the seventeenth century.

The Company has no charter of incorporation.

THE ARMORIAL BEARINGS (Pl. 20)

Sable a chevron or between three broad arrows also or headed and feathered argent.

> Granted[1] by William Hawkeslowe,
> Clarenceux
> 12th October 1467

Crest : On a wreath or and sable an angel proper vesture and wings endorsed or feathered of many colours holding with both hands a bundle of arrows also or, headed and feathered argent encircled with a band sable.

Mantling : Sable doubled or.

> Granted[2] by Sir Thomas Holme,
> Clarenceux
> 1486

Motto : True and sure.

---

[1] The original patent is in the possession of the Company. A transcript appears in *The Genealogist*, vol. 4, (1880), p. 127.

[2] The original patent has not survived, but the crest is given in colour, without blazon, in Coll. Arms MS. 1st H.7/59b.

Broad arrow   Crest

These arms were confirmed by Thomas Benolt, Clarenceux, on 12th October 1530, and entered by him in his visitation book. They were again entered at the 1634 visitation.

The blazon of the arms in the original patent of 1467 reads as follows : " sable a cheveron golde thre brode arowes of the same garnet silver ". From representations in the College of Arms it is clear that " garnet " means garnished, the arrows being depicted as or with the heads and feathers argent.

THE WORSHIPFUL COMPANY OF FOUNDERS

IN 1365 the men of the mistery of founders presented a petition to the mayor and aldermen stating that some of the mistery made "works of false metal and false solder", and requesting that ordinances be approved to regulate the trade. Articles specified in the ordinances were stirrups, buckles, spurs, candlesticks, lavers and pots. These were small wares of daily use and they no doubt constituted the staple products of the founders' craft which involved the casting of brass and copper objects as opposed to the work of the brasier whose implement was mainly the hammer. The founding of bells and guns are not touched on in the successive ordinances of the Founders. It is probable that some of the mistery were capable of producing such things, but there is evidence that their manufacture was not confined to that body.

During the sixteenth century the Founders acquired the right of sizing and marking brass weights and this privilege was confirmed to them in their first charter of 18th September 1614. This charter required all brass weights used within the City and three miles compass to be brought to Founders' Hall to be sized and marked, and enjoined

Taper candlesticks and laverpot

Tongs from an early woodcut of a founder at work

the appointment of searchers for the discovery of false weights. These powers gradually fell into disuse during the nineteenth century and the laſt entry concerning the sizing of weights in the Company's records occurs in 1908. The control of weights and measures is now governed by Aĉt of Parliament and although the rights of the Founders' Company were reserved to them they are not exercised.

THE ARMORIAL BEARINGS (Pl. 20)

Azure a laverpot between two taper candlesticks or.

Creſt : On a wreath of the colours a fiery furnace proper from which a melting-pot proper is being lifted by a pair of tongs sable held by two arms, veſted azure cuffed argent, and the hands carnat, emerging from the clouds proper.

Mantling : Gules doubled argent.

Granted[1] by Robert Cooke,
Clarenceux
13th Oĉtober 1590

Motto : God the only Founder.

The blazon in the original grant of arms reads as follows :

the field azure a Laverpott betwene two taper Candelſticks gold, And to

---

[1] Original deposited in the Guildhall Library, MS. 6362. A full transcript appears in *Misc. Gen. et Heraldica*, vol. I, p. 103, and in Hibbert (W. N.), *History of the Worshipful Company of Founders* (1925), p. 303.

the Creast uppon the healme on a wreathe golde and azure a feyrye furnes proper out of the cloudes proper two Armes the handes carnat the sleves azure holdinge a payer of Closing-tonges sables takinge holde of a meltyng-pott proper manteled gules doubled silver.

The arms were in existence before the letters patent were issued, and are recorded, without the crest, in William Smith's *Breffe description of the royall Citie of London*, 1575.[1] A yet earlier version[2] showing sable a laverpot within a bordure argent is given in an unofficial volume in the College of Arms, containing a collection of the arms of the London Companies and compiled about 1530.

The following extract from the wardens' account book[3] of the Company relating to the year 1590 records the payment for the confirmation of arms and " gifte " (i.e. grant) of crest :

> Also payd by the Auditors to Clarenciaux Kinge at armes by the handes of Norrey Heraulde for the Armes of the Company with a Creste thereunto added of the gifte of the sayde Kinge at Armes and confirmed to the Company under his seale of office .   .   .   . £3.2.8.

The laverpot—a ewer for filling a washing bowl—and the candlesticks are examples of the founder's art.

[1] Guild. Lib. MS. 2463.
[2] Coll. Arms MS. Vincent, " Two Ears of Wheat ".
[3] Guild. Lib. MS. 6330/2.

THE WORSHIPFUL COMPANY OF
FRAMEWORK KNITTERS

WILLIAM LEE, a member of the University of Cambridge and a Nottinghamshire parson, produced in 1589 a machine for knitting woollen stockings and later adapted it to knit silk hose. During his lifetime the inventor failed to get adequate support for the exploitation of his machine and he died in France a poor man. After his death, those who subsequently developed his stocking frame petitioned Cromwell for a charter. This was granted on 13th June 1657 and thereby the Framework Knitters of the City of London became an incorporated body. Cromwell's charter was succeeded by another of 19th August 1663 which widened the Company's powers and constituted it as the " Master, Wardens, Assistants and Society of the Company of Framework Knitters of our cities of London and Westminster and our kingdom of England and dominion of Wales ". Under the charter the Company was given powers of search for bad work and the prosecution of offenders. During the eighteenth century London lost its leading position as the centre of the stocking trade which became concentrated in the Midlands. This migration made remote control from the City increasingly difficult and a final attempt in 1809 to impose the Company's rights by process of law met with failure. Its influence today is mainly exercised through the consortium of members of the industry who form a large section of the Company.

THE ARMORIAL BEARINGS (Pl. 19)

Argent a knitting frame sable garnished or.

Crest : On a wreath argent and gules a lamb passant proper resting the dexter forefoot on a hank of silk fessewise or.

Mantling : Gules doubled argent.

Supporters : On the dexter side a student of the University of Cambridge in academical costume of the seventeenth century proper and on the sinister side a female figure also in seventeenth century costume habited azure, cuffs, cap, neckerchief and apron argent, holding in the dexter hand a knitting needle proper and in the sinister hand a like needle and a piece of worsted knit gules.

Motto : Speed, ſtrength and truth united.

Granted and confirmed[1] by Sir Gerald Woods Wollaſton,
Garter
Arthur William Steuart Cochrane,
Clarenceux
Algar Henry Stafford Howard,
Norroy
3rd February 1933

The earlieſt device adopted by the Company was as follows :

On a chevron between two combs and as many leads of needles in chief and an iron jack and lead sinker in base, a main spring between two smaller springs.

This uninſpired composition incorporates various vital parts of the knitting machine. It firſt appears in an engraving of 1708.[2] No tinctures are recorded.

Knitting frame from the grant of arms

Some thirty years later,[3] arms corresponding to those described in the 1933 grant were assumed, but about the middle of the nineteeenth century the Company reverted to the earlier device. Thereafter the

[1] Original grant deſtroyed by enemy action but a certified copy is now in the possession of the Company.

[2] Hatton (E.), *New View of London*, (1708), vol. 2 (folding plate).

[3] Maitland (W.), *History of London* (1739).

IN THE SWEAT OF

THY BROWS SHALT THOW

EATE THY BREAD

LUCEM TUAM DA NOBIS DEUS

Pl. 24

H.102

GARDENERS, p. 107
GLAZIERS, p. 115

old arms occur regularly on official documents until 1933, in which year the Framework Knitters eliminated doubts as to the correct form by seeking an official grant.

The dexter supporter is described in works of reference published during the nineteenth century[1] as a student of the University of Oxford. The supporter in question is, however, clearly meant to commemorate William Lee,[2] of St. John's College, Cambridge, who invented the

Early device

knitting frame in 1589. The inspiration for the supporters appears to derive from a painting formerly owned by the Company[3] but now lost. It was by repute the gift of George Balderston, one of the wardens appointed by the charter of Charles II, and purported to depict Lee showing the loom to a female knitter standing at his side. The painting is reported to have been in the Company's Hall[4] but its whereabouts

[1] Cf. Allen (Thos.), *History of London* (1828), vol. 2, and all eds. of Burke's *General Armory*.

[2] On the identity of Lee and the claims of Oxford and Cambridge, see Felkin (W.), *History of Machine Wrought Hosiery* (1867), ch. 3–4.

[3] Seymour (R.), *Survey of the Cities of London and Westminster* (1733), vol. 1, p. 603.

[4] Beckmann (J.), *History of Inventions* (1846), vol. 2, p. 370.

was unknown in 1851 when its loan was required for the Great Exhibition.[1]

The crest symbolizes the wool and silk which were the raw material of the trade.

[1] Funston (J.), *The Worshipful Company of Frame-Work Knitters* (1901), p. 8. A pamphlet by a former Clerk to the Company, privately printed.

THE WORSHIPFUL COMPANY OF FRUITERERS

A RECORD of the appointment of two wardens on 12th May 1416 to rule the mistery of " Friturers " may be an early reference to the Fruiterers' guild. It certainly existed in the fifteenth century for it is included in a list of misteries and trades compiled in 1422, and an ordinance of the mistery of Fruiterers was approved by the mayor and aldermen in 1463. This ordinance was mainly concerned to prevent the infringement of non-freemen upon the privileges of the enfranchised fruiterers in selling fruit about the City. On 9th February 1605/6 James I granted the mistery a charter of incorporation which gave it the right of supervision and search of the trade within the City and three miles radius, and other powers usual to the guilds.

In common with most other companies, the chartered powers are no longer used but the Company still identifies itself with the industry by co-operation with horticultural organizations and centres of research for the development and benefit of the trade.

THE ARMORIAL BEARINGS (Pl. 13)

Azure on a mount vert the tree of Paradise, environed with a serpent, between Adam dexter and Eve sinister, all proper.

Motto : Deus dat incrementum.

There is no authorized grant of arms to this Company. Arms have, however, been borne by the Fruiterers since the latter part of the sixteenth century and, apart from occasional variations in the positions of Adam and Eve, are identical with those now in use. The earliest certain example that has been found is contained in a manuscript of 1591.[1] A rough sketch which appears in William Smith's *Breffe description of the royall Citie of London*, 1575,[2] is probably a later insertion, and the fair copy of this work, dated 1588,[3] shows for the Fruiterers' arms only a blank shield.

The first motto adopted was *Arbor vitae Christus, fructus per fidem gustamus*. This is found in Wallis,[4] and according to the Company's

---

[1] Harl. MS. 2220.
[3] Harl. MS. 6363.
[2] Guild. Lib. MS. 2463.
[4] Wallis (R.), *London's Armory* (1677).

historian was in official use until 1835, in which year the Company's notepaper was altered to show the present motto.[1] Heraldic writers nevertheless continued to use the old form up to the publication of Burke's *General Armory* in 1884.

Holme's *Academy of Armory*, vol. 2 (*c.* 1690), printed in 1905 from the original manuscript in the British Museum, gives a variant of the arms of the " Fruiterers or Fruitsellers, Hucksters ", and records the motto as : *Cave Deus videt*, but this motto is not found elsewhere.

[1] Gould (A. W.), *History of the Worshipful Company of Fruiterers* (1912), pp. 60-2.

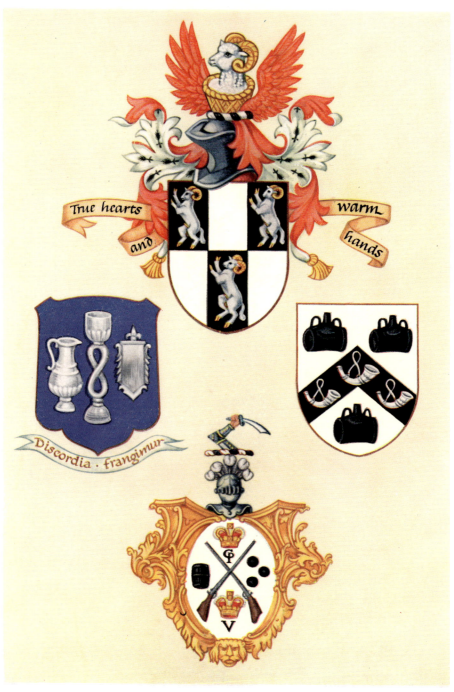

Pl. 25

I.107

GLOVERS, p. 119

GLASS-SELLERS, p. 113

HORNERS, p. 141

GUNMAKERS, p. 133

THE WORSHIPFUL COMPANY OF GARDENERS

THE first charter of the Gardeners' Company, dated 18th September 1605, indicates the wide range of the gardeners' activities in London at a time when both market and pleasure gardens were common. It incorporated all men of the craft in the City and six miles compass thereof and gave the Company control over " the trade, craft or mistery of gardening, planting, grafting, setting, sowing, cutting, arboring, rocking, mounting, covering, fencing, and removing plants, herbs, seeds, fruits, stocks, sets and of contriving the conveyances to the same belonging ".

The gardens of the City are now either municipal, or in the form of window-boxes, and the Company's powers, although unabated, are not exercised. Nevertheless it has successfully turned its attention to the encouragement of window-boxes to mitigate the severity of a concrete City, and, in association with other appropriate bodies, uses its funds for educational work in horticulture.

THE ARMORIAL BEARINGS (Pl. 24)

On a shield representing a landscape the figure of a man habited about the body with a skin delving the ground with a spade all proper.

Crest : On a wreath argent and vert a basket of flowers and fruit proper.

Mantling : Vert doubled argent.

Motto : In the sweat of thy brows shalt thow eate thy bread.

Granted[1] by Sir Alfred Scott Scott-Gatty,
Garter
George Edward Cokayne,
Clarenceux
William Henry Weldon,
Norroy
8th September 1905

Supporters : On either side a female figure [proper] vested argent wreathed about the temples with flowers and supporting on the exterior arm a cornucopia proper.

Granted[2] by Sir Alfred Scott Scott-Gatty,
Garter
8th September 1905

---

[1] Guild. Lib. MS. 3398.   [2] Guild. Lib. MS. 3399.

Cornucopia

The grant of arms, crest and supporters, from which the above blazon is transcribed, resulted from the Company's petition to the

king representing that in the margin of their second charter, dated 9th November 1616, was depicted a drawing of their arms which appeared not to have been recorded in the College of Arms. This charter is still extant[1] and shows a crude drawing of the arms, crest and supporters in pen and wash clearly contemporary with the document.

On 9th June 1905 a royal warrant[2] was issued permitting the Company to continue to bear arms as heretofore, provided that such arms were duly exemplified and recorded in the College. The ensuing grant blazoned the arms in the terms above and reproduced the original coat unchanged, apart from the addition of tinctures which are not indicated in the 1616 drawing.

Crest

[1] Guild. Lib. MS. 3402.   [2] Guild. Lib. MS. 3397.

THE WORSHIPFUL COMPANY OF GIRDLERS

In letters patent of 10th March 1326/7 by which Edward III confirmed certain ordinances of the Girdlers of the City it is laid down that no girdle of silk, of wool, of leather, or of linen thread be garnished with inferior metal. Similar provisions, set out in articles for the conduct of the trade agreed to by the mayor and aldermen in 1344, include garters as well as girdles, and these two items of apparel were the main products of the girdler's craft. The girdle was an essential feature of both male and female wear from early times until the Stuart period, providing a means not only for the girding of dress but also for the suspension of dagger or sword and for such domestic needs as purse, keys and ink-horn.

Before the Reformation the Girdlers of London were a fraternity devoted to the Blessed Virgin Mary and to St. Lawrence whose effigy and symbol of martydom are depicted in the Company's armorial bearings. Their first charter of incorporation was granted on 6th August 1449, and by a subsequent charter of 12 October 1568 Elizabeth I united the Girdlers, the Wire Workers and the Pinners as one Company, with the style of the Master and Wardens or Keepers of the art or mistery of Girdlers. The Pinners, who had been joined as a voluntary association with the Wire Workers since the time of Edward IV, later separated from the Girdlers and were incorporated by a charter of 20th August 1636; they became defunct in the eighteenth century.

Change of fashion and the end of the guild system as an economic instrument caused the trade functions of the Girdlers to be largely inapplicable after the eighteenth century and the Company's powers, although not removed, are now inoperative.

THE ARMORIAL BEARINGS (Pl. 20)

On a field of six pieces azure and or three gridirons or.

Crest : In a cloud with the sun issuing therefrom the figure of St. Lawrence, vested azure, and holding in his dexter hand a gridiron and in his sinister hand a book or.

Mantling : Azure doubled ermine powdered with suns issuing from clouds.

Granted by John Smert,

Garter

15th October 1454

Motto : Give thanks to God.

The original patent of arms has not survived but a full copy of the text is recorded in the College of Arms.[1]   In this John Smert recites that the " notables and worshipfull men of the sayd crafte all of one minde accorde and assent have funded one brotherhoode in the worshippe of god of our ladye and of the blessed gloryous martyr Seynt Lawrence " and at

> the desyre and will of the said worshipful maister and wardens and others of the said crafte . . . being at this tyme in the worshippe of the said glorious martyr Seynt Lawrence . . . I have devysed them one blason that is to wytt a schucheon of vi pointes of Azure & gold with iii gredyron of that same and the tymbre about the healme the bodye of Seynt Laurence in a clowde with sonnes issuing or pouryng owt holding in his right hande a gredyerne & a boke in his left hande of golde clothed of asure enmantelled of the same with that same dowblyd of Ermyns powdrid with celestiaulx that ys to wytt of clowdes with sones comynge owt or issuynge.

Arms of similar design were granted to the Glovers' Company and to the Tallow Chandlers' Company, also by John Smert, whose surviving patent of 1456 to the Tallow Chandlers describes their arms as " Ung escue de six pointz dasur et dargent a trois Coulombs de mesmes."   This division of the shield into six or nine pieces by vertical and horizontal lines was a fashion developed in the fifteenth century. Later works on heraldry have complicated the blazoning of such a shield, and the Girdlers' arms are now invariably found described as " party per fesse azure and or a pale counterchanged, three gridirons of the last . . ."[2]   It is simpler, and indeed more accurate, to revert to ancient practice, since the pale is an ordinary superimposed on a shield, and would be so shown if made in relief, whereas it is clear that a division of the field into six compartments is intended.   The term *point* which occurs in the Girdlers' and the Tallow Chandlers'

---

[1] Coll. Arms MSS. 1st H.6 and 2nd H.6. fo. 123b.   A trick of the arms, nearly contemporary with the grant, is given in Randle Holme's book (Brit. Mus. Harl. MS. 2169/63) ; this volume is described in Wagner (A. R.) *Cat. of English medieval rolls of arms,* 1950, p. 101/2.

[2] e.g. Smythe (W. D.), *An Historical Account of the Worshipful Company of Girdlers* (1905), p. 222.

GOLD AND SILVER WYRE DRAWERS, p. 121
INNHOLDERS, p. 143

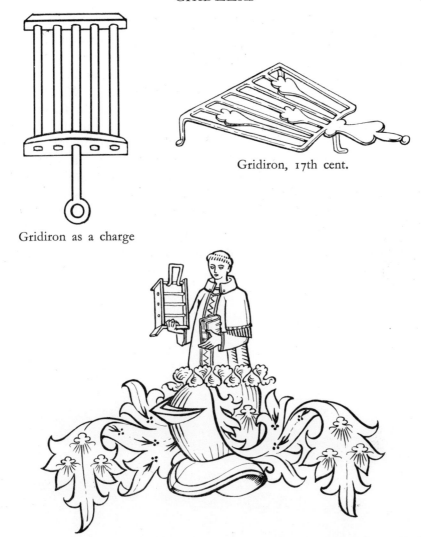

Gridiron, 17th cent.

Gridiron as a charge

Crest and mantling doubled ermine powdered with suns issuing from clouds

patents is still used in French blazonry in the sense of " piece " above, but its use in English is now limited to define those parts of the shield which are distinguished by such expressions as *dexter chief point*.

The foundation of the guild as a fraternity of St. Lawrence explains the use of gridirons on the shield, for these are symbols of the martyrdom of St. Lawrence whose effigy in the crest, holding gridiron and

Bible, is a further sign of the Company's devotion to that saint. A return of all guilds and brotherhoods made in 1389, on a writ of Richard II,[1] indicates that at that time the Girdlers were a company or fraternity of Our Lady. No mention is made of St. Lawrence, and it is possible that their religious vows were extended subsequently. Whether there was more than a happy coincidence in the choice of St. Lawrence as the Company's patron saint, it is not possible to say, but the gridirons provide an opportunity for punning which is so prominent a feature of armory from early times. The word " girdle " still survives in the north of England and in Scotland as a synonym for " griddle " or " gridiron ", notably in " girdle-cake ", and the appositeness of the gridirons in heraldry is hardly likely to have escaped the designer of this coat of arms.

[1] Westlake (H. F.), *Parish Guilds of Medieval England* (1919), p. 237.

THE WORSHIPFUL COMPANY OF GLASS-SELLERS

GLASSWARE in England before the sixteenth century was crude and simple, but with the accession of the Tudors imports of quantities of Venetian glass created a growing taste for delicate design and purity of material. Home production was stimulated by the work of Jacob Verzelini, an immigrant of Venetian origin, who settled in England with other Venetian glassmakers in 1571. The rapid expansion of trade in glass encouraged the growth of itinerant hawkers who peddled glassware, often of doubtful quality, throughout the land. To protect themselves and to maintain good standards the glass-sellers of London followed the course most familiar to them; they formed a guild and sought a charter of incorporation whereby they might control the trade. An abortive attempt to obtain a charter in 1635 was followed by success on 25th July 1664. The charter granted by Charles II constituted " the glass-sellers and looking glass makers " of London one body corporate under the name of the Master, Wardens, Assistants and Commonalty of Glass-Sellers of London. It gave them control of the " art, trade or mystery of grinding, polishing, casing, foyling and finishing of looking glasses and in selling of glasses and looking glasses " in the City and seven miles thereof, together with the supervision of the sale of hourglasses, stone pots and other earthen ware. A saving clause was inserted which was designed to safeguard the privileges in the making of " christall glasses and looking glass plates " given to Thomas Tilson by royal licence on 19th October 1662. Tilson was a nominee agent of the Duke of Buckingham. The latter had acquired, among his other enterprises, an almost complete monopoly of glassmaking but his interest in the administration of his licences appears to have been intermittent, and the Glass-Sellers' Company became eventually the dominant power in the trade. They played a prominent part in the development of English glass, notably by their patronage of such eminent makers as Ravenscroft whose experiments they encouraged and whose wares they sold. Their control of the trade survived into the eighteenth century by which time the guild system had largely ceased to operate. A late record of attempted enforcement occurs in the Company's minutes of 1830 when the Clerk reported that he had summoned upwards of twenty persons carrying on the trade of glass-sellers to show cause why they had not taken up the freedom of the Company.

THE ARMORIAL BEARINGS (Pl. 25)

Azure a Venetian glass cup between a laverpot of white ware on the dexter and a looking-glass on the sinister all proper.

Motto : Discordia frangimur.

The Company has adopted as its insignia the device of its seal but the arms are without authority and their details have consequently varied over the years. Early examples are to be found in an engraved almanac,[1] *c.* 1680, a copy of which is preserved in the Pepysian Library at Cambridge ; and in a manuscript collection of the arms of the City companies,[2] written in or about the year 1681, in the British Museum. In the latter the tinctures are shown in trick and from this the blazon is interpreted as follows : Or a Venetian glass cup proper between a laverpot of " white wair " on the dexter and on the sinister a looking-glass proper in a frame gules porfled or. The present usage of the Company is to depict the field as azure and the looking-glass frame is usually shown as argent or white.

The charges represent the three classes of goods with which the Glass-Sellers were concerned. In its charter of incorporation the Company is empowered to control the sale of " glasses, looking-glasses, hour glasses and stone potts, or bottles ", and in the bye-laws subsequently approved on 28th November 1664, reference is made to the penalties to be incurred for the " deceitful " sale of glasses, looking-glasses, hourglasses, stone pots, or earthen bottles, or " any other white or galley ware". It is clear from this that the laverpot, or ewer, of " white wair " is intended to be a jug of white earthenware and not, as might be supposed, of glass.

[1] *London Almanack for XXX years ;* by Morden and Lee (*c.* 1680).
[2] Harl. MS. 1098.

THE WORSHIPFUL COMPANY OF GLAZIERS

EARLY references to London glaziers term them " verrers ", and this is the usual name during the thirteenth and the beginning of the fourteenth centuries. It was then replaced by " glazier " which subsequently became the common title for craftsmen in this art. Ordinances were granted to the " Verrers " of the City of London on 28th February 1364/5 and new ones were sanctioned by the mayor and aldermen on the petition of those " enfranchesed of and in the crafte or mystere of Glasiers " on 27th July 1474.

In its first charter of incorporation, dated 6th November 1637, the Glaziers' Company is designated the Master, Wardens and Commonalty of the Art or Mistery of Glaziers of the City of London, and control was given over those who practised the art or mistery of glaziers and painters of glass within the City and three miles thereof. The preamble to the charter recites the petition of the men of the mistery who advanced as grounds for incorporation the fact that many persons using the trade of glaziers and painters of glass had abused their trade by " the draught of their lead beyond the proportioned length for the weight thereof ". This statement demonstrates the functions of the glaziers' art which was the glazing, leading and, as occasion required, painting of windows ; the abuse referred to was the attempt to economize in an expensive material by reducing the lead to insecure proportions. The use of lead was an essential feature in early glazing, since medieval sheet glass was produced only in small sizes. Until the sixteenth century the design was built up as a mosaic of coloured glass, stained in the process of manufacture, and the artist added mainly black outlines and shadows. The discovery about the middle of the sixteenth century of pigments in various colours suitable for painting white glass widened the scope of the glass painter, especially in his capacity to add small detail which had hitherto been difficult or impossible by the leading process alone. This change of technique was particularly valuable in the development of heraldic glass.

The Company's control of the trade had largely ceased by the eighteenth century but the Company of Glaziers is still an active force in fostering the art. Many of its members are prominent artists ; prizes are awarded for notable work ; gifts of windows are from time to time made ; and a close association is maintained with the British Society of Master Glass Painters.

THE ARMORIAL BEARINGS (Pl. 24)

Argent two " glazing " irons[1] in saltire between four closing nails sable, on a chief gules a demi-lion passant guardant or.

Crest : On a wreath of the colours a lion's head couped or between two wings azure.

Mantling : Sable doubled argent.

Supporters : On either side a boy proper holding in the exterior hand a torch or inflamed also proper.

Motto : Lucem Tuam da nobis Deus.

Certificate[2] by Sir Henry Farnham Burke,
Garter
5th March 1926

No record of a patent of arms to the Glaziers can be found, but arms were recorded in the Visitation of London conducted by Henry St. George, Richmond Herald, in 1634.[3] According to this document the arms of the Company, " testified under the hand of Robert Cooke, Clarencieux King of Armes, 1588, in a piece of vellam ", were " viewed and approved " by Henry St. George. No trace of this " piece of vellam " has been found. It is, however, quite clear from the wording that it was not a grant, and this view is substantiated by the absence of any record in the College of Arms. It was in all probability an exemplification of the arms as then used by the Company. Some confusion has arisen as to the exact form of these early arms, since the trick that appears in the record of the visitation differs from representations[4] prior to 1634 in rendering the lion in chief as a lion passant. Apart from one exception,[5] which depicts a demi-lion passant,

---

[1] Properly, " grozing irons ".

[2] Original in the possession of the Company.

[3] Coll. Arms MS. 2nd C.24 fo. 15.

[4] e.g. the earliest discovered example (*temp.* Hen. VI) in Foster (J.), *A Tudor Book of Arms* (1904). On the date of the MS. edited by Foster see Wagner (A. R.), *Catalogue of English Medieval Rolls of Arms* (1950) pp. xxix, 102. For other instances see Coll. Arms MS. Vincent, " Two Ears of Wheat " (*c.* 1530) fo. G ; B. M. Cotton MS. Tib. DX (*c.* 1613) ; Harl. MS. 6363 (1588) ; Harl. MS. 472 (1599) ; Harl. MS. 6860 (1617) ; Harl. MS. 1349 (*c.* 1618).

[5] Harl. MS. 2220 (1591).

the earlier tricks and blazons show a demi-lion passant gardant. None of these earlier records is of an official nature, but some are by reputable hands and it is unacceptable that an almost unanimous weight of evidence is in error. An enquiry conducted by the College of Arms in 1926 at the Company's request disclosed that the trick[1] in the 1634 visitation had originally been drawn with a demi-lion passant gardant in the chief, but this had been altered subsequently to a lion passant. As to when the change had been made there is no evidence, but it was reasonably inferred that, since the herald in 1634 specifically "viewed and approved" the arms as they existed in 1588, the trick must have reproduced those arms exactly. And those arms, as stated above, depicted without reasonable doubt a demi-lion passant gardant. Thus the conclusion was reached that the alteration was made at a later date than the visitation and is without authority.

A similar alteration is discernible in a manuscript collection of arms[2] made by Richard Price, arms painter, " in the tyme of the Visitaĉon of London " of 1634, and subsequently bought for £20 by John Withie a seventeenth-century herald painter and Master of the Painter Stainers' Company in 1657. In this case the demi-lion passant gardant has been changed to a lion passant gardant.

The demi-lion passant gardant appears to be the rule until about the year 1675.[3] Thereafter variations occur in the renderings of the charge upon the chief: of seven publications and one manuscript seen between 1677 and 1724, five show a lion passant gardant and two give the orthodox demi-lion passant gardant. It is to be noted that none gives the lion passant that occurs in the alteration of the 1634 visitation.

Subsequently the lion passant gardant is universal and this later practice appears to have originated, as far as it can be traced, with the publication of Wallis's *London's Armory* in 1677. It is probable that an error committed in this major work of its time was perpetuated by imitation. The incorrect arms were used by the Company until a true exemplification was authorized in 1926 and duly recorded in the books of the College of Arms.

[1] No blazon is given in the visitation.

[2] Harl. MS. 1464.

[3] Walton (R.), *New Table of the Tradesmen's Armes*. Engraving in Guild. Lib. (Bs. 6.154/8).

The glazing iron, so-called in Garter's certificate, is a misnomer for the grozing iron used by glaziers to break off small portions of glass when cutting curves. The term grozing iron is used in all blazons of the arms until it appeared in early editions of Burke's *General Armory* as " grazing iron ". It can only be assumed that " glazing " was a misconceived correction of Burke's version since glazing iron appears

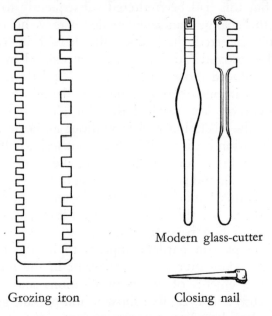

Modern glass-cutter

Grozing iron   Closing nail

to be a term unknown to the craft. The closing nails shown on the shield were nails used to hold loose glass in position during the leading process in the art of stained glass.

The supporters are probably inspired by cherubs which are common features of religious glass, as well as in church art generally,[1] and the torches they hold no doubt allude to the illumination provided by the windows made by the craft, a light whose divine source is implicit in the motto.

[1] Cp. these supporters with the unofficial ones of the Joiners and the Carpenters, both of which crafts would employ similar decoration in religious art.

Pl. 27

GOLDSMITHS, p. 125

THE WORSHIPFUL COMPANY OF GLOVERS

ORDINANCES were agreed in 1349 for the regulation of the craft of glovemaking in London, and wardens were appointed to enforce discipline and good workmanship. In 1498 the Glovers were united with the Pursers on a joint petition to the mayor and aldermen which represented that, owing to the decay of their trades, the two crafts were incapable of surviving as two separate misteries. Within a few years a further merger took place which incorporated the Glovers-Pursers in the Leathersellers' Company on 7th June 1502. Thereafter the Pursers lost their identity but the Glovers were incorporated as a separate company under a charter of 10th September 1639. This charter which gave them power to govern the trade in the City and within three miles thereof, was confirmed by an *inspeximus* of 21st March 1898, although by this time the Company's trade functions had ceased to operate. Its interest in the trade still obtains, however, and it seeks in co-operation with trade associations to encourage good craftsmanship.

THE ARMORIAL BEARINGS (Pl. 25)

On a field of six pieces sable and argent three rams salient argent armed and unguled or.

Crest : On a wreath argent and sable a ram's head argent armed and issuing from a basket or filled with wool argent between two wings erect gules.

Mantling : Gules doubled ermine.

Granted by John Smert,
Garter
20th October 1464

Motto : True hearts and warm hands.

From 1502 to 1639 the Glovers were united with the Worshipful Company of Leathersellers. In 1819 a fire at Leathersellers' Hall destroyed the fifteenth century patents of arms of both Companies. A record of these survives, however, in a scroll of arms[1] prepared at the 1634 visitation of London from the original grants, and certified

---

[1] At Leathersellers' Hall. For other details of the scroll see the chapter on the Leathersellers' arms.

by Sir Henry St. George, Richmond Herald. This document, which also records the arms of the Pursers who never regained a separate identity after union with the Leathersellers, gives no narrative blazon for the Glovers but depicts the arms in colour; the blazon given above describes the arms so depicted. From a note inscribed on the scroll it would appear that the original grant was in French.

The text of Smert's patent, wherein the arms are stated to be allowed, given and granted, is recorded in the College of Arms [1] but it does not include a blazon.

[1] Misc. Gts. 1/50; Vincent 169/70.

THE WORSHIPFUL COMPANY OF GOLD AND SILVER WYRE DRAWERS

THE art of making gold and silver wire by drawing out the malleable metal through holes of varying sizes in steel plates is said to have been invented in Nuremberg about 1350. The early evidences of its practice in London indicate that the craft was at first in the hands of immigrants from Europe, and such control as was exercised was claimed as the prerogative of the Goldsmiths' Company. The age of adornment during the Tudor and Stuart periods caused the trade to prosper to such an extent that stocks of bullion were affected. To reduce the trade and secure control, James I proposed to incorporate the craftsmen of the City. This measure was resisted by Parliament and proposals for the abolition of the trade were substituted. Nevertheless the trade continued to flourish and after repeated attempts to secure a charter, the men of the craft were finally incorporated as a company on 16th June 1693. The Company's powers were still to some extent effective in the early years of the nineteenth century but, although they have never been surrendered, these rights are inexpedient in modern times.

THE ARMORIAL BEARINGS (Pl. 26)

Azure on a chevron or, between two coppers in chief of the second and in base two points in saltire argent, a drawing iron between two rings sable.

Crest : On a wreath or and azure two arms embowed vested gules cuffed argent, holding between their hands proper an engrossing block or.

Mantling : Azure doubled or.

Supporters : The dexter an Indian proper, crowned with an eastern crown or, vested round the middle with feathers pendant alternately argent and gules, holding over the shoulder a bar of silver; the sinister a man vested proper, on his sinister arm a hank of silk argent.

Motto : Amicitiam trahit amor.

This is one of the few companies still using arms of no authority. The terms of the blazon given above are those adopted by the Company[1]

[1] See *A list of the Master, Wardens, Court of Assistants and Livery of the Worshipful Company of Gold and Silver Wyre Drawers* (1939), p. 38.

Copper (Diderot)

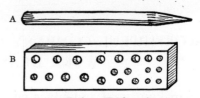

A. Point (Diderot).
B. Drawing-irons (Diderot)

and are based upon the device of its common seal. The Company's historian[1] asserts that this seal was the gift of Nicholas Cunliffe, master in 1743 ; this appears to be an error. According to the Court minute book, it was ordered on 17th January 1742/3 that " a common seal be forthwith made for the Company to be engraved on silver ".[2] On 26th January 1742/3 it is recorded that " according to the order of the last Court a seal was engraved and now produced ".[3] On 22nd April 1743 it is further entered that " the Master [i.e. Nicholas Cunliffe] this day presented to the Company a shagreen case set in silver (with his own arms engravd on the top and his name at the bottom) for the Company's seal and received the thanks of the Court for his present ".[4] It is apparent that Nicholas Cunliffe's gift was confined to the container for the seal.

The seal does not, however, mark the first use of the arms, for they appear, without supporters, in Maitland's *History of London* published in 1739, and may well have been used earlier. In designing them, their unknown author has drawn upon the tools of the craft. The process of wire-drawing was originally a manual operation in which wire was pulled through " drawing-irons ", or metal plates pierced with holes of various diameters. In the course of this operation, the holes in the drawing-irons became worn and were reset and repolished with small steel punches or bodkins of appropriate sizes ; these punches are the " points " shown in the arms.[5] When the proper fineness had been achieved the wire was annealed on the copper, " a large hollow copper bobbin, set upright, including small coal, and encompassed with lighted charcoal and small

Ring

[1] Stewart (H.), *History of the . . . Gold and Silver Wyre Drawers* (1891), p. 90.
[2], [3], [4], Guild. Lib. MS. 245/2.
[5] See Diderot, *Encyclopédie* s.v. *Tireur d'or.*

Pl. 28

I.122

GROCERS, p. 129

coal, communicating a gradual heat ".[1] The rings in the arms are gauges, and what is termed the engrossing block[2] appears to represent the wooden cylinder which functioned as a windlass in pulling the wire through the drawing-iron. One end was fitted with two staples into which long handles were inserted for turning the block.

The significance of the supporters is not clear. The Indian presumably is intended to represent the source of silver, a supposition reinforced by the bar of silver which he carries on his shoulder. But the other supporter has no ready explanation. In the official history of the Company this supporter is described as : " a man vested proper (called in the grant a silk throwster) on his sinister arm a hank of silk argent ".[3] The source of this statement is Edmondson[4] from whose work it is taken verbatim, but what the " grant " was to which Edmondson refers has not been discovered. It is certain that no grant of arms was ever made to the Company. There is, moreover, no obvious or likely connection between the wire drawers and the silk throwsters ; the latter were a separate incorporated company, now defunct, having

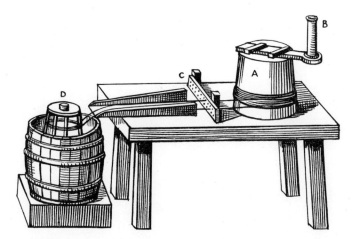

Manual wire-drawing : A. Degrossing block on which the wire is wound up. B. handle. C. Drawing-iron. D. Reel (Rees' *Cyclopaedia*, Plates IV, 1820)

---

[1] Rees (A.), *Cyclopaedia*, XVI (1819), s. v. Gold wire.
[2] ? " Degrossing " block. At no point in the process of wire-drawing was the wire *enlarged* but rather diminished in girth.
[3] Stewart (H.), loc. cit.
[4] Edmondson (J.), *Complete Body of Heraldry* (1780), vol. 1.

K

their own patent of arms granted by Sir Henry St. George, Clarenceux, in 1629.[1] It can only be concluded that Edmondson had seen a drawing of the arms and had described as a silk throwster what was in fact a freeman of the Company with a coil or hank of drawn wire over his arm. The two supporters would thus typify both the raw material and the finished product of the craft.

[1] Original patent in Guildhall Library, MS. 5819.

THE WORSHIPFUL COMPANY OF GOLDSMITHS

THE Goldsmiths' Company is among the most ancient of the City fraternities, a guild of goldsmiths being named as one of those paying a fine to the crown in 1180. A charter of 1327 confirmed to the Company its control of the trade together with powers of self-government. Incorporation as a perpetual corporation was obtained by letters patent dated 6th February 1393/4.

In addition to the powers of trade control which were granted by a succession of charters, the Company was given certain legal duties to perform under various acts of Parliament. The right of assay of gold and silver plate was first assigned to the Company by an act of 1300 which required goldsmiths throughout the country to submit their work to the Goldsmiths' Company of London to ensure that the quality of the metal conformed to the standards laid down. Articles of approved worth were thereupon stamped with the leopard's head and this royal emblem is incorporated in the Company's arms as a symbol of its ancient privilege. Current statutes still require the Company to assay and " hall-mark " plate at its hall, and to prosecute persons who in any part of England sell plate contrary to the law of the realm.

Assay of new coin is also the responsibility of the Company. It has been carried out by a jury of members since the thirteenth century at a ceremony known as the Trial of the Pyx. This now takes place annually at Goldsmiths' Hall to which the coin is sent from the Mint in a sealed casket, or pyx, to be tested against approved trial plates.

Although many of the Company's former activities have been adapted to the new conditions of trade, the continuity of the spirit of its original functions is a notable feature of its history. It cherishes the closest relationship with the trade and craft of precious metals and spends much money and effort to further the art in conjunction with government organizations and voluntary associations. And its finely equipped hall is from time to time the scene of important exhibitions of ancient and modern examples of the craft.

The Company takes precedence as the fifth of the Great Twelve.

THE ARMORIAL BEARINGS (Pl. 27)

Quarterly gules and azure, in the firſt and fourth a leopard's head or, in the second and third a covered cup between two buckles, the tongues fessewise, all or.

Creſt : On a wreath or and gules a demi-virgin, issuing from clouds proper, in a gown gules and kirtle or, arms extended holding in the dexter hand proper a balance or and in the siniſter hand a touchſtone both proper.

Mantling : Gules doubled argent.

Supporters : On either side a unicorn or, the mane, hoofs and tail argent.

Motto : Justitia virtutum regina.

Creſt and supporters granted[1] by Robert Cooke,
Clarenceux
8th November 1571

The creſt and supporters alone have a formal grant. In the letters patent assigning these to the Company, Clarenceux recites that the " art or miſtery hath of longe tyme borne armes " and have now required him " to assigne to these theyre auncient armes a Creaſt and Supportars ". He accordingly

> devised ordeyned and assigned . . . to these theyre auncient armes, that is to say quarterly gules and asur in the firſt a leopardes hed in the second a cuppe betwene two buckells golde, the creaſte and supportars hereafter followenge, Uppon the heaulme on a wreathe golde and gules, issuant owt of the clowdes a demy virgin her gown purple her kertell golde holdinge in her right hand a payre of ballance golde in her left hande a Tuche ſtone manteled gules dowbled argent. The supportars two unicornes golde mayned, clayed and tayled purple.

An inscription on the patent, signed by Henry St. George, Richmond Herald, indicates that it was approved and entered at the visitation of London, 1634, and adds that the " unicornes to be mayned, clayed and tayled argent, and the gowne of the creaſt gules ".

That the arms were ancient is demonstrated by a drawing in a manuscript of about 1480–1500[2] which depiĉts them, without creſt and supporters, in the same form as blazoned in the grant of 1571.

The charges on the shield symbolize the union of the delegated royal privilege of assay, of which the leopard's head was the emblem, with the trade of goldsmith as represented by the cup and buckles.

---

[1] Original at Goldsmiths' Hall.   [2] Brit. Mus. Harl. MS. 6163.

Pl. 29

HABERDASHERS, p. 136

In 1300 an act[1] provided that all arts of gold and silver should be assayed by wardens of the Company and stamped with the leopard's head to testify to the quality of the metal. In a later statute of 1363[2] this device is called the king's mark and is clearly derived from the heraldic leopard of the royal arms. In the crest the touchstone also refers to the Company's responsibility of assay, while the balance signifies the Trial of the Pyx which is still conducted by a jury of Goldsmiths at their Hall to determine whether coin of the realm are of proper weight and fineness. In earlier times assay was effected by means of the touchstone. This was usually a slab of black stone or slate upon which a streak was made by the gold or silver to be assayed.

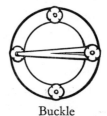

Covered cup   Buckle

The streak was then tested by comparison with streaks made by touch needles, or strips of gold or silver, of known quality.

Unicorns, which appear as supporters to the Company's arms, were frequently used as house signs of goldsmiths and probably were intended to symbolize wealth. Among the many fables associated with this mythical beast were the supposed powers of its horn to protect against poison.[3] These horns, which were in fact the tusks of narwhals, were highly prized, and consequently acquired a fabulous value. Because of the prophylactic properties with which their horns were credited, unicorns appear also as supporters for the arms of the Apothecaries' Company; those of the Wax Chandlers have a quite different significance.

[1] *Statutes of the Realm* 28 Ed. I c. 20.   [2] ibid. 37 Ed. III c. 7.
[3] Vinycomb (J.), *Fictitious Creatures in Art* (1906), p. 133.

The demi-virgin of the crest suggests an allusion to Elizabeth I in whose reign the grant of crest was made ; a further reference to the queen occurs in the motto.   An alternative motto—*Soli Deo honor et gloria*—is noted in the College of Arms,[1] and an English version thereof was entered at the 1634 visitation of London.[2]

In modern representations of the arms, the Goldsmiths use a peer's helm to bear the crest.   Authority for this practice seems to rest upon an exemplification of the arms authorized on 31st March 1891 by Garter King of Arms who certified beneath the painting that the " armorial bearings—arms, crest and supporters—above depicted do of right belong and appertain to the Wardens and Commonalty of the mystery of Goldsmiths of London . . ."   This is a quite definite statement about which there would appear to be no doubt.   But the original patent of crest and supporters, granted in 1571, shows an esquire's helm.   It is therefore surprising to find no reason given in the 1891 certificate for the exceptional introduction of a helm which is not considered proper to a corporation.   Since, however, such a helm appears in an authoritative document, it has been retained also in the illustration which accompanies this present work.   As in the case of the other three City guilds whose arms incorporate peers' helms,[3] the Goldsmiths' title to this distinction can only be settled by a ruling of the Kings of Arms.

[1] Vincent 183/90b.   [2] 2nd C.24/219.
[3] See Apothecaries, Clockmakers and Fishmongers.

THE WORSHIPFUL COMPANY OF GROCERS

THE Grocers' Company originated in a guild of Pepperers of which mention is first found in the Pipe Roll for 1180. Ordinances for the control of the Pepperers were established in the fourteenth century. Their trade comprised all manner of spices which they bought and sold in bulk. In 1365 the mistery is described as the mistery of Grossers, Pepperers and Apothecaries, and further ordinances in the following year indicate the extent of their trading activities : wax, soap, oil, flax, copper, iron, canvas, as well as spices are among items listed therein. This combination of varying trades was a common feature of early guild history ; at a later date some trades broke away to form separate guilds, and, in the case of the Grocers, the apothecary element became an independent society by royal charter in 1617.

Although many of the medieval grocer's wares are still to be found in the shop of the modern grocer, the latter's function merely as a retailer is only one aspect of the business of his earlier namesake. *Grosarii* were merchants who dealt in goods which were bought and sold " in gross ", or heavy weight, as opposed to costly articles which were weighed by the pound rather than by the hundredweight. Such heavy, or bulk goods were required to be weighed by the " great beam ", a weighing apparatus which tested merchandise for correct weight, and which in London was controlled on behalf of the king by the Grocers' Company. Weighing was compulsory and the fees charged for the service, which are specified in the Company's ordinances, produced a handsome revenue for the crown.

The Grocers' Company was incorporated by royal charter on 16th February 1428/9, and today ranks second to the Mercers as one of the Great Twelve. Among the many benefactions administered by the Company perhaps the most famous is Oundle School which owes its birth to a trust committed to his Company by a former member and sixteenth-century Lord Mayor, Sir William Laxton.

THE ARMORIAL BEARINGS (Pl. 28)

Argent a chevron gules between nine cloves sable.

Supporters : On either side a griffin per fesse gules and or, the underwing azure, beaked and clawed or.

Granted[1] by Thomas Benolt,
Clarenceux
1532

Crest : On a wreath argent and gules a camel statant or, bridled sable, on his back two bags of pepper argent powdered with cloves and corded sable.
Mantling : Azure doubled argent.

Granted[2] by William Hervey,
Clarenceux
14th October 1562

Motto : God grant grace.

The 1532 patent has not survived and the College of Arms possesses only an incomplete docquet,[3] the text of which gives neither blazon nor date. The latter is, however, given in the 1634 visitation of London[4] as 1532, and this receives some support by the statement in the docquet that the grant was made at the request of " Syr Wyllym Butler Knyght, Alderman, Rauffe Alayne & Thomas Person Wardaynes or kepers of said company ", all of whom held office together during the period 1530–1. The authority for the blazon of the arms and supporters is Hervey's grant of crest in 1562, and the 1568 and 1634 visitations.[5] Hervey mentions Benolt's grant with " two griffons for their supporters, and so bearinge them destytute of the chefest mater to the said Armes appendant " ; he accordingly grants an " Augmentation of healme and Creaste with th'appurtynannces ". The absence of a crest in the 1532 coat is also specifically referred to in an abstract of Hervey's grant in the British Museum[6] wherein it is stated that " the armes and supporters were graunted and Alowed " by Benolt, and " having no healme creaste nor mantells ", Hervey granted the same " to make perfect and augment " them.

---

[1] Coll. Arms MSS. L.1 " Alphabet "; 2nd C.24/187 ; Vincent 169/52 ; Misc. Gt. 1/49.
[2] Coll. Arms Hervey's Gts. ff. 38–41.
[3] Coll. Arms MS. L.1 " Alphabet ".
[4] Coll. Arms 2nd C.24/187.
[5] Coll. Arms G.10/120 (1568) ; 2nd C.24/187 (1634).
[6] Brit. Mus. Add. MSS. 14295. This is partly compiled by Richard and Henry St. George, Norroy and Clarenceux Kings of Arms.

The College of Arms text of Hervey's blazon reads as follows :

Uppon the Healme a Camell golde, brydle sable, bearinge two [" pepper Baggs "—deleted] bagys of p̄pyr argent powdered with cloves and corded sable [" powdred and corded sable "—deleted] [" spangled with Cloves Argent "—deleted] on a wreath argent and sable mantelled gules dubled argent.

It will be observed that the common mantling of this period, gules and argent, is here given, but this was altered to azure and argent at the 1634 visitation, and is so recorded in two other manuscripts in the College of Arms ; [1] this mantling, with argent and gules for the crest wreath, was adopted in the official exemplification certified by Norroy King of Arms on 8th June 1927,[2] and has also been followed here.

Crest

In making the unusual grant of arms with supporters but no crest, Benolt may have been influenced by the Grocers' pre-grant usage of a similar device. The charter of incorporation, granted to the Company by Henry VI on 16th February 1428/9, permitted them, as was customary, the right to use a common seal. It is probable that the purchase of the seal in that year, as recorded in the Company's accounts,[3] was also accompanied by the adoption of heraldic insignia, for ten years later is an entry in the same source [4] of the payment for " ii Getons

---

[1] Coll. Arms Vinc. 169/52, and Misc. Gts. 1/49.
[2] Original in the possession of the Company.
[3] Kingdon (J. A.), ed. *Facsimiles of the MS. archives of the Grocers' Company, 1345–1463*, pt. II (1886), fo. 204.
[4] ibid. fo. 260.

[i.e. guidons] of wosted w^t Groceris Armes ". In the period of account for 1450–1 tapestries and cushions " w^t our Armes " were bought,[1] and it is significant that in 1454 three more tapestries were bought " w^t the sayd Armes and grefonis ",[2] thus clearly indicating that the griffins were then in use either as a badge or, as is likely, supporters to the arms.

What form the arms then took is uncertain, but it is probable that they were similar to those granted by Benolt in 1532. An example of these pre-grant arms does, in fact, survive in the fifteenth-century glass in the church of St. Helen, Bishopsgate. This is identical with the shield today, but how far it exactly represents the arms as originally portrayed is doubtful since the glass is said to have been much restored.[3] Two other instances of what may be pre-grant arms exist in two documents [4] in the College of Arms, both considered to date about 1530. Each shows a minor deviation from the current arms in filling the shield with ten cloves, four being in base.

While the griffins probably have the conventional significance of guardians of treasure, the cloves and the pepper bags allude to the fraternities of Spicers and Pepperers whose union under the above-mentioned charter of 1429 first constituted the " Mistery of Grocers ". The camel symbolizes the East whence came the products of their trade.

---

[1] Kingdon (J. A.), ed. *Facsimiles of the MS. archives of the Grocers' Company, 1345–1463* pt. II (1886), fo. 315.

[2] ibid. fo. 353.

[3] *L.C.C. Survey of London*, vol. IX : St. Helen, Bishopsgate, pt. 1 (1924), p. 45 ; *Royal Comm. on Hist. Mon :* The City (1929), p. 23.

[4] Coll. Arms 1st H.7/6lb, and Vincent, " Two Ears of Wheat ".

THE WORSHIPFUL COMPANY OF GUNMAKERS

THE Gunmakers' Company is one of the few City guilds still exercising full statutory powers. Its functions are concerned solely with the viewing and proving of small arms and handguns, and it shares this process of testing with the more recently constituted Proof House at Birmingham.

Prior to the formation of the Company by its charter of 14th March 1637/8, working gunsmiths of the City were enrolled as freemen of either the Armourers' Company or the Blacksmiths' Company. The charter, when obtained, was for some years an empty document, for the former parent companies bitterly opposed its enrolment by the Court of Aldermen, without which formality the powers of the new company were ineffectual. It was not until 1656 that enrolment was secured. Numerous Acts of Parliament have subsequently enlarged the Company's powers under its charter.

THE ARMORIAL BEARINGS (Pl. 25)

Argent two guns in saltire proper between in chief a monogram formed by the letters GP in base the letter V, both regally crowned, on the dexter side a powder barrel and on the sinister three bullets, all sable.

Crest: On a wreath of the colours a dexter arm embowed vested with steel armour garnished or, the hand holding a scimitar, all proper.

These arms, which are without authority, were assumed in the seventeenth century. Their genesis is probably to be found in a passage from the Company's court minute books, dated 5th July 1694,[1] which reads as follows:

Ordered that a Seale be made for the Company's use to seal all Publick writings of the Company and particularly that the assignment aforesaid be sealed with such seale which said seale to be made to have engraven the Cross Guns, GP and Crowne, the letter V and Crowne with a powder barrell and three bullets.

The symbols listed are precisely those used in the arms, and the terms of the order suggest that the device upon the seal antedated

---

[1] Guild. Lib. MS. 5220/6.

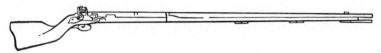

Long-barrelled flint-lock gun, *c.* A.D. 1660

the arms : for if arms were then existent it would have been simpler
and natural to have required the seal to have been engraved with them,
rather than to itemize the symbols in detail.

The crest appears to have been a later addition ; an entry in the
court minute books for 1794[1] indicates that it was not adopted until
that year. This entry, dated 27th February, is as follows :

> Ordered also that a new copper plate of the Company's arms be cut for
> the Court Summonses of the same pattern . . . with the alteration only
> of making the shield an oval and the addition of the crest of an arm armed
> over the helmet.

The inference that this records the crest's first assumption is supported
by the absence of any crest in all examples of the arms seen before
1794.

The arms are usually displayed, when used by the Company, on a
shield encompassed by an array of banners and weapons of all periods

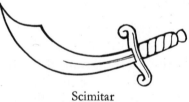

Scimitar

ranging from the primitive war mace
to the bayoneted musket. The heraldry
of official representations of the device is unorthodox in other respects :
the helm resembles that now reserved
for the sovereign and princes of the
blood royal ; no mantling is shown
but ostrich feathers decorate the helm, above which the crest and
wreath float unattached.

The cipher GP signifies " Gunmakers Proof " and is the proof mark
with which all handguns passed at the Proof House are required to be
marked under the charter of 1638, together with the letter V meaning
" viewed ". Proving is concerned with testing the barrel of the gun
by firing a charge in it, while viewing appears to have been a further
test of the barrel for correctness of bore and straightness of barrel,

[1] Guild. Lib. MS. 5220/11.

GOD IS OUR STRENGTH

ASSHER · DURE

Pl. 30

IRONMONGERS, p. 148

etc. The two processes were at one time separate inspections, for on 7th August 1670 the minute book of the Company records the appointment of Oliver Wadland as View Master, as distinct from the office of Proof Master.

Shield encompassed by an array of banners and weapons

THE WORSHIPFUL COMPANY OF HABERDASHERS

THE origin of the word "haberdasher" and the early activities of the trade of haberdashery have provoked much speculation without reaching certainty. City records, however, throw some light on the subject which, in conjunction with the investigation of the eminent etymologist, W. W. Skeat (*The Academy*, vol. 72, pp. 513/14), suggests a solution.

In two lists of custom dues on cloths and furs coming into London in the reign of Edward I appears the term "hapertas" in one and "haberdassherie" in the other. Apart from the obvious similarity of these two words, the context makes it probable that they are two renderings of the same word, or are at least allied in meaning. Since hapertas is said to have been a coarse thick cloth or fustian used beneath armour, it would appear that the haberdasher's original function was that of a dealer in this material, and later, by extension, a seller of underwear of all kinds together with other articles of apparel and personal wear. The wide variety of a haberdasher's wares is revealed by an inventory of a haberdasher's shop made in 1378. This lists such goods as leather laces, numerous caps and hats, purses, spurs, beads, pencases, children's woollen boots, linen thread, etc. Of these, the most prominent articles mentioned are caps and hats, and the existence of separate misteries of cappers, hatters and hurers indicates that they were the manufacturers who supplied the haberdasher with these wares.

By a charter of 6th July 1502 the successors of the hatters, cappers and hurers were united with the haberdashers, and incorporated under the title of the fraternity of St. Katherine of Merchant Haberdashers. This new dignity of "Merchant", which the Haberdashers shared with the Taylors of the City, marks a change in the functions of the members of the guild from small-scale shopkeeping to merchant trading. But whereas the Merchant Taylors retained their new style against much opposition both from the Court of Aldermen and the other City guilds, the Haberdashers were forced to relinquish the title of "Merchant" under a charter of 2nd November 1510.

The Company now concerns itself, in addition to its ceremonial observances, with the administration of many charitable endowments largely for the support of schools and university scholarships.

THE ARMORIAL BEARINGS (Pl. 29)

Barry wavy of six argent and azure on a bend gules a lion passant guardant or.

Crest : On a wreath argent and azure issuing from clouds two naked arms embowed holding a laurel wreath all proper.

Mantling : Azure doubled argent.

Supporters : On either side a goat of India argent flecked gules membered or.

Motto : Serve and obey.

Confirmation of arms and grant of crest and
supporters by Robert Cooke,
Clarenceux
8th November 1570[1]

Two earlier patents of arms to the Haberdashers are also in the possession of the Company. The first of these was issued by Roger Legh, Clarenceux, to the " Churche Wardeyns of the . . . Craft of Haberdasshers " on 16th July 1446, and granted a " feld of silver three brosshes of Gowlys bound of the feld betwene a Cheveron of Asure in the Cheveron three Kateryn wheles of gold ". The dominant religious interest of the Haberdashers at this period is evident from " Churche Wardeyns " being named as the principals negotiating the grant on behalf of the Company. Moreover, Roger Legh in making his grant says that he was moved to do so " for the good entent observaunce and worship to holy Churche and to Sainte Kateryn Virgin and Martyr " ; and in the illuminated initial of the patent is painted the figure of the saint with a wheel and a sword. This fraternity was in fact the antecedent of the guild which two years later was incorporated by a charter of 1448 under the name of the Fraternity of St. Katherine the Virgin of the Haberdasshers in the City of London. The " Kateryn wheles " in the arms therefore represent the instrument on which St. Catherine of Alexandria was condemned to die. The significance of the brushes is not so clear, but it is likely that they allude to one of the many former activities of the Company. Before the process of amalgamation had united it into one body, the Haberdashers' trade comprised several fraternities, amongst which was the Hurers, *alias*

---

[1] Original document in the possession of the Company.

Arms of A.D. 1446

Arms of the Merchant Venturers

Arms of the Merchant Staplers

Cappers. As the Hurers seem to have been makers of rough wool or hair caps,[1] brushes were probably used in the finishing process.

On 13th December 1503 Roger Machado, formerly Richmond Herald to Henry VII and at this time Clarenceux King of Arms, issued a new patent of arms to the Haberdashers. Machado blazoned these

[1] Riley (H. T.), *Memorials of London* (1868), pp. 402 ff., 558 ff.

Within the certificate banner:

I certify and declare that the Armorial Bearings Arms, Crest and Supporters above depicted do of right belong and appertain to the Wardens and Commonalty of the mystery of Goldsmiths of the City of London. In testimony whereof I have hereunto set my hand at the College of Arms, London this thirty first day of March, 1891.

Albert W. Woods
Garter

On the scroll: JUSTITIA VIRTUTUM REGINA

Pl. 31   K.138

CERTIFICATE OF ARMS TO THE WORSHIPFUL COMPANY OF
GOLDSMITHS, 31ST MARCH 1891, SHOWING A PEER'S HELM
IN THE EXEMPLIFICATION

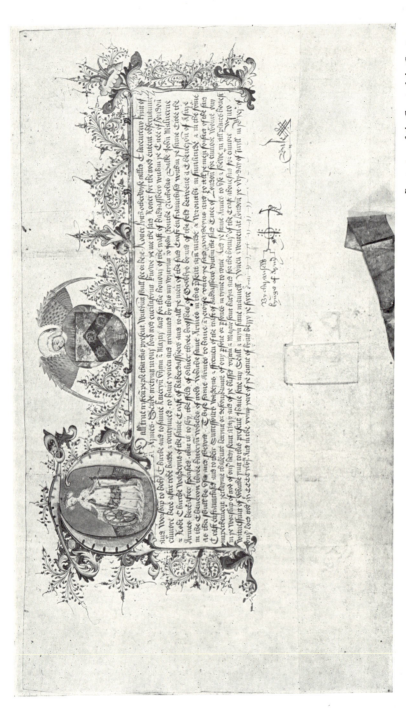

L.139

Pl. 32

LETTERS PATENT GRANTING ARMS TO THE WORSHIPFUL COMPANY OF HABERDASHERS,

16TH JULY 1446

arms as a "feld of Asur and Silver owndey a bend gowlys with a lyepard passaunt on the bende gold armyd asur". This new grant was occasioned by the charter of 6th July 1502 which united the fraternity of Hurers with the mistery of Haberdashers. The newly constituted body had now become the "Craft of Marchauntt Haberdashers" in the patent of arms, but the figure of the saint still decorates the initial letter as in the earlier patent of 1446.

The arms granted by Roger Machado were later confirmed by Robert Cooke, Clarenceux, in the current grant of 8th November 1570 which added thereto crest and supporters. This patent recites that

> whereas the freemen of the art or mistery of haberdashers . . . was first incorporate by the name of . . . the fraternytie of Sainct Katherine the Virgin of haberdashers . . . to whom aunclent armes were given . . . which saide corporacion hathe ben by letters patentes of the quenes majesties progenitors altered into the name of marchantes habardashers to whom the armes hereafter mencioned was given, yet notwithstandinge for the further honor of the sayd arte or mistery by the name of haberdashers to which they be now lastly translated and reduced for avoydeng of contencions and other inormities whereunto they might fall by reason of the unaccostomed name of marchant habardashers . . . I the said Clarencieulx . . . [have] given and graunted . . . to these their aunclent armes that is to saye onde silver and asur on a bende gules a lion passant golde, the creast and supporters hereafter followenge viz. uppon the heaulme on a wreathe argent and asur issuant out of the cloudes two naked armes holdinge a lorell garlande all in proper coollar, the armes supported with two Goates of India silver, flecked gules, membred golde mantled asur, dowbled argent.

The Company's former title of Merchant Haberdashers is only paralleled among the craft guilds of the City by that of the Merchant Taylors, and the designation "Merchant" was clearly intended to recognize the greater dignity and importance of the Companies concerned. The distinction was due to their trading activities extending beyond small shopkeeping into wholesale buying and selling, especially trading beyond the seas. The point is well illustrated in the charter of 1503 which conferred upon the Merchant Taylors' Company its new style. This charter recites that because the men of the mistery of Taylors traded in all and every kinds of merchandize in all quarters and kingdoms of the world, the king was pleased to change their name to the Guild of Merchant Taylors. Among the great trading corporations, the Merchant Venturers and the Merchant Staplers are notable examples of the use of the term "merchant".

L

By their charter of 6th July 1502 the Haberdashers had acquired a similar distinction a year before the Merchant Taylors, and no doubt the wavy field of their arms was intended to represent their ocean-wide commerce,[1] with the leopard of England, or lion passant gardant, symbolizing the royal patronage which had gained for them their new style. It appears, however, that the more imposing title was not generally acceptable, giving rise, in the words of the 1570 patent of arms, to " contencions and other inormities ". In consequence a further charter of 1510 reduced the Company in name to that of Haberdashers only, but their arms were unchanged and remain as a witness to their former merchant status. That the City itself played some part in this incident is evident from a single entry in the Repertories of the Court of Aldermen,[2] dated 1st April 1511, which ordered the Chamberlain of London to pay 40 marks to the wardens of the Haberdashers towards the cost of their new charter by which " their name ys chaunged from the name of merchaunthaberdasshers unto the name of haberdasshers ". Why the City intervened and subsequently agreed to pay part of the costs is not revealed.

The significance of the crest is obscure but it follows a pattern favoured by Cooke and it is repeated with minor variations in the crests granted by him to the Bakers, Curriers and Pewterers. The supporters allude to the source and origin of the raw material of some of the haberdashers' wares.

[1] Compare similar fields of the arms of the Merchant Venturers and Merchant Staplers.
[2] Corporation of London Records Office, Rep. 2 fo. 110.

THE WORSHIPFUL COMPANY OF HORNERS

THE making of articles of horn is a craft of great antiquity. Apart from its natural formation which made it readily adaptable for the production of such things as drinking cups, powder horns, ink-horns, and hunting horns, horn was easily worked and provided a durable and cheap substitute for domestic metal ware such as spoons and platters. It was also processed to form translucent sheets for lantern and window coverings.

A reference to " Statutes of the Horners " in the City records of 1284 suggests that those who followed this craft may already have been organized at that date. Formal ordinances for the government of the mistery are recorded in 1391 and give powers to elect wardens " like wardens of other misteries " and to search for bad workmanship. On 5th March 1475/6 the Horners and the mistery of Bottle-

Hunting horn

Leather bottle

makers, or makers of leather bottles and other vessels of leather, were united at their own request as one mistery; the armorial bearings of the Horners Company symbolize this union. This act of union seems to have been a measure of economy partly due to the decline of the trade at this period. New materials were beginning to replace leather for bottles, and the parallel trade of the Horners was similarly threatened by the increasing use of glass. About a hundred years later, Harrison in writing of Elizabethan England reported that " Horn in windows is now quite laid down ". Glass, was however, still too dear for commonplace articles and for such objects as lanterns which were subjected to rough usage. The lantern indeed contributed to a revival of the horner's trade in the growing London of the seventeenth century, a revival which was encouraged by a new demand for snuff and tobacco boxes, and by the development of the horn-book which presented for the education of children durable copies of the alphabet, the Lord's prayer, etc., protected by thin transparent sheets of horn. During this period of relative prosperity the Company acquired a charter of incorporation on 12th January 1637/8 which confirmed to them their control of the trade and set out the limits thereof. Economic factors were, however, to undermine this control and by the reign of George III the Company's powers had become ineffective. Although successful proceedings were taken in 1745 against infringement, this was the last recorded attempt at enforcement. The Company's interest in the craft is nevertheless not extinct, and it has in addition become associated with the development of plastics through the numerous members of the livery who are prominent in that industry.

THE ARMORIAL BEARINGS (Pl. 25)

Argent on a chevron between three leather bottles sable as many hunting-horns stringed of the first.

These arms, for which there is no authority, have been used by the Company at least since the end of the sixteenth century.[1] Union with the Mistery of Bottlemakers, which occurred in 1476, is commemorated by the inclusion of the three leather bottles as charged.

The Company has no motto.

[1] Guild. Lib. MS. 2463 (*anno* 1575)

THE WORSHIPFUL COMPANY OF INNHOLDERS

On 28th October 1473 the wardens and good men of the mistery of Hostelers successfully petitioned the mayor and Aldermen that all those of the craft who were freemen of the City and kept inns therein should thenceforth be called innholders to distinguish them from their servants who were hostelers "indede". Previously, hostelers and "hay-mongers" had been associated in regulations issued for the conduct of the hosteler's trade, of which an essential service was the provision of feed for the traveller's horse. The subsequent restriction of the term "ostler" (a corruption of hosteler, or hostel keeper) to describe the stableman is indicative of the emphasis on this aspect of the inn-holder's early activities.

Ordinances for the self-government of the mistery of Hostelers were granted in 1446. These required all those enfranchised in the craft to be obedient to the rules of the wardens appointed, and set out various regulations empowering the wardens to search "hostries" in the City and to report guests of ill-fame and their "harberers" to the mayor or the chamberlain. Every hostry was to display an "opene sygne" and hostelers were to bring any alien, who sought lodging, before the mayor so that the "maire may have knowleche of the cause of his comyng" to the City. Numerous other obligations were from time to time laid upon the hosteler or innholder for the maintenance of peace and the good conduct of the City. Among these regulations were orders that every hosteler was to warn his guests not to carry arms and to remove them from those that did so ; he must warn his guests not to wander abroad after curfew ; no one was to be lodged beyond a day and a night ; no hosteler might bake bread but buy it from a baker, nor might he sell ale except to his guests ; and prices of hay and the standard of measures were also regulated.

The Innholders were first incorporated by royal charter on 21st December 1514. A later charter of 1663 extended the Company's jurisdiction over the trade to a radius of three miles from the City, but legal opinion in 1757 considered that this was not then capable of application.

The Company no longer exercises any of its former trade functions.

143

THE ARMORIAL BEARINGS (Pl. 26)

Azure a chevron argent between three oatsheaves or, on a chief argent a " St. Julian's cross " sable.

Crest : On a wreath argent and azure a star or appearing out of a cloud proper.

Mantling : Gules doubled argent.

Supporters : On either side a horse regardant argent.

Granted[1] by Sir Richard St. George,
Clarenceux
2nd December 1634

Motto : Hinc spes affulget.

The Innholders had assumed arms more than a century before the date of their grant. In the illuminated border of the Company's first charter,[2] dated 21st December 1514, there appears in two places a shield of arms which is clearly the precursor of the present coat armour. These early arms show : azure a chevron per pale and per

Impaled arms from the Charter of A.D. 1514   Oat sheaf

chevron gules and argent between three oatsheaves or, impaling argent a saltire formy. The next record of the arms, in a manuscript compiled about 1530,[3] omits the impalement and it does not appear again, in any of the examples seen, until 1633.[4] A similar impalement occurs in the fifteenth-century grant to the Brewers' Company, in the margin of which the Company's arms are depicted impaled with the insignia

---

[1], [2] Originals at Innholders' Hall.
[3] Coll. Arms MS. Vincent, " Two Ears of Wheat ", p. I.
[4] Stow (J.), *Survey of London* (1633), p. 631.

attributed to St. Thomas Becket, their patron saint ; in both cases the religious association was prudently concealed with the onset of the English Reformation and Henry VIII's break with Rome. In 1588[1] the tinctures of the chevron are found transposed and thereafter this rendering becomes the usual custom ; no significance appears to be attached to the change which was probably fortuitous and due to the absence of a controlling grant. When in 1634 the Company sought a grant, no doubt because the visitation of that year revealed the lack of authority for the arms then in use, Clarenceux incorporated the existing devices in a new form, modified the parti-coloured chevron to one of plain argent, and added the crest and supporters.

A further minor change was the probably unconscious transformation of the saltire formy into a saltire crosslet, an alteration which has increased the obscurity surrounding it. For this cross sets a problem. In the blazon of the grant it is described as a *St. Julian's cross*, a description that is used for the saltire crosslet by most subsequent manuals of heraldry. It seems certain, however, that this is a misnomer, since in neither form is the cross known in the iconography of St. Julian the Hospitaller, and hagiographical literature does not mention it in association with him. Indeed the most that is said on the subject of the symbolism of this saint is that no emblem is commonly ascribed to him ; on occasion he may be seen in company with a stag, an oar or a boat.

Common oat

Clues to the reasoning that led to the false attribution are to be found in two features of the 1514 charter. Therein the Company is described as " artis sive mistere Sancti Juliani le Herberger de Inholders civitatis nostre London : ", and the illumination also includes a painting of the figure of " Sanctus Julianus " clad in armour and bearing the cross symbol on his breastplate. It would seem that the obvious but erroneous inference has been drawn by the herald when devising the grant of 1634.

[1] Harl. MS. 6363 fo. 18.

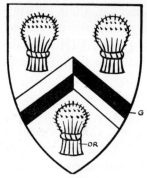

Arms, after the drawing in Harl. MS. Brit. Mus. 6363 fo. 18, A.D. 1588

Few facts are known about St. Julian the Herberger, or Hospitaller, and there is some confusion with him and the many saints of the same name in the martyrology. The legend of his life was a popular one in the Middle Ages, notably in Belgium and Spain. In penance for the unwitting murder of his parents, as foretold by a stag that he had hunted, he set up a hospice on the bank of a river, and there succoured the pilgrim and wayfarer, ferrying them as need required across the stream. Hence he became the patron saint of the innkeeper, but the cross that he bears in the Innholders' charter is in all probability simply a hospitaller's cross. It was a common practice for those who did charitable work for the sick in hospitals, or who cared for the way-

Arms of the Brewers' Company impaled with St. Julian's cross, after the drawing in Harl. MS. Brit. Mus. 472/9, A.D. 1599

farer and pilgrim, to wear such a device. It would be a natural symbol for the Innholders to have adopted, or for the artist who designed the illumination of the charter to have attributed to them as a symbol of their patron's vocation. There may be some support for this interpretation in one example of the arms of the Brewers' Company, found in a manuscript of 1599,[1] where that Company's arms also have been impaled with this same cross; the possibility of an artist's error is to some extent discounted by the presence on the same page of the exact arms of the Company as rendered in their current grant. The similar activities of the Brewers and the Innholders would explain the use for both Companies of the symbolic cross of hospitality.[2]

Interesting drawings of the impaled arms and the arms as afterwards granted are to be found in a manuscript volume[3] compiled at the time of the 1634 visitation by Richard Price, arms painter, and subsequently bought from him by John Withie.[4] In this volume the artist has superimposed upon the unauthorized arms a sheet of paper bearing a drawing of the official arms; the crest is added upon the original page. Beneath the earlier drawing appears the motto " Come ye blessed, when I was harborles, ye lodged me." This early motto has clearly influenced the choice of the crest which recalls the lodestar by whose light the travellers were guided to Christ in the stable; there was no room for Mary and Joseph at the inn. It is a reminder of the duty of the innholder to succour the wayfarer as exemplified by the legend of St. Julian, and this tradition of hospitality is succinctly conveyed in the present motto: *Hinc spes affulget* (Hope shines from here).

The oatsheaves represent the staple sustenance provided by the innholder for the traveller's horse.

In the original patent the blazon reads as follows:

Azure a chevron argent between three Oatsheaves or on a cheife Argent a St. Julian's cross Sable and for there Crest a starr or appearing out of a cloude proper supported wth two horses regardant Argent.

---

[1] Brit. Mus. Harl. MS. 472.

[2] I am indebted to Fr. Philip Hayes, C.P., for help in arriving at this conclusion.

[3] Brit. Mus. Harl. MS. 1464 fo. 113/93.

[4] An arms painter employed by the College of Arms and Master of the Painter Stainers' Company in 1657.

THE WORSHIPFUL COMPANY OF IRONMONGERS

THE early ironmonger made his living by selling iron in rods and bars to blacksmiths, farriers and other workers in metal, and although his wares included manufactured goods they were not his sole concern as in the case of his modern successor.

London ironmongers are recorded as an organized body in 1300 when overseers were appointed to ensure proper standards of iron for cartwheels and generally to administer the trade. The mistery first became an incorporated company by a charter of 20th March, 3 Edward IV (1463), and its powers of trade control, now lapsed, were confirmed by a succession of charters of which the latest is dated 19th November 1688. The Company is one of the Great Twelve and is the tenth in order of precedence.

THE ARMORIAL BEARINGS (Pl. 30)

Argent on a chevron gules between three gads of steel azure three swivels or.
Crest : On a wreath azure, gules and argent two lizards erect face to face proper coupled with a chain gules.
Mantling : Gules doubled ermine.

Granted[1] by William Tyndale,
Lancaster King of Arms
1st September 1455
Ratified and confirmed by letters patent[2]
issued by William Hervey,
Clarenceux
28th May 1560

Supporters : On either side a lizard erect proper.

Granted[3] by Sir Henry Farnham Burke,
Garter
10th July 1923

Mottoes : God is our strength ; *Assher dure.*

---

[1] Original grant at Ironmongers' Hall. Coloured facsimile with transcript in *Catalogue of the antiquities and works of art exhibited at Ironmongers' Hall,* vol. 1 (1869), p. 262.

[2] Original at Ironmongers' Hall. Transcript in Nicholl (J.). *Some Account of the Ironmongers* (1866), p. 27.

[3] Original at Ironmongers' Hall.

The 1455 grant of arms to the Ironmongers was confirmed by Thomas Benolt, Clarenceux, on 16th October 1530. The authority of Lancaster's patent was later rejected by William Hervey who issued a new patent, dated 28th May 1560, which left the arms, however, in the same form as they had hitherto been borne.

The 1455 patent blazoned the arms as follows:

> We Lancastre Kyng of Armes sende gretyng . . . Know ye us the forsaide Lancastre to have yeven and graunted unto the honurable crafte and felasship of the fraunchised men of Iremongers of the Citee of London a token of Armes that is to sey Silver a cheveron of gowles sette bytwene three Gaddes of Stele of Asure on the cheveron three swevells of golde with two lizardes of theire owne kynde encoupeled with Gowlys on the helmet.

The patent is signed "Lancastre", the official name alone being used without indication of a personal name. Originally the office of

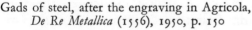

Gads of steel, after the engraving in Agricola,   Swivel
De Re Metallica (1556), 1950, p. 150

Lancaster was that of a herald in the service of the earls or dukes of Lancaster, but with the accession of Henry IV the title was given to a crown officer. From then until the reign of Edward IV, Lancaster was a King of Arms and had charge of the northern province.[1] His position in the southern province appears to have been that of an agent to Clarenceux. This is to be inferred from a trick of the Ironmongers' arms included in the 1530 visitation of Surrey[2] to which is added a note stating that the arms were given "by Lancaster King at Arms, Mareschall under Clarenneux [*sic*] King at Armes". The 1568

---

[1] See Wagner (A. R.), on the officers of arms in *Complete Peerage*, vol. XI (1949), appx. p. 73, and London (H. S.), in Burke's *Landed Gentry* (1952), p. cxiii.
[2] Coll. Arms MS. 1st H.7/60b.

visitation of London[1] similarly enters the arms. Why Hervey in 1560 should question the authority of this grant is uncertain, for Lancaster clearly had a lawful status when he made it. In his letters patent Hervey says :

> Whereas one Lancaster, by the name of Lancaster King of Armes, hathe heretofore assigned unto the Worshipfull Company and fellashipe of the Iremongers of the Citie of London, armes and crest . . . And fyndyng the same to be without good auctoryte I . . . being requyred . . . to ratefye and confyrme the saide armes helme and crest . . . as they heretofore have used and borne the same . . . In consyderacon whereof . . . I, the said Clarencieulx King of Armes by power and auctoryte to myn office anexed and graunted by the quenes majesties letters patents . . . have ratyfyed and confyrmed . . . the saide armes helme and crest in the same manner and forme as in the old patent is depicted.

The jurisdiction of Lancaster was not disputed by Clarenceux Benolt when he confirmed the grant on 16th October 1530 ; and Benolt was not accustomed to be complacent when he considered his powers of office threatened. It can only be surmised that while Benolt was admittedly aware that Tyndale had made his grant by licence from, or with the agreement of Clarenceux, this arrangement may not have been appreciated by Hervey, who would therefore conclude that Lancaster had infringed Clarenceux's authority in issuing letters patent to the Ironmongers. The great controversy of 1530 between Benolt and Garter King of Arms in which Benolt challenged the right of Garter to grant arms within Clarenceux's province of the south,[2] must have been fresh in Hervey's mind. The order of Charles Brandon, Duke of Suffolk, Earl Marshal 1524–33, which required " all craftes and companyes of this noble Cittye of London "[3] to bear arms only with the authority of Clarenceux, would reinforce Hervey's rejection of Lancaster's authority if Hervey himself were in fact unaware of the latter's position *vis-à-vis* Clarenceux at the time of the grant. Whatever may have been the reason for Hervey's objection, it is evident that he did not dispute the patent on heraldic grounds since he confirmed and ratified the arms without alteration.

---

[1] Coll. Arms MS. G.10/121.

[2] Wagner (A. R.), *Heralds and Heraldry in the Middle Ages* (1939), ch. IX.

[3] Anstis Collns. in the *College of Arms*, vol. 2, p. 552, cited by Dallaway (J.), *Inquiries into the Origin and Progress of Heraldry* (1793), pp. 170–1.

Supporters in the form of lizards had been adopted by the Iron-mongers some time in the sixteenth century and are shown with the arms in the account book of the Company for the year 1572. No formal grant was made until 1923.

Unless the use of lizards for crest and supporters is merely decorative, it can only be assumed that they are intended to represent salamanders. The salamander was described by naturalists of old as a form of lizard which was alleged to have the capacity to withstand the hottest fire without harm. The lizards could thus be held to symbolize the tempering process of the steel represented in the arms by the gads, or wedge-shaped bars of steel. This theme is further emphasized by *Assher dure*, the older of the Company's two mottoes, and a phonetic rendering of the French *Acier dur*.

THE WORSHIPFUL COMPANY OF JOINERS

A MISTERY of Joiners appears to have been a voluntary association in London in the fourteenth century, and there is evidence that it was associated or identified with a religious guild of St. James the Apostle in the church of St. James Garlickhithe. The trade first became a fully organized community, with powers to elect wardens to govern the craft, on 18th March 1400/1. The petition which sought these powers stated that deceits were practised in the trade because the mistery had no wardens or governing body. Ordinances were accordingly granted by the mayor and aldermen, and the Company was later incorporated by royal charter on 14th April 1571 by the name, in translation, of the Master, Wardens and Commonalty of the faculty of Joiners and Ceilers.

The various trades concerned in working wood were highly specialized in the Middle Ages, and specialization then, as now, was fraught with potential friction. Carpenters, turners, sawyers, joiners, and others from time to time brought their complaints of infringement of their respective crafts before the mayor and aldermen for settlement. The original function of the joiner was the joining of timber by mortice and tenon. Large-scale work on the construction of houses involving frames and roofs was the prerogative of the carpenter who employed the joiner to fit doors, window frames and wainscoting. The joiner's use of the chisel and plane in these processes and in the making of furniture led him to acquire the art of carving which is recognized in the 1571 charter by the Company's secondary title of " ceilers " (Lat. *caelatores* : carvers).

Attempts to resolve differences between the Carpenters, Turners and Joiners were made by the mayor and aldermen by the restriction of turner's work to " whatsoever is done with the foot as have treddle or wheele for turning wood ", and the joiner's craft to work involving mortices and tenons, and the employment of planes and chisels. The jurisdiction of the Joiners' Company was further defined by the Lord Mayor in 1613 who agreed that its powers of search should cover the trades also of coachmaker, trunkmaker, gunstock, flask and touch box maker, and box maker.

The Company's powers of search were regularly carried out during the seventeenth century but appear to have been discontinued after 1748. Thereafter the Company ceased to exercise trade control.

THE ARMORIAL BEARINGS (Pl. 35)

Gules a chevron argent between in chief two compasses extended, points downwards, and in base a globe or ; on a chief argent a pale azure between two roses gules, on the pale an escallop argent.

Crest : On a wreath or and azure a demi-man carnation, with a laurel garland vert about his head and waist, holding with his dexter hand a lance or at rest upon his shoulder.

Mantling : Gules doubled argent.

Granted[1] by Robert Cooke,
Clarenceux
10th August 1571

Motto : Join loyalty and liberty.

Arms were in use by the Company before a formal grant was achieved and there is an early trick of them included at the end of a record of the visitation of Surrey of 1530.[2] The latter conforms to the terms of the grant which blazons the arms as follows :

gules a cheveron silver betwene too Compasses a globe in poynte gold, on a pale azure (betewene to rosses of the fyrste) in Cheffe a Scalope of the seconde and to their Creste upon a heaulme on a wreath golde and asur a demy man charnu holdinge a Lanse golde withe a garlande of [Laurel][3] aboute his hed and waste vert manteled gules dowbled argent.

Although only arms and crest have been granted to the Joiners, the Company has adopted supporters which appear to have originated at the beginning of the eighteenth century. According to the Company's minute book,[4] a committee of enquiry was instituted on 1st February 1842 to consider the question of the Company's right to supporters. On 11th February the Committee submitted that supporters were found engraved in a work dated 1708,[5] and were also shown in other literary sources of a later date. On this evidence it was decided that the supporters were " Two naked boys proper the dexter holding in his hand an emblematical female figure crowned with a mural coronet

[1] Original patent deposited in Guildhall Library, MS. 8039.
[2] Coll. Arms MS. 1st H.7.
[3] Word partly illegible.
[4] In the custody of the Company at the time of writing.
[5] Hatton (E.), *New View of London* (1708), vol. 2 (folding plate).

Compass

Scallop

sable; the sinister holding in his hand a square." These supporters have continued to be used but they have no authority.

The ancient seal[1] of the Company, bearing the date 1571, shows the authorized arms and crest encircled by the motto " God grannte us to use justice withe mercye ". This motto was succeeded by " Join truth with trust " which in turn was replaced by the current motto.

Although not so blazoned, the crest is in fact a " wild man " or " woodman ", an ancient figure of pageants and heraldry, and was no doubt chosen for the sake of the canting allusion to the Joiners as men of wood, or woodmen.

Arms with unauthorized supporters

----

[1] Preserved in the Guildhall Museum. For an article on its recovery by the Company see *City Press* (22nd August 1900), p. 4.

Pl. 33   L.154

LETTERS PATENT GRANTING ARMS TO THE WORSHIPFUL COMPANY OF IRONMONGERS,
1ST SEPTEMBER 1455

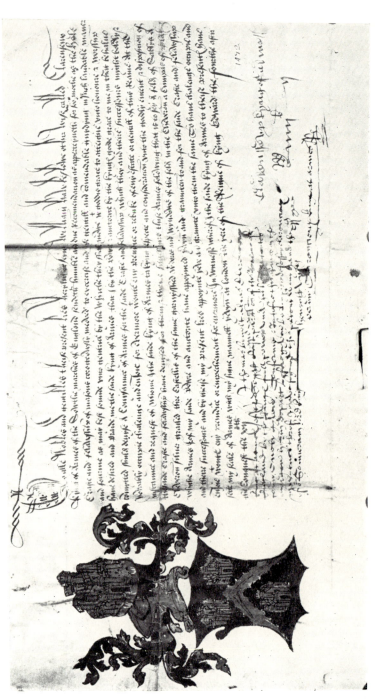

Pl. 34   M.155

By courtesy of the Court of the Company

LETTERS PATENT GRANTING ARMS TO THE WORSHIPFUL COMPANY OF MASONS, 1472–3

(12 Ed. IV—no day and month given)

THE WORSHIPFUL COMPANY OF LEATHERSELLERS

An organization of leathersellers appears first to have been established by a grant of ordinances in 1372 which gave to the mistery powers to control the trade. Hitherto control had been effected by the direct rule of the Court of Aldermen. The ordinances laid down standards of workmanship, both for the leathersellers and the pursers, and ordained that two men from each of the misteries be elected yearly to oversee the crafts. Additional ordinances were made in 1398 and 1440, and on 19th August 1444 the Company of Leathersellers was incorporated by royal charter.

The pursers' early association with the leathersellers was revived on 7th June 1502 when, by an order of the Court of Aldermen, the mistery of Glovers-Pursers, who had united in 1498, were merged with the Company of Leathersellers. The pouchmakers were similarly absorbed by the Leathersellers on 17th November 1517. No reference is made to these absorbed misteries in the Leathersellers' later charter of 24th June 1604 in which the Company is described as the Wardens and Society of the Mistery or Art of the Leathersellers of London. The Glovers, however, regained their independence by a charter of 10th September 1639.

From the early ordinances of 1372 it would appear that the Leathersellers originally dealt only in finished leather after it had left the hands of the tanner and currier. They were not then manufacturers of leather articles, but their subsequent absorption of the misteries mentioned above extended their activities to include the sale of all leather goods other than those which were the province of the Companies of Glovers, Girdlers, Saddlers and Cordwainers.

The Company's powers are known to have been exercised up to the year 1679, but there is no record of any supervision of the trade after that date. Although its control of the craft has lapsed, the Leathersellers' Company is closely associated with educational and technical development in the leather industry, notably through the Leathersellers' College in Bermondsey which was built at the Company's expense.

THE ARMORIAL BEARINGS (Pl. 36)

Argent three roebucks passant regardant gules attired and unguled sable.

Crest : A demi-roebuck gules, attired and unguled sable, standing on a wreath of the colours.

Mantling : Gules doubled ermine.

Supporters : Dexter a roebuck or attired and unguled sable ; sinister a ram argent armed and unguled or.

Motto : Soli Deo honor et gloria.

The above is transcribed from the blazon testified by Sir Alfred Scott Scott-Gatty, Garter, on 3rd April 1905.[1]

The Company was first granted arms by John More, Norroy, on 20th May 1479. This fifteenth century patent was burned in a fire at Leathersellers' Hall in 1819[2] but a record of the grant is preserved on a scroll of arms[3] " viewed proved and confirmed " by Sir Henry St. George, Richmond Herald, at the visitation of London in 1634. In that year the Company exhibited all the grants then in their possession and the careful transcription of the relevant parts of the grants together with painted copies of the arms, has preserved a historical record of the development of the arms that might otherwise have been lost. The scroll displays in addition to the transcript of the 1479 grant, a translated abstract of the 1464 grant to the Glovers, at that time united with the Leathersellers ; the 1505 grant impaling the arms of the Glovers quartered with the now defunct Pursers ; and a certification of the 1505 arms by Thomas Benolt, Clarenceux, on 11th October 1530.

The 1479 arms were identical with the present coat apart from the absence of the supporters which were not added until 1505. According to the transcript made in 1634, the original patent stated that the Company of Leathersellers had " required me [i.e. John More, Norroy King of arms] inasmuch as I had weded a wife of the same company to testifie and affirme the Armes ", and they were accordingly certified in the following terms : " Silver three Roe bucks passant gules looking backwards armed sables, more plaine the hornes and clewes black, the creast the foreparte of a Roe bucke from the midle upwards sheweinge the forefeet standing in a wreath silver and gules, the mantells

---

[1] At Leathersellers' Hall.
[2] Black (W. H.), *History of the Worshipful Company of Leathersellers* (1871), p. 36.
[3] At Leathersellers' Hall.

gules and ermin." That Norroy was permitted to intrude in Clarenceux's province of the south was obviously a courteous concession
on the latter's part in view of More's family connection with the
Company.

On 7th June 1502 the Leathersellers absorbed the united companies
of Glovers and Pursers, and on 7th November 1505 the triple union
was formally marked by the grant of new arms by Roger Machado,
alias Richmond, Clarenceux King of Arms. The record of these arms
on the 1634 scroll is confined to a coloured exemplification which
depicts the arms of the Leathersellers impaling quarterly 1 and 4 the
Glovers' arms and 2 and 3 those of the Pursers (sable two goats argent
tongued gules armed or); no crest is shown, but the supporters as
now borne are for the first time added. An entry in the College of
Arms of the blazon of Machado's grant reads as follows :

> they bere party per palle sylver thre Roes coward gowles clowed and
> horned sable the second party quarterly the fyrst six peces sable and
> sylver thre ramys montaunt of the same horned and clowed gold the
> second quarter sable two cheverelles combatans silver clowed and horned
> gold.

These arms were confirmed to the Leathersellers on 11th October 1530
by Thomas Benolt, Clarenceux.

In 1639 the Glovers, under a new charter of incorporation, separated
from the Leathersellers, who thereupon readopted their old arms but
retained the 1505 supporters with the ram as a reminder of their former
association with the Glovers ; these arms were confirmed by Sir Henry
St. George, Clarenceux, on 29th January 1687.[1]

The Company's motto is taken from the Vulgate text of 1 Timothy
i. 17.

---

[1] Original in the possession of the Leathersellers' Company.

THE WORSHIPFUL COMPANY OF LORINERS

THE Loriners' ordinances of 1260/1 are among the oldest known rules of self-government granted by the mayor to the City misteries or guilds. They set out the terms of apprenticeship, stipulate that all members obey the overseers, and include a survival of feudalism by requiring the mistery to do annual service to the mayor of London by providing him with a bridle and bit every Easter. Further ordinances of 1313 and 1393 permit the election of wardens to survey the craft of " lore-merie ", and in 1488 the ordinance book, submitted to the mayor for approval, exhibits concern for the spiritual and bodily welfare of mem-

Manage-bit

Boss

bers which was a feature of the medieval trade fraternities. In addition to rules for apprenticeship and the conduct of the craft, provision is made therein for masses for dead members and for alms for the poor.

Trade control appears to have been lost at an early date and the Company's only charter of incorporation, dated 3rd December 1711, deals solely with its domestic and internal government.

The loriner was a maker of bridle bits and other metal work for horse trappings. Although at one time the mistery of loriners was responsible for the supervision of the craft of spurriers, or makers of spurs, the latter became an independent company until it was united with the Company of Blacksmiths in 1571.

Join loyalty and liberty

GOD IS OUR GUIDE

THE ARMORIAL BEARINGS (Pl. 35)

Azure on a chevron argent, between three manage-bits or, as many bosses sable.

There is no authority for these arms. In the earliest known instances of their use the field is recorded as gules,[1] and indistinguishable objects not resembling the later bosses appear upon the chevron, but azure is generally adopted thereafter and bosses become established.[2]

Manage is an archaic term for the schooling of a horse and is employed in the blazon as a synonym for riding. The bosses on the chevron are the metal caps, often elaborately engraved or incised with decorative patterns, which cover the junction of the bit's mouthpiece with the sidepieces.

There is no crest, supporters or motto.

[1] 1588 : Harl. MS. 6363 ; and 1591 : Harl. MS. 2220.
[2] 1599 : Harl. MS. 472.

THE WORSHIPFUL COMPANY OF MAKERS OF
PLAYING CARDS

ALTHOUGH playing cards are of great antiquity, evidence suggests that they were not made in England until the first half of the fifteenth century. Attempts were made to restrict or forbid their use, both on moral grounds and in the interests of the preservation of archery which was said to suffer from the indulgence in card playing. But by the end of the sixteenth century the pastime was a favourite with all classes of the community, and during the reigns of Elizabeth I and James I monopolies of both imported and home-produced cards were granted to various individuals with the right of searching, sealing and exacting import duties. The London card makers first sought a charter of incorporation from James I but were not successful until 22nd October 1628. The charter constituted the Master, Wardens and Commonalty of the Mistery of Makers of Playing Cards of the City of London as a perpetual corporation with control of the trade of paste board making as well as of playing card making in the City and within ten miles distant from it. The principal reason for seeking a charter was stated as being the uncontrolled import of foreign cards to the hurt of the home trade. In return for the prohibition of imports allowed by the charter, the Company was required to pay to the king's receiver certain specified duties on each pack.

Pasteboard makers were originally included within the Company's jurisdiction since, as it was stated, they were at that time all playing card makers. The expanding use of pasteboard for other purposes made its manufacturers unwilling to accept control by the Company. Towards the end of the eighteenth century the Company instituted proceedings against recalcitrant makers but the actions failed, and the powers of trade control thereafter became ineffective.

Today many leading makers of playing cards are members of the Company and by this means it still retains its association with the trade.

THE ARMORIAL BEARINGS (Pl. 42)

Gules on a cross argent between the four ace cards proper, the aces of hearts and diamonds in chief and of clubs and spades in base, a lion passant gardant gules.

Crest : On a wreath of the colours an arm embowed in armour erect, holding in the hand an ace of hearts, all proper.

Mantling : Gules doubled argent.

Supporters : On either side a man in armour proper, garnished or, over his left shoulder a sash gules.

Motto : Corde recto elati omnes.[1]

These arms, of which the earliest example found occurs in 1739,[2] are without authority.

[1] All are exalted by a good heart.
[2] Maitland (W.), *History of London* (1739), p. 603.

THE WORSHIPFUL COMPANY OF MASONS

ALTHOUGH domestic buildings in medieval London were mainly timber structures, the mason's art was required for the larger public edifices. Masons in considerable numbers were needed for such buildings as Westminster Abbey, the Tower of London, the churches and for the first stone bridge across the Thames begun by Peter of Colechurch in 1176. References in the City archives to the regulation of the trade at the beginning of the thirteenth century indicate its importance at an early date. The first direct reference to a trade association of masons occurs in 1376 when four masons were elected to represent the mistery on the Common Council of the City. Thereafter the Company became firmly established and the pattern of its development follows that of other medieval guilds, with ordinances, of 1481, showing its concern both for the control of the craft and the religious devotion of its members.

The decline of guild powers was precipitated in the case of the building trades by the Great Fire of 1666. The restriction of labour to freemen, which was the essence of the guild, was opposed to the rapid reconstruction of the devastated City, especially as new fire regulations required the use of stone and brick in place of timber. In the emergency the guilds' privileges were ignored, and Parliament enacted that nonfreemen be employed throughout the City. The grant of a charter of incorporation on 17th September 1677 could not arrest the decay of its trade functions. The last known exercise of the Company's powers of search for faulty work occurred in 1704, and the Company has since concentrated on its ceremonial and benevolent purposes.

THE ARMORIAL BEARINGS (Pl. 35)

Sable on a chevron engrailed between three castles argent, garnished with doors and windows sable, a pair of compasses extended also sable.

Crest : On a wreath of the colours a castle argent.

Mantling : Sable doubled argent.

> Granted by William Hawkeslowe,
> Clarenceux
> 12 Edward IV, 1472–3[1]

Motto : God is our guide.

---

[1] Only the regnal year is given in the original patent, which is preserved in the British Museum : Add. ch. 19135. A collotype facsimile is given in Conder (E.), *Records of the Hole crafte and fellowship of Masons* (1894).

This is one of the few surviving fifteenth century patents of arms. At some period it was alienated from the Masons' archives, but was subsequently purchased by the Company in 1871 and presented by them to the British Museum. To its loss are due the corrupt arms that are generally found during the seventeenth, eighteenth and nineteenth centuries, and which appear to be traceable to the engraving in the 1633 edition of Stow's survey.[1] In these exemplifications the castles become towers and the chevron is plain. Conder[2] is troubled

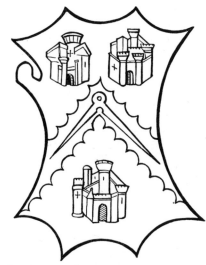

Crest and arms after the patent of A.D. 1472–3

by this change and theorizes at length as to its cause. He advances the possibility that the adoption of the plain chevron was due to a preference for an emblem more reminiscent of the symbolic square of the speculative masons, or Freemasons, who, as he says, were active within the ranks of the operative masons. There seems to be, however, no necessity to seek for a deliberate act in this alteration, since it is far more probable that the change was the unconscious result of that indifference to heraldic detail which has similarly corrupted other arms on numerous occasions.

A former motto of the Company was " In the Lord is all our trust ". It was observed, however, that in the church of St. Helen Bishopsgate

[1] Stow (J.), *Survey of London* (1633), p. 630.
[2] Conder, op. cit. p. 92 ff.

was a tomb of a member of the Masons' Company, one William Kerwin, who died on 26th December 1594, which bore the correct arms of the Company together with the motto " God is our guide ".   By a decision of the Court this motto was, therefore, adopted in 1894.[1]

The original patent of arms states that William Hawkeslowe " Devysed . . . a feld of Sablys a Cheveron silver grailed thre Castellis of the same garnysshed with dores and wyndows of the feld in the Cheveron a Cumpas of Blak . . ."   An exemplification in the margin of the patent shows the crest, which is not mentioned in the text, as described above. The crest wreath, however, appears to be wholly of argent slightly high-lighted by yellow pen-shading.   In view of this indeterminate colouring the conventional practice of using the main colour and metal of the arms (sable and argent) has been followed in the modern blazon given above.   Notes on the document indicate that the arms were confirmed by Thomas Benolt, Clarenceux, in 12 Henry VIII (1520/1) and entered at the visitation of London in 1634.

Arms granted in comparatively modern times to various lodges of Freemasons have been based on this coat.

[1] Conder, op. cit. p. 86 n.1.

THE HONOURABLE COMPANY OF MASTER MARINERS

THIS is one of the few companies of very recent origin whose constitutions are based upon the organization of a City guild.   It was formed on 25th June 1926 and was granted a charter of incorporation in August 1930.   Its distinctive appellation of " Honourable " was conferred by George V in June 1928.

Objects of the guild are, in general, to maintain and enhance the professional status of senior officers of the Merchant Navy, and to promote education and research in all matters relating to the nautical profession.   Membership is limited to duly qualified master mariners who are elected by the Court of the Company.

THE ARMORIAL BEARINGS (Pl. 36)

Argent on waves of the sea a representation of the ship " Golden Hind " in full sail all proper, on a chief arched azure a terrestrial globe also proper between two mullets of the field.

Crest : On a wreath of the colours in front of a sun in splendour proper a quadrant or.

Mantling : Azure doubled argent.

Supporters : On either side a seahorse proper gorged with a naval crown or, that on the dexter supporting a staff proper headed or flying therefrom the Union flag, and that on the sinister supporting a like staff flying therefrom the Red ensign also proper.

Motto : Loyalty and service.

Granted[1] by Sir Henry Farnham Burke,
Garter
Gordon Ambrose de Lisle Lee,
Clarenceux
Arthur William Steuart Cochrane,
Norroy
26th April 1927

The Master Mariners' Company shares with the newer Company of Farmers and the older Company of Plumbers the distinction of having been granted a badge in addition to a coat of arms.   This is described as :   In Front of an anchor or a fountain fimbriated of the first thereon

---

[1] Original in the possession of the Company.

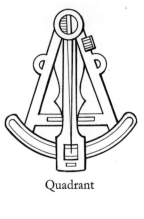

Quadrant

Naval crown

Badge

Standard

Pl. 36

M.166

LEATHERSELLERS, p. 155
MASTER MARINERS, p. 165

a seahorse proper gorged with a naval crown also of the first. The date of the grant is 8th November 1951.

It is of interest to note that two of the most recently established companies have resorted to this ancient practice of using badges. The badge as heraldic ensign is at least as old as the armorial shield, and as a personal device antedates it. The function of the heraldic badge is distinct from that of the coat of arms. The latter is peculiar to the bearer thereof and, in the case of a company, may only be used by that body as a corporate whole. The badge, on the other hand, may be worn by whomsoever its owner pleases and is properly so used on livery or uniform, or in such other ways as may indicate adherence or ownership.

The patent granting the badge of the Master Mariners is illuminated with a painting of the Company's standard which is of four panels bearing : 1, next the staff, the arms ; 2, the badge ; 3, the quadrant of the crest ; and 4, in the fly, the badge.

THE WORSHIPFUL COMPANY OF MERCERS

MERCERY was formerly a generic term, derived from the Latin *merx* (merchandise), which covered a wide variety of small goods, mostly for apparel and personal use. In the Middle Ages these were hawked by the pedlar and chapman who sold them from village to village and displayed them at fairs. Fine fabrics, damask, satin, silk, linen, hats and trinkets were originally among their stock-in-trade. The precise province of the London guilds dealing in such articles was in early times neither well defined nor legally determined, and it was restricted only so far as the guilds could enforce it. The activities of the Mercers impinged especially upon those of the Haberdashers, to an extent that their wardens are found jointly challenging the *bona fides* of a freeman of another guild who had used the " art of Mercers and Haberdashers ".

With increasing wealth and power, many of the Mercers of the City became merchant importers and exporters, notably of silks and other fine textiles ; and from their ranks stemmed the Company of Merchant Adventurers, while the Merchant Staplers included eminent Mercers among their members.

The earliest mention of the Mercers is the appointment of the fraternity, about 1190, as patrons of the Hospital of St. Thomas of Acon, upon the site of which the Company's Hall still stands. On 13th January 1393/4 the " men of the Mistery of Mercery of the City of London " were incorporated by royal charter. Thereafter the Company achieved pre-eminence among the City guilds, and now ranks as the first of the major companies which are known as the Great Twelve. Although its trading function has long ceased, the Company administers great estates and numerous benefactions among which are St. Paul's School, Mercers' School, Gresham's Royal Exchange and Gresham College.

THE ARMORIAL BEARINGS (Pl. 37)

Gules issuant from a bank of clouds a figure of the Virgin couped at the shoulders proper vested in a crimson robe adorned with gold, the neck

encircled by a jewelled necklace, crined or and wreathed about the temples
with a chaplet of roses alternately argent and of the first, and crowned with
a celestial crown, the whole within a bordure of clouds also proper.

Crest : On a wreath of the colours issuant from a bank of clouds proper
a figure of the Virgin as in the arms.

Mantling : Gules doubled argent.

Motto : Honor Deo.

Granted[1] by Sir Alfred Scott Scott-Gatty,
Garter
George Edward Cokayne,
Clarenceux
William Henry Weldon,
Norroy
2nd April 1911

These arms, without the crest, were recorded in the visitations of
1568, 1634 and 1687,[2] but the Company had no formal patent of arms
until 1911, when the crest was added. The blazon given above is
transcribed from this patent.

The preamble to the patent states that records in the College of Arms
show the figure of the Virgin with an uncrowned head ; but on the
representation of the Company that the crown had always been present
in the arms as used by them, the Kings of Arms accordingly assigned
the crown and blazoned the arms in the terms given above in order
to remove all doubts as to their correct form. That the conflict was
recognized much earlier is established by the entry of the arms at the
1687 visitation. The trick there shown gives an uncrowned head
accompanied by a trick of the Company's seal depicting the crowned
Virgin. The entry records that the arms were entered at the 1634
visitation and " now again approved and entered ". Although the
1634 visitation provides no details of the arms but merely records their
entry, it is of interest to note that in a manuscript collection of the arms
of eminent Mercers in the archives at Mercers' Hall, there is inserted
a painting on vellum of the arms of the Company showing the crown
and bearing the signature of Henry St. George, Richmond Herald,
the herald who conducted the 1634 visitation.

The device of the Virgin derives from the Company's common seal,
a cast of which is preserved in the British Museum.[3] This seal depicts

[1] Original patent at Mercers' Hall.
[2] Coll. Arms MSS. G.10/120 (1568) ; 2nd C.24/1 (1634) ; K.9/433 (1687).
[3] British Museum. *Catalogue of Seals,* vol. 2 (1892), p. 119.

a female full-face, the head wearing a crown of five points. Doubts have been expressed as to the identity of the female thus portrayed, and the Company's historian concludes that there is no evidence to support the assertion that the figure represents the Blessed Virgin Mary.[1] No alternative suggestion of merit has, however, been offered, and this negative conclusion is based upon the absence in the Company's archives of any direct identification of the figure. But in spite of the lack of any positive evidence there are strong grounds for making the inference that the Virgin Mary is, in fact, intended.

In the first place it would appear improbable that this figure is of secular origin. Were this the case, the presence of a crown would signify a queen, but it is unlikely that the Mercers adopted as their emblem the head of the wife of Richard II, whose charter to the Company empowered them to use a common seal. If a royal symbol were adopted the king himself would have been the natural choice. But the bust depicted on the seal is clearly that of a female and the persistent designation of the figure as the " maiden " from early times confirms this. Failing, therefore, the identification of the head as of royal origin, the only acceptable alternative is that it is of religious significance. Since all the medieval City guilds probably derived from religious fraternities —many of their pre-Reformation arms incorporate symbols of devotion to their patron saints—the use of a religious emblem by so ancient a company as the Mercers is not unexpected. The crown, however, would eliminate all female saints other than the Blessed Virgin Mary who is customarily portrayed crowned.

Although the Company is not associated in its charters or other instruments with a religious fraternity from which it can establish a direct origin, the Mercers have been closely connected with the Hospital and Chapel of St. Thomas of Acon, a foundation dedicated to the Blessed Virgin. At the inception of this hospital in the twelfth century the Mercers were specifically constituted its patrons. Thus the absence of any female patron, and on the other hand the early and continuous association with the Blessed Virgin Mary through the Hospital of St. Thomas of Acon, make at least a strong case for assuming that the figure on the seal represents the Virgin.

Turning to such references as exist in the archives concerning the Company's device, it is found that the figure is invariably called the

---

[1] Watney (Sir J.), *Account of the Mistery of Mercers* (1914), p. 27.

HONOR · DEO

Pl. 37   N.171

MERCERS, p. 168

"maiden" or the "maidenhead". The use of these terms for the Virgin is frequent in both devotional and secular literature of the Middle Ages,[1] and it may well be that the Mercers had turned a common usage into an habitual custom for so important a symbol in their life, thereby obscuring in later times the true origin of their emblem. The importance attached to the figure is borne out by a series of incidents that occurred in the latter half of the sixteenth century. In accordance with the political stigma adhering to Thomas Becket at this time, his effigy which stood above the gateway of the Hospital of St. Thomas of Acon was removed by the Mercers at the order of Thomas Cromwell, and a "maidenhead" in stone was erected in its place.[2] With the turn of the religious tide under Mary, Becket's image was reinstated, only to be supplanted once more by the maiden in the reign of Elizabeth. It might be supposed that the substitution of the "maiden" for Becket would discredit the theory that she represented the Virgin Mary, on the grounds that both at this period would be unacceptable religious emblems. But the period was one of great confusion with strong iconoclastic feelings running counter to the supporters of the ancient ritual, while both factions tended to misconstrue the various orders for the prevention of religious abuses. One such order to permit the reinstatement of images that had been removed contrary to the Injunctions of Edward VI was suspended lest the replacement should "engender contention".

Further evidence for the homage that the Middle Ages paid to the Virgin Mary is to be seen in the widespread use of the words Maiden and Maidenhead in early street names and house signs in London ; [3] and in the popular design of "maidenhead" spoons which, as precursors of apostle spoons, are often to be found among testators' goods in early wills.[4] That these spoons, now notable collectors' pieces, ceased to be produced much after the sixteenth century may probably be indicative of the disfavour into which devotion to the Virgin fell.

Final support for the attribution of the figure in the arms to that of

---

[1] Cp. *Speculum Christiani* (Early English Text Society, original series, vol. 182) ; glossary s.v. Mayden.

[2] Watney, *Account of the Mistery of Mercers* (1914), p. 28 ; Watney, *Some Account of the Hospital of St. Thomas of Acon* (1906), pp. 119, 159.

[3] Cp. Harben (H. A.), *Dictionary of London* (1918), s.v. Maiden and Maidenhead.

[4] Rupert (G.), *Apostle Spoons* (1929), p. 3 ; Gask (N.), *Old Silver Spoons* (1926), pp. 47–9.

N

the Virgin Mary is the presence of the clouds which there surround her and which may symbolize her Assumption. The Assumption was a favourite tableau in City pageants, and in a recently published work on City dramatic records[1] it is seen that the Assumption occurs more frequently than any other feature ; its complete absence after 1540 is a significant comment on one effect of the Reformation. The " maiden " however, continued as a spectacular feature of the Mercers' pageants well into the seventeenth century but it is apparent that the main character had by then lost its original significance.

From the available evidence it would seem that the identification of the female head by the Kings of Arms in their grant of 1911 is correct. It is difficult, indeed, to believe that any representation of a crowned female head in the Middle Ages could be intended to portray any other than one whose cult pervaded medieval life and to whom was accorded a veneration above all the saints.

[1] Malone Society. *Calendar of Dramatic Records in the Books of the Livery Companies of London, 1485–1640* (1954).

THE WORSHIPFUL COMPANY OF MERCHANT TAYLORS

IN 1327 the tailors and armourers of London presented a petition to Edward III seeking the right to govern their own mistery and to ensure that none be permitted to " hold table or shop of the mistery " unless he be free of that mistery. The king granted the suppliants their request, naming them in the ensuing letters patent the Tailors and Linen Armourers (" Cissores et Armurarii Linearum Armaturarum civitatis Londonensis "). This expanded designation makes it clear that one of the functions of the tailor at this time was the lining and quilting of armour in addition to the making of male garments. Restriction to the manufacture of male apparel is referred to in the present operative charter of the Company, dated 6th January 1502/3, which states that none shall engage in the " working, cutting or making of men's garments within the said City, the liberties and suburbs of the same " unless he be first admitted to the guild. But from the same charter it appears that the activities of many members had already deviated from the narrow confines of the tailoring trade and had for some time embraced wholesale trading in many commodities. In consequence of this enhanced merchant status the king renamed the guild the " Merchant Taylors of the fraternity of St. John the Baptist " since its members " exercised the sale and purchase of all and singular whatsoever goods and merchandise and especially woollen cloths both wholesale and retail ". The Company had sought this new dignity because, as the author of the *Great Chronicle of London* asserts, " the name of Taylours was nott correspondent to theyr worshypp ". This move had excited " grete dysdayn of alle the worshypffull Felyshyppis " of the City as well as the hostility of the Court of Aldermen. But whereas the combined forces of the City had successfully suppressed the similar dignity conferred in the previous year upon the Haberdashers, the Taylors retained their new title against all opposition. From this date the merchant activities of the Company overshadowed its original functions and today members are drawn from diverse occupations and callings. As one of the Great Twelve companies it is richly endowed and contributes large sums towards educational establishments, notably for the administration of Merchant Taylors School.

THE ARMORIAL BEARINGS (Pl. 38)

Argent a pavilion imperial purple garnished or lined ermine between two mantles also imperial purple lined ermine, on a chief azure a lion passant guardant or.

Crest : On a wreath argent and azure on a mount vert a lamb argent in sunbeams or.

Mantling : Gules doubled argent.

Supporters : On either side a camel or.

Motto : *Concordia parvae res crescunt.*

Granted[1] by Robert Cooke,
Clarenceux
23rd December 1586

This grant superseded an earlier one granted by Sir Thomas Holme, Clarenceux, on 23rd October 1481, to the " laudable and right honourable craft of Taylors and Linge Armourers ".[2] The reason for the new grant is given in the text of Cooke's patent which recites that the Art or Mistery of Merchant Taylors of the Fraternity of St. John the Baptist was incorporated under this style and title in the eighteenth year of the reign of Henry VII

> which fraternety have of longe continuance borne Armes healme and creast, which Armes and Creast to the knowlege of suche as be skilfull in that facultye, beinge fownde to be over muche intrecate with confused mixtures of to many thinges in one shilde contrarye to the loweid and comendable manor of bearinge of Armes, I theirfore . . . have thought good to yelde them my helpe onlye reformynge and alterynge of the same armes and creast : but for a further declaration of the worthines of the said fraternety do graunte unto them these supporters hereafter folowinge : which Armes Creast and Supporters is thus Blased ; That is to saie the field Silver a pavilion with two mantells imperiall purpell garnyshed with golde on a chiffe azure a Lyon passant golde, and to the Creast upon the healme on a wreathe silver and azure on a mount vert a Lame silver in the sonne beames gold mantled gules doubled Silver, and Supported with two Cameles golde.

The " over muche intrecate " arms to which exception was taken was blazoned by Holme as follows :[3]

---

[1] Original at Merchant Taylors' Hall.

[2] Original not now extant. Transcript in Clode (C. M.), *Memorials of the Merchant Taylors Company* (1875), p. 96.

[3] Clode, loc. cit. Clode has modernized the language of the original patent which was evidently accessible to him at that time.

Pl. 38

N.175

MERCHANT TAYLORS, p. 173

Silver a pavilion between two mantles imperial purple garnished with gold in a chief azure an holy lamb set within a sun. The crest upon the helm a pavilion purple garnished with gold being within the same our Blessed Lady St. Mary the Virgin in a vesture of gold sitting upon a cushion azure, Christ her son standing naked before her holding between his hands a vesture called tunica inconsutilis his said mother working upon that one end of the same vesture set within a wreath gold and azure, the mantle purple furred with ermine.

The effect of the new patent was to substitute a lion of England for the holy lamb on the chief, and to replace the crest of Virgin and Child with a secular version of the holy lamb : " a lame silver in the sonne beames golde " ; supporters were also added at this time. While it is possible that suppression of the religious symbols was a late effect of the Reformation, it is at least equally likely that the change was due to a desire to conform to a more austere taste in heraldry. A number of guilds had expediently secularized their arms during the period of the Reformation, and as late as 1582 the Parish Clerks had sought a new grant because their arms were " over muche charged with certayne superstition ". But other guilds had retained emblems of their religious origins and still continue to exhibit them in their current arms.[1]

Cooke's justification for the new patent to the Merchant Taylors was that the " Armes and Creast to the knowlege of suche as be skilfull in that facultye, beinge fownde to be over muche intrecate with confused mixtures of to many thinges in one shilde contrarye to the loweid and comendable manor of bearinge of Armes." On its face value this suggests no more than a desire for a simpler device. But that the religious aspect was present in the minds of the members of the guild seems to be implied in an entry in the Company's minute book for the year 1583[2] which records the appointment of two Assistants of the Company to " talk with the Harolds, concerning the crest of the Company's arms, for the altering of the same in such convenient manner *as may stand in good form of heraldry*, and *as shall be best considered of for the worship of the Company*". Concern for the Company's prestige, or " worship ", may have been due only to a desire to avoid a loss of tradition by a too drastic reform of the arms. But, coupled with what seems a calculated elimination of any specific religious symbol in the new patent, it suggests a desire to escape any implication of devotion

[1] e.g. Fishmongers, Mercers, Drapers, Girdlers, Broderers, Upholders.
[2] Herbert (W.), *History of the Twelve Great Livery Companies*, vol. 2 (1836), p. 392.

to papist rule. The matter had evidently been deliberated for some time and it is unlikely that the religious issue would not have been considered, as well as the heraldic.

Although the arms were modified, the Company's seal of 1502, which bears the old arms without crest, remained unchanged and is still in use today.

Both the ancient crest of Virgin and Child, and the holy lamb allude to the Company's origin as a fraternity of St. John the Baptist, deriving as religious emblems from the Gospel of St. John.[1] The " tunica

Pavilion, after the woodcut from *De Re Militari Valturius*, Verona, A.D. 1483

inconsutilis " is the coat " without seam ", woven by the Blessed Virgin Mary, for which the soldiers cast lots after the Crucifixion. The pavilion which survives in the current arms was no doubt inspired by the similar canopy in which the Virgin sits in the 1481 crest ; such canopies of dignity are familiar accompaniments to religious personages in art, and are similarly used in the arms of the Upholders. The mantles in the shield symbolize the tailor's craft.

In placing a lion of England on the chief, Clarenceux Cooke follows the course he took in the case of the Haberdashers. Both companies had received the distinctive epithet of " Merchant "[2] in royal charters

[1] St. John i. 29, 36 ; xix. 23.
[2] See the notes on the Haberdashers for the significance of this term.

granted by Henry VII, and in each case the royal patronage is alluded to by this royal charge.

The camels firſt appear as supporters in Cooke's patent, but it is clear that the animal was already an eſtablished symbol of the Company. In the expenses of the pageant of 1556, provided for the mayoral celebrations of Sir Thomas Offley, a Merchant Taylor, the Company paid the sum of 4*s* 2*d*. for " hym that rode upon the camyll " and a further sum of £1 " to Southwall for the kamyll hyer ".[1]   A camel was in faċt an habitual feature of Merchant Taylors' pageants in the sixteenth century,[2] and it may be that the beaſt was intended as a reference to the eaſtern trade of the Merchant Company, as was the camel creſt of the Grocers, but no evidence has been found to confirm this.

The Company's motto is a quotation from Salluſt :[3] *Concordia parvae res crescunt, discordia maxumae dilabuntur*—with harmony small things grow, while with discord the mightieſt are ruined.

[1] Sayle (R. T. D.), *Lord Mayors' Pageants of the Merchant Taylors' Company* (1931), p. 30.

[2] Malone Society. *Calendar of Dramatic Records in the Books of the Livery Companies of London, 1485–1640* (1954), p. xxxviii.

[3] *Jugurtha* x. 6.

THE WORSHIPFUL COMPANY OF MUSICIANS

ORDINANCES dated 1350 indicate that a fellowship of minstrels of London existed in the fourteenth century. The fellowship was then concerned solely with mutual benevolence and charity. Contemporary with this small association was an influential body attached to the Court and known as the King's Minstrels, to whom a royal charter was later granted by Edward IV on 24th April 1469. The King's Minstrels thereby were given control of all musicians, including those of the City. Nevertheless in 1500 the City minstrels obtained from the mayor and aldermen authority to govern their own affairs. Further acts of Common Council confirmed their powers and on 8th July 1604, a royal charter was granted, giving the City guild government over all minstrels and musicians within the City and within three miles thereof. This charter trangressed that which Edward IV had given to the King's Minstrels, and a conflict ensued between the two bodies. In 1634 the Westminster guild secured the revocation of their rivals' charter, and in the following year obtained for themselves a new charter. Meanwhile the City company continued to exercise control within the City under various acts of Common Council, culminating in that of 1700. By the middle of the eighteenth century, however, the company, in common with other guilds, ceased to function as a craft guild, and turned to those benevolent and educational works in the cause of music which it now fosters.

On 29th December 1950 a new charter was granted by George VI to replace that revoked by Charles I.

THE ARMORIAL BEARINGS (Pl. 35)

Azure a swan with wings expanded argent within a double tressure flory counter-flory or, on a chief gules a pale between two lions passant gardant or, thereon a rose gules barbed and seeded vert.

Crest : On a wreath of the colours a lyre or.
Mantling : Azure doubled or.

Granted by William Camden,
Clarenceux
15th October 1604

The original patent of arms has not survived and the above blazon is derived from records in the College of Arms.[1]

Evidence that the Musicians were using arms before this grant is to be found in a manuscript of about 1590 in the British Museum.[2] This compilation includes the " armes of the several companies within the City of London " and gives a trick of the " Minstrells " showing : Azure a swan argent within a double tressure flory counter-flory also argent ; a chief with a pale thereon is also given but without tinctures, and the compiler has added a note " No arms ".

A Fellowship of Minstrels of London had been formed in the year 1500, with the consent of the Court of Common Council. Its members had formerly been under the governance of the King's Minstrels, a body incorporated by Edward IV in 1469, and this early association no doubt explains the presence in the arms of the royal emblems of the lion and the rose. In 1604, the year of the grant of arms, the London Minstrels achieved incorporation by royal charter under the name of the Master, Wardens and Commonalty of the Art or Science of the Musicians of London. The powers assigned to them included control over musicians in the City of London and within three miles of the City. Since this was territory which had been the province of the King's Minstrels, the new Company felt itself to be the lineal descendants of the chartered body of 1469, and the royal emblems set the seal upon this assumption. Another royal allusion may be the tressure flory counter-flory. This, tinctured gules, is a feature of the ancient royal arms of Scotland which were marshalled with those of England and Ireland on the accession of James VI of Scotland to the English throne in 1604. If its introduction into the arms of the Musicians' Company were out of compliment to King James who gave the Company its first charter, then the date of 1590 accepted for the manuscript referred to above must be an error. This date is based upon the inclusion in the manuscript of the arms of Sir Christopher Hatton, " lorde Chanselur ", with the date of 1589 added. Hatton died in 1591, but it is by no means impossible that further additions were made to the volume after his death, and that the sketch of the Musicians' arms may well be a suggested design prepared in the year 1604. The association of this notable royal device with the Musicians' Company in the very year

[1] Camden's Grants I. 4. and 2nd C.24/213.
[2] Harl. MS. 2220 fo. 11.

Crest and arms after Coll. Arms 2nd C.24/213

of James's accession seems to be beyond mere coincidence. On the other hand it must be noted that the double tressure flory counter flory is known in English arms of an earlier date.

The swan and, in the crest, the lyre probably allude to the legend which has many variations but commonly tells how the soul of Apollo, the god of music, passed at death into a swan ; swans are therefore said to sing at the approach of death because they are inspired by Apollo.

The arms now usually appear without motto, but an early motto was *A Deo et caelo symphonia* with a later substitute of the word " Harmony ".

THE WORSHIPFUL COMPANY OF NEEDLEMAKERS

JOHN STOW, in his *Annales*, says that needles were first made in England during the reign of Queen Mary by a Moor dwelling in Cheapside. Signs of a developing needle industry in London and the organization of the craft may be seen in a petition of 1629 made by the needlemakers of London against the manufacture of needles by an " engine " worked by aliens. The " engine " was suppressed because it was held that it made faulty products, was dangerous to those working it and deprived many of their means of livelihood. Full corporate status was achieved by the needlemakers by a charter granted by Cromwell on 10th November 1656, and reincorporation took place after the Restoration on 9th February 1664. The provisions of the latter charter were similar to those made by Cromwell, and constituted the needlemakers as the Master, Wardens and Commonalty of the art or mistery of Needlemakers of the City of London, with control of needlemaking in the City and ten miles compass thereof.

By the eighteenth century London had ceased to be a centre of the trade which had become established in its present home at Redditch. The Company still maintains a close association with the industry and is intimately linked with the Needlemakers Association, the modern trade organization.

THE ARMORIAL BEARINGS (Pl. 39)

An escutcheon of azure, with three needles palewise in fesse argent crowned or, displayed in front of an apple-tree environed with a serpent proper.

Supporters : Dexter the figure of Adam, sinister the figure of Eve holding in her dexter hand a needle argent, both wreathed about the waist with fig-leaves proper.

Motto : They sewed fig-leaves together and made themselves aprons.

There is no authority for these arms and the absence of a grant is no doubt responsible for the variations which have occurred in the Company's device since the first discovered example of its use in 1680.[1] From that date until about 1875[2] the colour of the field is invariably

---

[1] *London Almanack for XXX years*, by R. Morden and P. Lee (1680).

[2] The *City of London Directory*, 1875, gives *vert*; 1876 gives *azure*. Welch (C.) in his *Coat Armour of the London Livery Companies*, published 1914, still gives *vert*.

given as *vert*; no explanation can be given for the change to *azure*, and it may well be that the alteration was merely fortuitous.

The original crest was a fruit-tree with no serpent entwined around it.[1]   This gave place, *c.* 1780,[2] to a Moor's head couped at the shoulders in profile proper, wreathed about the temples argent and gules, vested round the shoulders argent and in the ear a pearl; at the same time the supporters appear.   The Moor's head is recorded in unofficial sources as being still in use at least until 1915,[3] but the practice had earlier developed of omitting the crest entirely and placing the shield in front

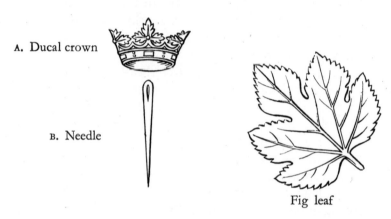

A. Ducal crown

B. Needle

Fig leaf

of an apple-tree environed with a serpent.   These are the arms accepted by the Company today.

The Moor's head was probably chosen in reference to the tradition that fine Spanish needles were first introduced into England during the reign of Queen Mary by a negro (i.e. a Moor) who lived in Cheapside,[4] while the tree and serpent allude, as do the supporters and motto, to the Biblical story of the fall of man in the garden of Eden.

It has been suggested that the charges on the shield are a rebus for Threadneedle Street (formerly Three Needle Street), and from this the inference has been drawn that this street was the centre of the needle

[1] Maitland (W.), *History of London* (1739).
[2] Edmondson (J.), *Complete Body of Heraldry*, vol. 1 (1780).
[3] The *City Directory*, until it ceased giving this information in 1915, quotes the Moor's head crest.   It is of interest to note that the official history of the Company, first published in 1874, gives (p. 10) the Moor's head, but the arms on the title-page and on the publisher's cover show the present form of the device.
[4] Stow (J.), *Annales* (1615), p. 948.

They sewed fig leaves together and made themselves aprons

Amor *queat* *obedient-* *iam*

Pl. 39

N.182

NEEDLEMAKERS, p. 181
PAINTER-STAINERS, p. 184

trade in the City. There is, however, no documentary evidence to support this ingenious theory, and it is more probable that the needle was adopted solely as a proper symbol of the industry, three of them being used with a natural regard for artistic symmetry. It is true that Threadneedle Street probably derives from Three Needle Street, but since this area is known to have been an enclave of tailors and drapers, the street may well have come by its name from a sign of The Three Needles, a likely device for a tailor.

THE WORSHIPFUL COMPANY OF PAINTER-STAINERS

As indicated by its title, the Company of Painter-Stainers is the result of the union of two separate guilds. Painters worked upon wood, metal and stone, while the Stainers produced stained or painted cloth and decorated hangings. Both crafts were represented by organized misteries in the thirteenth century, but were united as one guild in 1502, acquiring a charter of incorporation on 19th July 1581, which was succeeded by a new one in 1686.

Apart from the production of painted house signs, house-decoration and hangings, the Painter-Stainers found considerable use for their art in the provision of painted tableaux during the great age of pageants. Portraiture and the painting of shields of arms also fell within their province. The latter activity was the cause of some acerbity between the Company and the College of Arms, whose officers claimed a monopoly of this work. Amicable arrangements were generally reached by the appointment of certain members of the Painters' Company to be employed for the painting of escutcheons of arms, and the presence of these symbols in their arms demonstrates the Company's insistence on their right to regulate this particular craft.

THE ARMORIAL BEARINGS (Pl. 39)

Quarterly first and fourth azure three escutcheons argent, second and third azure a chevron between three phoenix heads erased or beaked gules.

Crest: On a wreath or and gules a phoenix proper.

Mantling: Azure doubled ermine.

Supporters: On either side a panther argent spotted with various colours, ducally crowned, collared and chained or.

Motto: *Amor queat obedientiam.*

The blazon given above represents the arms as now used by the Company. They take the place of earlier arms granted to the Painters by Sir Thomas Holme, Clarenceux, in 1486; these are blazo ed in the original patent[1] as follows:

The feld asure a Chevron betwene thre Fenyx hedes rased golde membred Goules the Creste upon a helme a Fenyx in his propre nature and coloure set with a wrethe gold and gowles the mantell asure furred with ermyn.

---

[1] Original patent deposited in the Guildhall Library, MS 5672

This 1486 grant was confirmed by Thomas Benolt, Clarenceux, on 6th October 1530.

The current arms have no grant and the only entry for them in the College of Arms occurs in the 1634 visitation of London.[1] The official history of the Company,[2] however, bases the claim to them on an unspecified entry of Benolt's confirmation in the College of Arms which is said to show a painting of the quartered coat and crest.[3] It is further asserted that this drawing " should, of course, have appeared in the margin of Benolt's confirmation of 1530 [i.e. on the letters patent of 1486] but was apparently omitted in error ".[4] Elsewhere the writer states that the 1530 confirmation on the original grant " refers to a blazon [vere exemplification] in the margin which does not, however, exist ".[5]

A re-inspection of the documents in question does not confirm the writer's conclusions on these points. The official record of Benolt's visitation of 1530 in the College of Arms[6] shows only the 1486 arms without quarterings, as indeed does the 1568 visitation.[7] The quartered coat is, however, shown in a manuscript in the College, probably compiled about 1530.[8] It may be that this is the document to which the Company's historian refers, but as this is an unofficial collection without authority, it can only be regarded as recording the usage at that time.

On the question of the " missing " exemplification of 1530, an examination of the letters patent of 1486 clearly establishes that there is no possibility of a second painting having been " omitted in error ". Benolt's confirmation, which is added at the foot of the letters patent, refers in fact to the original painting thereon. Benolt says : " I . . . confirme and rateffye this Armes in the Margen herin depict before graunted be my Predesessor Clarenceux . . ."

Thus the only evidence for claiming the quartered coat rests on the entry in the 1634 visitation of London. This entry is accompanied by a statement signed by Richard Bryan, then Clerk to the Painter-Stainers, which reads as follows : " The arms, crest and supporters of the . . . Painters Steners . . . wch are said to bee granted by Sr. Thomas

---

[1] Coll. Arms 2nd C.24/215.
[2] Englefield (W. A. D.), The History of the Painter-Stainers Company (1923) ; Supplement, (1936).
[3, 4, 5] op. cit. p. 49.   [6] Coll. Arms 1st H.7/59b.   [7] Coll. Arms G.10/123.
[8] Coll. Arms Vincent, " Two Ears of Wheat ", H.

Holme . . . in the first year of King Henry the VIIth wch pattent it seems at this time was mislaide[1] . . . but is affirmed by some of the ancient of this Company that they have seene it and at this present visitation was thus entered." From the evidence examined above it appears that the " ancient of the Company " were not testifying to the arms as in the 1486 patent—the sole grant—but were in fact merely recalling the adopted arms which incorporated the quartered coat and supporters.

The significance of the escutcheons in the first and fourth quarters, which were probably adopted early in the sixteenth century, has been explained as commemorating the union of the Painters with the Stainers in 1502. There is, however, no evidence to support this assumption ; the Stainers are not known to have borne arms, nor would the escutcheons have any symbolic reference to their trade. There can be no doubt that the introduction of the shields is accounted for by the Painters' claim to pursue the craft of arms painting independently of the College of Arms. The College contended that it held a monopoly of this craft, and a long dispute ensued between the two bodies. A similar device of three shields is to be found in the arms of fraternities of shield painters in various European countries.

In most blazons of the arms the supporters are termed leopards. As only a trick of the arms, without verbal description, exists in official records, identification cannot be certain, but it seems much more probable that the supporters are in fact panthers. Although the panther and leopard of nature are identical, they are different beasts in heraldry. One mark of the heraldic panther is the spots of colour upon its hide. These are not found upon the leopard for whom, in any case, no explanation can be found to account for its use as part of the Painters' achievement. On the other hand, there are good reasons for believing that the beasts were intended for panthers. In animal mythology the phoenix was regarded as a symbol of the Resurrection, and since the art of the heraldic designer is inspired by allusion, the phoenix of the ancient arms and crest may well have suggested the supporters in the form of panthers which medieval bestiaries describe as a type of Christ.[2] It is also to be noted that the arms of the Dyers'

[1] The letters patent were not returned to the Company's custody until they were found and presented in 1827 by a liveryman, George Bishop.
[2] White (T. H.), *Book of Beasts* (1954), p. 15.

JUSTICIA · ET · PAX

Recipiunt foeminae sustentacula nobis

Unitas societatis stabilitas

Company have panthers as supporters ; in each case the coloured spots as tokens of the craft are most appropriate. If further support is needed in favour of the panther, it may be recalled that these beasts have in the past been called " panters ",[1] an earlier phonetic English version either of the Latin *panthera* or the Old French *pantère*. Such a pun on the word " painter " would be wholly in keeping with the humour of the armorist, and may indeed be the simple explanation of the supporters.

A translation of the motto of the Company as now used is difficult to provide, and corruption of an original seems certain. The only

A. and B. Crest and Fenyx head erased from original patent, A.D. 1486 Guild. Lib. MS. 5672. C. and D. Crest and Phoenix head erased from Guild. Lib. MS. 5667/2

English version that is possible is " Let love achieve obedience ", but the rendering of *queo* in the sense of " achieve " so strains the use of that word that it is not readily acceptable.

The current form of the motto is first noted in the entry of the arms in the 1634 visitation of London ;[2] it appears, however, as *Amor queat obediencia* (both nouns in the nominative) as early as 1599 in a collection of pen and ink drawings of the arms of the City companies.[3] The latter rendering is also given in literary sources of the eighteenth and nineteenth centuries. During this time the Company itself seems regularly to have used the unexceptionable *Amor et obedientia* on official

[1] *N.E.D.* s.v. Panter. The term " painter " is still current in the U.S.A. for the American leopard or puma.
[2] Coll. Arms MS. 2nd C.24/215.
[3] Brit. Mus. Harl. MS. 472.

O

publications,[1] and it was not until this century that the present usage appears to have been adopted, probably as a result of the researches carried out for the Company's history in which the 1634 rendering is noted.[2]

If the motto is corrupt, two possible alternatives are suggested which would at least accord with the meaning of the earlier usage of *Amor et obedientia* : the words might have been intended to read *Amorque et obedientia* (Both love and obedience) ; or *queat* may be an ignorant transposition of letters for *atque*. Although the former is stylistically repugnant to the classicist, it is an accurate construction which could have come from the pen of a maker of mottoes.

A third possibility is that *queat* should read *querat* (a medieval form of *quaerat*), the *r* having been omitted by accident ; in this case the motto would be in translation " Let love demand obedience."

The solution which carries the most conviction, however, is that *queat* is a scribal error for *creat*.[3] Such an error could easily have been committed either by a *lapsus auris* during dictation, or by faulty copying of letters that in earlier hands could bear a superficial resemblance to *q* and *u*. *Amor creat obedientiam* (Loves creates obedience) has the ring of a good motto and is eminently suited to a fraternal guild.

These suggestions are no more than conjectural, but it is certain that the motto, as it stands, is without sense.

[1] *Amor et obediencia* appears as early as 1649 beneath a painting on vellum of the quartered coat in the Company's court minute book (Guild. Lib. MS. 5667/2) with the note : " This peece given by Mr. John Withie, 1649 ".

[2] Englefield (W. A. D.), *The History of the Painter-Stainers Company* (1923), p. 50.

[3] I am indebted to Professor E. H. Warmington for this suggestion.

THE WORSHIPFUL COMPANY OF PARISH CLERKS

UNSUPPORTED tradition, based apparently upon a statement of John Stow, claims that the parish clerks of London were an incorporated body as early as 1233, but the first established charter to the Company is that of 22nd January 1441/2. Under this charter the chief parish clerks of the collegiate and parish churches of London, hitherto a brotherhood in honour of St. Nicholas, were formed into a perpetual corporation. During the Reformation the Company had the melancholy distinction of being the only London guild which suffered total confiscation of its property on the grounds that it was not a trade organization as the other guilds had successfully claimed on their own behalf. A new charter was granted on 9th January 1611/12 to the "Master, Wardens and Brethren of the Parish Clerks of the City of London and liberties thereof". The Company's present operative charter is dated 27th February 1638/9.

In the Middle Ages the parish clerk was a clerk in minor orders who assisted the priest in the preparation and conduct of church services, including the leading of the choir. After the Reformation his duties were confined to those of a lay nature, but he acquired the additional role in London of recording the numbers of births and deaths of parishioners. His returns of deaths were assembled by the Company and published as mortality bills. The compilation of these returns is recorded as part of the parish clerk's duties in the Company's ordinances of 1536. These bills continued to be published until the middle of the nineteenth century; the introduction in 1837 of a national system of registration had by then rendered them unnecessary.

The Company is now a guild of parish clerks, churchwardens and other parish officers.

THE ARMORIAL BEARINGS (Pl. 40)

Azure a fleur-de-lys or, on a chief gules a leopard's head or between two "prick-song books" of the same laced vert.

Crest: On a wreath gules and azure a cubit arm vested azure cuffed ermine holding an open "prick-song book" all proper.

Mantling : Dexter : gules and azure doubled ermine ; siniſter : gules and azure doubled or.

Granted[1] by Robert Cooke,
Clarenceux
30th March 1582

Motto : Unitas societatis ſtabilitas.

These arms superseded a grant by Thomas Holme, Clarenceux, dated 16th July 1482, which in turn had replaced a yet earlier grant of 1469 or 1470. Of this firſt grant nothing is known apart from the information conveyed in the patent of 1482.[2] This recites that

> Whereas Walter Bellenger othrewise called Ireland King of Armes . . . had yeven and graunted . . . unto Symon Mayew and Henry Empson Maiſters for the time being of the confraternitie founded in the chapell of the Guyldhall within the Citie of London in the honeur of our Lord God, our blessed Lady Marie the Virgin his modre and of Seint Nicholas the Armes heraftre folowing havyng noon auctoritie by vertue of his said office . . . to diſtribute or yeve to eny personne or personnes fraternitie or place within the precinĉte of my Jurisdiccion . . . I . . . have utterly adnulled and dampned the same . . . And at thinſtaunce requeſt & desire of the said Maſters I . . . have yeven & graunted unto them & their successors the same Armes . . . before yeuven & graunted as above, That is to say A sheld asur a chefe goules a flour de lice gold in the chefe the hede of a Leoparde of the same tonged goules two halywat[r] sprencles of gold & silver ensauter upon all. The Creſte upon ye helme sex halywater sprencles newed w[t] gold and silv[r], the mantell asur & goules furred w[t] Ermyn.

When Bellenger made his grant is not ſtated and no other record of it appears to have survived. A date may, however, be assigned to it with reasonable certainty from a contemporary manuscript in the Company's archives. This is a bede roll[3] which, in addition to liſting deceased members, also includes the names of those annually admitted to the Company. At the beginning of each yearly liſt is given the names of the maſters then in office. Since Symon Mayhew [*sic*] and Henry Emeson (or Empson) occur together as maſters only in the year

---

[1] The original was deſtroyed by enemy action in 1940. A full transcript appears in *Harleian Society Publications*, vol. 77, pp. 166–7.

[2] Formerly in the cuſtody of the College of Arms but reſtored to the Company in 1941. At the time of writing this patent could not be produced by the Company. A reduced monochrome facsimile is reproduced in the *College of Arms Commemorative Exhibition Catalogue* (1936), pl. 36 ; a transcript is given in *Harleian Society Publications*, vol. 77, p. 165. See also Wagner (A. R.), *Heralds and Heraldry in the Middle Ages* (1939), pp. 74–5.

[3] Guild. Lib. MS. 4889.

God can raise — to Abraham — Children of stones

IN·GOD·IS — ALL·MY·TRUST

Pl. 41

O.191

PAVIORS, p. 195
PEWTERERS, p. 197

Creʃt

1469, it is probable that the grant was made in that year or at the lateʃt during the end of their joint office in 1470.[1]

In spite of Clarenceux's resentment of the intrusion of Ireland King of Arms into his province and the infringement of his jurisdiction, his grant in effeƈt allowed the Company to retain the arms as previously devised by Bellenger.

These arms continued in use until 1582. The reason for their alteration in that year is supplied by the new patent, in which Robert Cooke, Clarenceux, ʃtates that

> Wher as Thomas Clarencieulx . . . by his Lr̄es Pattentt dated the xxijth yeare . . . Edward the fourth dyd geve and graunt unto the Confrater-nitye . . . of the Parrishe Clarkes . . . new armes with healme and Creaʃt, which Armes being over muche charged with certayne superʃtition . . . I . . . at the requeʃt of . . . the sayde Companye have thought good to reforme and alter the sayde Armes and Creaʃt . . .

The resulting arms were blazoned as follows :

> the feyld azur a flower delice goulde, on a chieffe gules a leopardes head betwene two pricke songe bookes of the seconde, the laces that bynde the bookes vert. And to the creaʃt uppon the healme on a wreathe gules and azur an arme from the elbow upward houlding a pricke songe booke [open][2] all propper Mantelled goulde Ermyn gules and azur.

---

[1] Ebblewhite (in his *Hiʃtory of the Parish Clerks* (1932), p. 15) failed to see this entry. He assigns the grant to the year 1479 when Mayhew was again maʃter, but in company with Henry Crane. He assumes that Empson, who served a second term in 1478, had aƈted for Crane whose death in office is also assumed by Ebblewhite.

[2] Word illegible in the patent, but supplied from the record in the College of Arms.

The effect of the new grant was to remove the " halywater sprencles " and substitute therefor the " pricke songe bookes ", that is service books pricked or scored for melody.　One of the duties of the medieval parish clerk was the carrying of holy water, and this office is symbolized by the brush or " sprencle " with which the ritual of sprinkling is still effected in the Roman Catholic Church.　It is perhaps surprising that the brush survived for so long in the arms, especially in those of a fraternity so close to the church, when most other companies had purged their arms of " superstition " some years before.　No doubt the severer penalties imposed in 1581 upon recusants and upon those who attended mass were the immediate cause of its removal ;　no body of men who were so dependent upon the orthodox church could afford to appear other than blameless.　Appearance, however, and not conviction seemed to have been their motive, for the fleur-de-lys, symbol of the Virgin their patron saint, remained ; probably because it was a less evident manifestation of superstition.

Arms A.D. 1482, a contemporary tilting shield, based on Coll. Arms records, 1st
H.7/60

THE WORSHIPFUL COMPANY OF PATTENMAKERS

PATTENS and "galoches" of wood were popular and inexpensive forms of footwear when leather was too costly for the common man and woman. The distinction between the two kinds is not clear but it is likely that the patten's sole was ironshod, or otherwise raised above the ground, as depicted in the Company's arms; the use also of the word "patten" or "patine" for a skate seems to support this view. The medieval galoche was probably a clog or a shoe with a wooden sole and leather upper tied with thongs.

In the fourteenth century there were separate misteries of pattenmakers and galochemakers, but both were also closely connected with the Mistery of Pouchmakers, no doubt because of the use of leather for ties and uppers in the making of this form of shoe. In 1488 a petition for ordinances was presented to the mayor and aldermen by the "good folkes of the crafte of pouchemakers, galeggemakers and patynmakers . . . now enfraunchised by the name of Powchemakers". Pouchmakers were eventually united with the Company of Leathersellers but the Pattenmakers remained independent and achieved a charter of incorporation on 2nd August 1670. This charter constituted the Company as the Master, Wardens, Assistants and Fellowship of the Company of Pattenmakers of the City of London with powers to regulate the trade of all concerned with the making of "pattens and cloggs".

Patten making ceased at the end of the eighteenth century and the company's powers of search and trade control fell into disuse. The Company now uses its influence to further the manufacture and sale of rubber footwear of all kinds in association with the modern trade organizations.

THE ARMORIAL BEARINGS (Pl. 40)

Gules on a chevron argent between three pattens or, tied argent, the ties lined azure, two cutting knives conjoined sable; in the middle chief two knives in saltire or.

Crest: On a wreath of the colours a patten as in the arms.

Mantling : Gules doubled argent.
Motto : *Recipiunt foeminae sustentacula nobis.*

These arms are without authority and the above blazon is that assumed by the Company.[1]   An early example of the arms is engraved upon a silver chalice[2] bearing an inscription dated 1693.   Subsequent examples are usually found without the two crossed knives in the middle chief, but these knives are now accepted as part of the insignia.

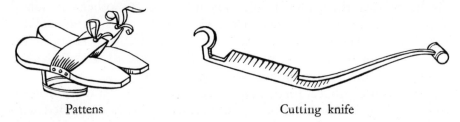

Pattens   Cutting knife

The pattens shown in the arms are wooden clogs raised upon iron rings and secured to the feet by wide leather straps tied across the instep. The wooden soles were shaped by means of the cutting knives which are the charges on the chevron ; examples of these knives are preserved in the Guildhall Museum.

The motto, which in translation means " From us women receive support ", is, of course, a reference to the benefits of the patten on wet and muddy roads.

[1] Fitch (C.), *The History of the Worshipful Company of Patten-makers* (1926), ch. 8.
[2] *ibid.* pl. facing p. 62.

THE WORSHIPFUL COMPANY OF PAVIORS

THE occupation of the pavior was that of a roadmaker or paver of streets. His activity involved surfacing the roads mainly with sand and stones consolidated by a rammer as depicted in the Paviors' arms. Such cobbled streets were the common form of surface in spite of the flagstones which also appear as charges in the arms, and the process of beating the roads gave to the pavior his name which derives from the Latin *pavire*, to ram or beat.

References to the paviors' activities in London occur very early in the City records, but the mistery or craft of paviors first appears as an organized body in 1479 when ordinances to regulate the trade were approved by the Court of Aldermen.

In 1673 the Company sought a charter of incorporation from the king but the move was opposed by the Court of Aldermen. A renewed attempt in 1724 to secure incorporation also failed, and the Paviors' Company has remained an unincorporated guild.

During much of the nineteenth century the Company became moribund but was revived in 1889, and today, with many of its members prominent in the road engineering and allied trades, it exercises a considerable influence in the industry.

THE ARMORIAL BEARINGS (Pl. 41)

Argent a chevron between three paving stones sable.
Crest : On a wreath of the colours a dexter arm embowed vested azure cuffed argent the hand grasping a pavior's pick the handle fessewise all proper.
Mantling : Sable doubled argent.
Supporters : On the dexter side a master pavior of the reign of Edward I resting the dexter hand on a measuring rod, and on the sinister side a pavior of the reign of Edward I holding in the sinister hand a rammer both proper.
Motto : God can raise to Abraham children of stones.

Granted[1] by Sir Henry Farnham Burke,
Garter
Arthur William Steuart Cochrane,
Clarenceux
Gerald Woods Wollaston
Norroy
4th November 1929

[1] Original grant lost by enemy action, 1941. A new certificate is in the Company's possession. For full transcript of the original document see Welch (C.), *History of the Worshipful Company of Paviors*, 2nd ed. (1932), pp. 133–5.

The Paviors' arms are known to have been in use, without supporters, as early as 1575 ;[1] they corresponded to the present arms. In 1929 the Company obtained its first grant of arms and supporters from which the blazon given above has been transcribed.

The reference to the reign of Edward I in the description of the supporters alludes to the hypothetical origin of the Company based upon the earliest known records of paving in the archives of the Corporation of London.[2]

The motto derives from the New Testament, St. Matthew iii. 9.

[1] Guild. Lib. MS. 2463. A matrix of the Company's seal, mid-sixteenth century, is in Guildhall Museum ; the arms are shown with the Paviors' motto as legend.
[2] Cal. Lett. Bk. A p. 183 (*anno* 1280) ; Lett. Bk. C p. 115 (*anno* 1302).

THE WORSHIPFUL COMPANY OF PEWTERERS

THE formation of the London pewterers into an organized body with disciplinary powers sanctioned by the mayor and aldermen is to be seen in ordinances made in 1348. These also clearly indicate both the composition and the extent of the medieval pewterer's wares. The makers of pewter vessels represented to the mayor and aldermen that the good name of their craft depended upon a high degree of skill which many who practised the art did not possess ; that such vessels as saltcellars, platters, chargers, pitchers and cruets " which are made square or ribbed " should be of fine pewter of tin and copper alloy, while all other things such as candlesticks, pots and " other rounded vessels " ought to be wrought of tin alloyed with lead in proper proportion. Articles for the regulation of the trade were accordingly approved and two wardens were elected to enforce them on behalf of the mistery.

On 26th January 1473/4 the Pewterers were incorporated, as a fraternity or guild in honour of the Virgin Mary, by a royal charter which gave the Company power to examine and assay all merchandise belonging to their craft throughout England.

The skill of the native craftsmen as fostered by the Company was such that English pewter has been unequalled, and William Harrison in his contemporary *Description of England* during the reign of Elizabeth I asserted that in foreign countries " English pewter . . . is esteemed almost so pretious as . . . fine silver ".

The craft declined in the eighteenth century and the powers of the Company are not now exercised. The last table of assays was made by the Company in 1772.

THE ARMORIAL BEARINGS (Pl. 41)

Azure on a chevron or between three strikes argent, as many roses gules, stalked, budded and leaved vert.

Granted[1] by Thomas Benolt,
Clarenceux
26th May 1533

[1] Original patent in the possession of the Company. A coloured facsimile is given in Welch (C.), *The Pewterers' Company* (1902), vol. 1.

Crest : On a wreath of the colours a mount vert, thereon two arms embowed vested argent, holding in both hands erect proper a pewter dish argent.

Mantling : Gules doubled argent.

Supporters : On either side a sea-horse or with tail proper.

Granted[1] by Robert Cooke,
Clarenceux
1573

Motto : In God is all my trust.

The earliest record of arms in use by the Company is found in a confirmation of arms by Roger Legh, Clarenceux, dated 13th August 1451.[2] These arms are reproduced in colour in a manuscript of about 1480-1500,[3] and an Elizabethan copy[4] of the patent, headed " The confirmacon of the Peauterers ", blazons the arms as follows :

> goules a cheveron of sable betwen iii lylly pottes of silver, in the cheveron iiii strakes of tynne in theyre kynde and in the poynt of the cheveron vi aungells in cloudes holdyng up our Lady of gold crouned under the handes of her blessed fader in a clowde.

Apart from some minor differences of spelling this corresponds with the authority in the College of Arms.

The representation of the Assumption in the arms recalls the Company's origin as a fraternity in honour of the Virgin Mary, and the lily pots, i.e. pots of lilies, are emblematic of her purity. As in the case of other companies, the Pewterers found it politic to eliminate any religious symbolism that might compromise their security during the Reformation, and the grant of 1533 was obtained accordingly. In this connection it is significant that in an unofficial collection of coats of arms,[5] dated *c.* 1530, the figure of the Virgin had already been dropped from the Pewterers' arms, which there show : gules on a chevron sable between three lily pots argent three strakes proper.

In his new patent Benolt states that he has

> gyven graunted ordeyned and assigned . . . the blason and armes folowyng. That is to say asure a chiveron gold betwene iii strykes silver. Upon

---

[1] Coll. Arms MS. 2nd C.24/383. The day and month of the grant is nowhere stated. Coll. Arms G.10 shows crest wreath argent and azure and this has been followed in the illustration.

[2] Coll. Arms MS. R.21/97.

[3] Brit. Mus. Harl. MS. 6163/49. For a description of this MS. see Wagner (A. R.), *Catalogue of English Medieval Rolls of Arms* (1950), p. 109.

[4] Brit. Mus. Cotton MS. Faustina E. 1/26.

[5] Coll. Arms MS. Vincent, " Two Ears of Wheat ", fo. H.

LET · BROTHERLY · LOVE · CONTINUE ·

CORDE · RECTO · ELATI · OMNES

Pl. 42

O.198

PLAISTERERS, p. 201
MAKERS OF PLAYING CARDS, p. 160

the chiveron three roses gueules their ſtalkes buddes and leves vert . . .
and in their ſtremer our Lady assumpcion powdred with lyllyepottes and
ſtrykes with their worde accuſtomed.

It is intereſting to note that while their arms were cleansed of offence,
their banner retained the symbolism of their devotion.

A problem that has hitherto not been satisfactorily solved is the
meaning of the word " stryke " or " ſtrake ". Welch made a careful
inveſtigation of its occurrence in the Pewterers' records, and concluded
that the object was an ingot of tin.[1] Apart from the fact that ingots
were unlikely to have been caſt in so complicated a shape, this theory
is unacceptable for a number of reasons.

Early arms, after Harl. MS. 6163

After the painting of the arms in
the margin of the 1533 grant

The word in its variant form of ſtrake is ſtill extant in denoting the
flat iron tire of a cart wheel, and it also had formerly a more general
application in meaning any flat band of metal. An inſtance of the
latter use is found in Stow[2] who, in describing the interior of a church,
says " there were tombs of alabaſter and marble, invironed with ſtrikes
of iron in the quire, and one tombe in the body of the church, also
coped with iron ". There is reason to believe that the ſtryke of the
pewterer is of like derivation and has a similar connotation; that is
to say, it is a flat ſtrip of tin. The elaborate pattern in which it occurs
may well be capricious.

[1] Welch, op. cit. p. 99.
[2] *Survey of London*; ed. C. L. Kingsford, vol. 1 (1908), p. 322.

Definite evidence of the association of these objects with the pewterer's craft is given by Diderot. Accompanying a detailed description of pewter manufacture is an engraving of the interior of a workshop ;[1] hanging on the wall thereof are three objects which, though circular in shape, are clearly identical of purpose with the strykes in the Pewterers' arms. In the relevant text[2] these are called " *étain en treillis ou en grilles* " and are said to be made from pure tin as obtained from ingots or from " saumons " (i.e. pig-tin). These " *treillis* ", according to the author, are sold to mirror-makers, glaziers, tinsmiths, plumbers, organ-builders, spurriers and copper smiths ; they are fashioned in the shape they bear since they are, he says, thus easier to sell than in ingots or pig.[3] It is further stated, significantly, that such devices are used as signs to advertize pewterers' shops. Why the peculiar shape should facilitate its sale, as Diderot asserts, is not easy to explain. Nevertheless it is likely that these strips of soft tin, so latticed, would be more manageable than when loose or in bundles ; moreover the natural instinct of the old craftsman to present his wares in attractive form, an art paralleled in other trades, might be an additional reason for the fanciful shapes of the strykes becoming conventional symbols of pewterers' shops.

Whatever may be the reason for their form, it seems certain that the basis of these objects was strip tin which the pewterer, as a prime consumer of that commodity, was able to sell as a sideline to those in other trades who needed it only in small quantities.

---

[1] Diderot, *Encyclopédie, planches*, VIII, s.v. *Potier d'étain*, pl. 1.

[2] ibid. *tome* 6 (1756), p. 9.

[3] From evidence in the accounts of the Company, each stryke weighed about 8 oz. ; a further objection to Welch's contention that the object was an ingot.

THE WORSHIPFUL COMPANY OF PLAISTERERS

THE plasterer's employment in the past was little different from today. Plaster was used extensively for the finishing of exterior and interior walls, and for rendering the inner surfaces of fireplaces and chimneys. An indication of a plasterer's work is to be seen in an entry in the City archives for 1317 which records an agreement by Adam le Plastrer, citizen of London, to supply plaster of Paris and to repair therewith the walls within and without, and also the flues of the Earl of Richmond's hall in the neighbourhood of St. Paul's Cathedral.

The plasterers of London were incorporated by a charter of 10th March 1500/1. The charter established the Company as the Master and Wardens of the Guild or Fraternity of the Blessed Mary of Pargettors

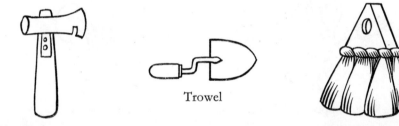

Trowel

Plasterer's hammer

Plasterer's brush

in the City of London, commonly called Plaisterers. The final charter of 19th June 1679 extended the Company's powers to cover an area three miles distant from the City and, in order to prevent poor work due to the heavy demand for labour in the rebuilding of London after the Great Fire, forbade any person to carry on the trades of mason, bricklayer or plasterer simultaneously.

The Company's power of search for bad work is said to have been observed, at least by the appointment of annual search days, up to the year 1832, but no control of the trade is now exercised.

THE ARMORIAL BEARINGS (Pl. 42)

Azure on a chevron engrailed argent a rose gules budded or, ſtalked and leaved vert, between two fleurs de lys azure ; in chief a trowel fessewise between two plaſterer's hammers palewise all argent handled or, in base a plaſterer's brush of four knots tied argent handled or.

Creſt : On a wreath argent and azure an arm veſted bendy of four gules and or, holding in the hand proper a plaſterer's hammer as in the arms.

Mantling : Gules doubled argent.

Supporters : On either side an opinicus vert winged, membered and eyed gules, the throat and belly purfled or.

Granted[1] by Thomas Hawley,
Clarenceux
20th January 1545/6

Motto : Let brotherly love continue.

Rose, slipped and leaved

Fleur-de-lis

The text of the blazon in the original patent, which in part is worn and difficult to decipher, reads as follows :

Asur on a cheveron engrailed silver a Rose geules budded golde ſtalked and levyd vert betwene two Flower delices asur in chef a Trowell in fece betwene two hamers of the saide crafte in pale silver hafted golde under the sayde cheviron a hery brusshe of Fower knottes tyed silver handled golde upon a helme on a torse silver and asur an Arme the sleve geules and golde bende of Fower peces holding in the hande one of their saide hammers with two beſtes callid Opimacus half serpent and half beſte vert wynged membrid and eyed geules the throte and bely purfled golde supporting the said armes manteled geules dobled silver.

On a billhead of Bishop & Tait, " Herald painters to His Majeſty ",

---

[1] Original patent : Guild. Lib. MS. 6131.

Remember your oath

HOLD · FAST, ❧ SIT · SURE ·

OUR · TRUST · IS · IN · GOD ·

Pl. 43

P.203

POULTERS, p. 207
SADDLERS, p. 211

attached to the original grant and dated January 1837, is the following note in manuscript:

> George Bishop having searched in the books of the Heralds College and found that this grant was not registered and on C. G. Young Esq., York Herald (Registrar) seeing this said grant he kindly consented to enter it in the office books which was done.

This statement is not correct, for there is in the College of Arms a sixteenth-century docquet[1] of the grant contemporary with the patent. A more perfect copy was, however, entered in the records on 29th November 1836 at the instance of C. G. Young, York Herald.

Opinicus, after the grant of A.D. 1546
(Guild. Lib. MS. 6131)

Opinicus, modern

---

[1] Coll. Arms MS. 2nd H.5/45.

THE WORSHIPFUL COMPANY OF PLUMBERS

ORDINANCES were granted to the mistery of Plumbers of London by the mayor and aldermen in 1365. The purpose of these was to ensure that none but skilled plumbers, free of the City, should engage in the craft, to regulate apprentices, and generally to maintain good workmanship and honest conduct, including the use of accurate weights.

Further ordinances of 1488 and 1520 reiterated and expanded the powers of the wardens of the mistery, and on 12th April 1611 it was constituted a corporate body by the name of the Master, Wardens and Commonalty of the Freemen of Plumbing of the City of London. By its charter of incorporation the Company was granted the governance of all persons using the art of plumbing within the City and the precincts and suburbs thereof. Such supervision is not now practised by the Company but its concern for the trade is still shown in its support for technical instruction and the maintenance of a register of qualified plumbers who have attained proficiency by examination.

THE ARMORIAL BEARINGS (Pl. 40)

Or a chevron sable between in chief a Jacob's staff fessewise sable between two sounding leads proper and in base a water-level sable ; on the chevron two soldering irons in saltire between a cutting-knife on the dexter and a shaver on the sinister argent.

Crest : On a wreath or and sable a fountain argent surmounted by the figure of an archangel holding in the dexter hand a sword and in the sinister hand a balance or.

Mantling : Sable doubled argent.

Motto : Justicia et pax.

Granted[1] by Robert Cooke,
Clarenceux
24th November 1588

Second motto : In God is all our hope.

The blazon of the letters patent reads as follows :

Or on a cheveron sable towe soodring irons in saultor with a cutting knyfe and a shaver argent ; in cheife between two sounding leades proper a Jacobs staffe of the seconde ; and in poynt a water levell of the same. And

---

[1] Original deposited in Guildhall Library, MS. 2224.

for their creaſt upon a heaulme on a wreath or and sable a fountayne argent garnisshed on the toppe with an archangell holding a sword and a ballance or with this their ancient worde or device Juſticia et Pax. Mantled sable dubled argent.

Pre-grant arms attributed to the Plumbers are to be found in a manuscript of about 1530 in the College of Arms[1] and are repeated in another of 1575 ;[2] these show gules a chevron argent between in chief two cutting-knives and in base two soldering irons in saltire argent.

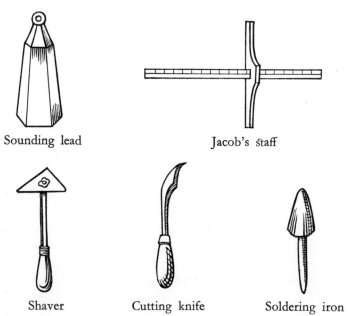

Sounding lead   Jacob's ſtaff

Shaver   Cutting knife   Soldering iron

The charges on the chevron in the current arms are tools of the plumber's trade, but the other charges seem to be merely rather remote puns on the Company's name. The sounding leads, or plummets, refer both to the material used by the craft and to the use of these objeðts in " plumbing ", or sounding, a depth ; while the Jacob's ſtaff and the water level are included as allusions to the process of levelling. No doubt the ingenious contriver of the arms was aware that the word " level " derives from the Latin *libella* with its secondary meaning of " plumb line ". The apparatus called a Jacob's ſtaff was

[1] Vincent, " Two Ears of Wheat ".   [2] Guild. Lib. MS. 2463.

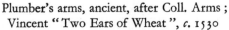

Plumber's arms, ancient, after Coll. Arms ;
Vincent "Two Ears of Wheat", *c.* 1530

Badge

a surveying inŝtrument for taking levels, and comprised a graduated rod with a cursor cross-piece. It acquired its name from its resemblance to the crutched ŝtaff of the pilgrim which was similarly called in allusion to the ŝtaff of the patriarch Jacob in the Book of Genesis.

Of the two mottoes used by the Company, the Latin one is unusual for this period in that it is mentioned in the patent of arms ; it is not, however, noted in the 1634 visitation when the arms were confirmed. In the painting in the margin of the patent, the motto is shown above the creŝt which is no more than an allegorical illuŝtration of the motto itself.

This company shares with the Maŝter Mariners' and the Farmers' Companies the diŝtinˆction of the grant of a badge in addition to a coat of arms. The Plumber's badge was granted on 9th February 1925 in the following terms :[1]

On a pellet a fountain argent garnished or surmounted by a representation of the Archangel Michael holding in the dexter hand a sword and in the siniŝter hand a balance or between two sounding leads proper.

The unnamed archangel of the 1588 creŝt has thus been identified in the badge as St. Michael who is claimed as the Company's patron saint. No evidence has, however, been found to support the possible implication that the guild originated in a religious fraternity of St. Michael.

[1] Coll. Arms MS. Standards I/270–1.

SAL SAPIT OMNIA

THE WORSHIPFUL COMPANY OF POULTERS

In 1299 poulterers were one of the trades of the City of London which elected men to supervise their respective trades in accordance with a proclamation for the regulation of food prices. Such indication of early organization is a feature of the victualling trades of the City. Ordinances for the government of the Poulters are first mentioned at the election of wardens of the craft in 1370, and it is clear from the reference that these had existed for some time before. Incorporation of the Company is said to have been achieved on 23rd January 1503/4 but no contemporary evidence of this has been discovered. The first recorded charter of incorporation is dated 13th June 1665, and this constituted as a corporation all those persons within seven miles of the City who used the trade of " meere poulters or selling poultry wares ", styling them the Master, Wardens and Assistants of Poulters.

The London poulter bought his supplies mainly from breeders in the nearby countryside and rarely reared his own. In addition to a wide variety of table birds, his stock-in-trade included rabbits, butter and eggs. The prices of these goods were regulated by lists set by the central government or by the mayor and aldermen, and it was one of the functions of the Company to be answerable for infringements of them. Rigid control was imposed on the trade in numerous other ways which the wardens of the Company were required to enforce ; these included rules relating to hours and places of sale and the quality of goods. This supervision ceased during the eighteenth century but the Poulters' Company is still associated with the trade through leading members of the industry who are also members of the guild.

THE ARMORIAL BEARINGS (Pl. 43)

Argent on a chevron azure between three cranes [?] proper three swans argent.

Crest : On a mural crown gules a crane [?] rising proper.

Mantling : Gules doubled argent.

Supporters : On either side a pelican wings displayed and addorsed or, vulning itself gules.

Granted by Sir Richard St. George,
Clarenceux
1634

Motto : Remember your oath.

The original letters patent have not survived and only a trick, without a blazon, exists in the College of Arms.[1] This trick, while satisfactorily establishing the tinctures of the arms, gives no clue to the identity of the birds therein other than what may be gathered from the sketches. No doubts arise as to the swans on the chevron, or the pelicans which form the supporters, but the other three birds on the shield do raise a question. To the Company these birds are storks and are so called in the official history of the Poulters.[2] Nevertheless there are substantial reasons for believing that cranes are really intended.

Mural crown

Evidence in favour of storks is meagre. The earliest blazon in which they are introduced appears to be that given by Edmondson in 1780,[3] and Edmondson is not a reliable guide to the arms of the City guilds. The fact that all subsequent blazons follow him is doubtless due to the absence of any other printed blazon to copy. It is true that Holme describes the arms, but this description is in a volume of his work which, although written at the end of the seventeenth century, was not printed until 1905.[4] In any event his description of the birds as peacocks entirely discredits his blazon, for peacocks they certainly are not.

Before Holme only one blazon has been found. This is in a manuscript dated 1587,[5] wherein the birds are termed cranes. There is, of course, no necessary probability that the earlier blazon is the correct one, but since the only explanation of the presence of the birds on the shield is that they represent the more distinguished articles of fare supplied by the Company, the crane on these grounds is more acceptable. The stork was a far less popular article of food than the crane : of fifteen lists of poultry prices given in the Company's records between 1507 and 1633,[6] thirteen include the crane but only three give the stork. Moreover, cranes are known to have bred in England at least up to the sixteenth century, whereas there is no evidence that the stork was a native bird.[7] There is, therefore, a good case for believing

---

[1] Coll. Arms MS. 2nd C.24/417.
[2] Jones (P. E.), *The Worshipful Company of Poulters* (1939), p. 8.
[3] Edmondson (J.), *Complete Body of Heraldry* (1780), vol. 1.
[4] Holme (R.), *Academy of Armory*, vol. 2 (*c.* 1690), pub. 1905, p. 407.
[5] Brit. Mus. Harl. MS. 839/50b.
[6] Jones (P. E.), op. cit. pp. 128–135.
[7] Seebohm (H.), *History of British Birds*, vol. 2 (1884), pp. 525, 570.

that the blazon of 1587 is an accurate record of the device then in use by the Company. The device was, however, unauthorized and in 1634 formal authority was obtained to bear arms, no doubt as a result of the visitation of that year revealing the absence of a grant. In March 1636 the Company paid £18 " to the King of Heraulds for the

Stork   Crane

adding of crest and supporters to our armes and confermacon thereof ".[1] This wording suggests that the Poulters regarded the grant of arms in the light of a confirmation of their existing arms incorporating cranes, not storks.

Additional support for accepting cranes is to be found in the manner of drawing these birds. The stork and the crane have superficial resemblances but the characteristic stance of the crane is quite different from that of the stork in being more upright, with the neck elongated, as opposed to the stork's habit of curving its neck and sinking its bill into its breast feathers. In all examples seen, the bird in question approaches in appearance more to the crane than to the stork. Heraldic art is, however, traditionally not noted for realism, and complete reliance upon it for nature notes is unsafe. More reliable guides are provided by two delightful border paintings that accompany illuminated armorial initials in two ordinance books of the Poulters' Company compiled about 1670 and 1688.[2] In these drawings swans are seen in sylvan settings together with other birds strongly resembling cranes.

Although swans and cranes, or storks, can be explained as representing former merchandise of the Poulters, the presence of the pelicans

[1] Wardens' Account Book: Guild. Lib. MS. 2150/1.
[2] Guild. Lib. MSS. 5071 and 5072.

as supporters cannot be similarly accounted for. The heraldic pelican is a fabulous and symbolic creature with little likeness to its natural namesake. It is usually depicted, as here, wounding its breast, by which means it is said to have revived its young by feeding them with its own blood. It is an emblem of the Eucharist and thus symbolizes charity and family piety, and these birds may have been added for supporters as emblematic of the charitable and pious objects which members of guilds were sworn to foster ; in this context the Company's motto is wholly appropriate. The choice of the pelican may, at the same time, have satisfied the herald's feeling for homogeneity in design.

THE WORSHIPFUL COMPANY OF SADDLERS

AN agreement concerning religious observances, which the canons of St. Martin's convent in London addressed to the guild of Saddlers in the twelfth century, establishes the existence of the guild at a very early date in London guild history. The " Saddlery ", where the saddlers' shops were located, was at the west end of Chepe in the vicinity of St. Martin's convent, and this religious connection of a trade fraternity with a neighbouring church is an early example of the dual aspects of spiritual and commercial interests which were a common feature of guild life.

A tradition that the Saddlers were given some form of charter in the year 1272 is unsupported by any surviving contemporary evidence, and the first recorded charter to the guild is dated 1st December 1363. The latter gave the Saddlers of London power to elect overseers of their trade. These overseers or wardens were entitled to search for faulty goods not only in the City but in association with those similarly appointed in other towns and boroughs, wherever saddle making was carried on. Ordinances made in the same year and ratified by the mayor and aldermen give a very full picture both of internal government of the trade and of details of saddle making in the Middle Ages.

The mistery of Saddlers first became a corporation by royal charter dated 20th March 1394/5 and successive charters have confirmed or extended its powers. These powers are now little exercised but the full prerogative of search was operated as late as 1882 when sixteen faulty saddles were condemned by a jury of London Saddlers and subsequently destroyed.

THE ARMORIAL BEARINGS (Pl. 43)

Azure a chevron between three saddles furnished or.

Crest : On a wreath of the colours a horse passant argent, bridled, saddled and trappings or, on its head a plume of three feathers carnation.

Mantling : Gules doubled argent.

Supporters : On either side a horse argent, hoofed and bridled or, on its head a plume of three feathers carnation.

Mottoes : Hold fast, sit sure.
　　　　　Our trust is in God.
　　　　　　　　　　Confirmation of arms and grant of crest
　　　　　　　　　　and supporters by Robert Cooke,
　　　　　　　　　　Clarenceux
　　　　　　　　　　20th October 1585

A sketch of the pre-grant arms, which were those confirmed by
Clarenceux, is given in a manuscript of 1575 ;[1] no tincture is there
shown for the field but the chevron and saddles appear as or.　Clarenceux's letters patent have not survived and the authority for the above
blazon rests on two early seventeenth-century entries[2] in the College
of Arms.　In these two documents the blazons are unfortunately incomplete, the same lacuna occurring in each as follows : " azure a
cheveron betwene 3 . . . saddells furnished d'or ".　A copy of the
patent, or an abstract thereof, contained in a collection of " Guiftes

Saddle

and confirmations " made by John Withie in 1620,[3] is similarly deficient.
In the official history of the Company[4] the word is supplied as " manage ", but the source of this addition is uncertain, and no instance of
the term has been found before 1780.[5] Holme[6] calls the saddles
" warre " saddles ; and the earliest blazon seen, in a compilation dated
1587,[7] reads " B (i.e. azure) on a chevron or betw. 3 sadels or sturops
or ".　" Manage " is an archaic word for the schooling or training of

---

[1] Guild. Lib. MS. 2463.
[2] Coll. Arms MS. Vincent 169/69, and Misc. Gts. 1/49b.
[3] Brit. Mus. Harl. MS. 1359/73b.
[4] Sherwell (J. W.), *History of the Guild of Saddlers* (1937), p. 36.　The word " manage " is also used in the blazon of the Loriners' arms.
[5] Edmondson (J.), *Complete Body of Heraldry* (1780), vol. 1.
[6] Holme (R.), *Academy of Armory*, vol. 2 (c. 1690), pub. 1905, p. 406.
[7] Brit. Mus. Harl. MS. 839/50b.

a horse, and the saddles as depicted in the official records of the College of Arms do appear to be of the early type of manage saddle,[1] but in the absence of good authority, the word has not been included in the blazon given above. This blazon differs also from that given in the Company's official history in two other particulars : the plumes on the heads of the horses are there given as argent, and their manes are described as or. Argent is probably a misreading of the tricks in the College of Arms which clearly indicate the feathers as " car." i.e. carnation, or flesh-coloured. In the case of the manes, the 1634 visitation[2] does trick them as or, but as the earlier tricks do not so show them, this is considered to be an error.

Two mottoes are attributed to the Company in the 1634 visitation : " Hold fast, sit sure " is shown on a scroll above the crest, while " Our trust is in God " occupies the more usual position beneath the coat. Vincent[3] asserts that the former motto was included in the original patent of arms. Mottoes are usually the choice of the grantee, but when they are specifically assigned, they form an integral part of the armorial bearings and are not alterable at will. The Company's practice has varied, one or other of the mottoes being shown beneath the arms, but two mottoes together have not been used in recent years. Since, however, they were entered in the record of the 1634 visitation, this is sufficient to settle their form and make both a part of the armorial bearings.

---

[1] The design has been closely followed for the illustration in this volume ; cp. also Winter (G. S.), *Bellerophon* (1678), p. 13 and pl. 2.

[2] Coll. Arms MS. 2nd C.24/391.

[3] Coll. Arms Vincent 169/69.

THE WORSHIPFUL COMPANY OF SALTERS

SALTERS were originally those who either produced and sold sea-salt, or preserved food by its application.

Salting was one of the oldest forms of preserving meat and fish. In the Middle Ages when the supply of food in the off-seasons was dependent upon prudent storage, the use of salt was of prime importance, and it was needed in great quantities. Some was produced in England but much was also imported from Europe. So vital was an adequate supply of this mineral that the severe restrictions on the export of bullion were relaxed to allow its being shipped to England.

Salt was a term formerly used, as now, not only for common salt but also for other chemicals. With the development of the dyeing industry, some of these other salts assumed increasing importance and became the predominant commodity of the trade of the salter, or dry salter as he was also known, probably from his use of dry salt in the curing of food as opposed to pickling in brine. In addition to vegetable and mineral dyes, his stock-in-trade included resins and shellacs, and from him the dyer obtained the raw materials of his craft.

An organized fraternity of salters is mentioned in 1394 when Richard II granted letters patent on 13th April to a guild of Corpus Christi in the Church of All Hallows, Bread Street. This fraternity was subsequently incorporated as the Art or Mistery of Salters of London by a charter of 20th July 1558, and today is the ninth of the Twelve Great companies. The Company's functions of trade control are no longer used but it maintains its interest in the chemical industry. By grants and scholarships it encourages the training of chemists and research in chemistry, in particular through the Salters' Institute which was founded in 1938 for this purpose.

Pl. 45

SCRIVENERS, p. 217
SPECTACLE MAKERS, p. 229

THE ARMORIAL BEARINGS (Pl. 44)

Party per chevron azure and gules three covered salts argent garnished or, the salt shedding on both sides of the salts argent.

Granted[1] by Thomas Benolt,
Clarenceux
17th November 1530

Crest : On a wreath argent and gules issuing from the water proper an arm embowed carnation holding in the hand a salt as in the arms.

Mantling : Gules doubled argent.

Supporters : On either side an ounce sable besantee with a crown about its neck and a chain all or.

Supporters and crest granted[2] by Robert Cooke,
Clarenceux
25th September 1591

Motto : Sal sapit omnia.

The original patent of arms records the blazon as follows :

Gueulles and asur party per cheveron three saltes coveryd sylver garnysshed gold the salt shedyng on both sydes of the saltes silver.

Salt, after the 1530 grant

It is of interest to note that, although the 1530 patent gives " gueulles and asur " for the field, the exemplification in the margin shows azure in chief and gules in base. Modern practice requires such a painting to be blazoned as azure and gules. This reversal of the order of the tinctures is an example of a former rule, at least as old as the fourteenth century, which asserted that the tincture, be it of the field or of a charge, which ran down to the base point must be named first.[3]

The patent of the crest and supporters has not survived and the authority for these is the record of the 1687 visitation of London[4] which enters them as follows :

---

[1] Original patent in the possession of the Company. A reproduction in colour, from a contemporary record in the College of Arms (L6/17), appears in the *Heralds' Commemorative Exhibition Catalogue* (1936), pl. 32, and in Wagner (A. R.), *Heraldry in England* (1946), pl. xii.

[2] Original patent has not survived. College of Arms entries are : 2nd C.24/375 and K.9/435.

[3] This is discussed by H. Stanford London in " Some medieval treatises on English heraldry " (*Antiquaries Journal*, vol. 33 (1953), p. 179).

[4] Coll. Arms K.9/435.

On a wreath silver and gules out of the water proper an arm carnation holding in the hand a saltcellar silver garnished gold

and the supporters,

2 ounces sable besantee with crowns about their necks and chains gold.

The trick that accompanies this blazon does not in fact depict any water in the crest, and in an unofficial collection in the College of Arms[1] the arm is shown emerging from clouds, drawn nebuly in the conventional manner. This feature of the crest may, however, be a misinterpretation of water which is, in any case, difficult to differentiate from clouds in a crest of this nature. Clouds are common in heraldry as an allusion to the divine origin of all things, but it seems likely that, despite the problem set for the artist, the designer of the crest introduced water to refer to the natural source of salt. For many years sea-salt was the only variety available and the arm rising from the water brandishing a salt cellar is a plausible allusion to this.

[1] Vincent 154/6.

THE WORSHIPFUL COMPANY OF SCRIVENERS

In the middle of the fourteenth century the Scriveners, or Writers of Court Letter, were associated, apparently as one guild, with the Writers of Text Letter. In 1373 the Scriveners acquired ordinances for their self-government, while the Writers of Text Letter in conjunction with the Illuminators founded in 1403 a guild which later became known as the Company of Stationers. The common origin of these two guilds may be indicated by the similarity of their armorial bearings.

Since the term "scrivener" by derivation means merely a writer, it is probable that the preparation of legal documents, which became the scrivener's province, was a later effect of the specialization demanded by an increasing complexity of legal deeds. An acquired knowledge of the law subsequently extended the scrivener's business to include conveyancing and acting as a financial agent. By the middle of the eighteenth century the scrivener had assumed the functions of the present-day notary, and the humbler role of writer of deeds was mainly taken over by the law-stationer.

Under its charter of incorporation, dated 28th January 1617/18, in which the Company is described in Latin as the Society of Writers of the City of London, the jurisdiction of the Scriveners encompassed the City and within three miles therefrom. All notaries who today practise within these boundaries are required by an act of 1801 to be free of the Company whose membership is confined to those of the legal profession.

THE ARMORIAL BEARINGS (Pl. 45)

Azure an eagle volant or, holding in its beak a penner [i.e. a pen-case] and ink-horn sable stringed gules, standing upon a book gules garnished or.

Crest : On a wreath or and azure a dexter hand proper, holding a pen argent, the sleeve or turned up argent, issuing from a cloud proper ; over all a scroll bearing the motto—*Scribite scientes.*

Mantling : Gules doubled argent.

Supporters : On either side a counsellor proper standing upon a scroll beneath the arms, also bearing the motto as over the crest.

Confirmation of arms and grant of crest and supporters by Sir Richard St. George, Clarenceux

11th November 1634

Additional motto : Littera scripta manet.

In the wardens' accounts of the Scriveners[1] is an entry of 12th January 1739 which records the payment of £3. 3s. 0d. to " Mr. Peters . . . for his trouble in procuring and drawing out the Armes of the

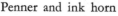

Penner and ink horn

Early arms, originally a seal device

Company on vellum ". This drawing with an accompanying copy of the 1634 patent of arms is the only full record of the grant now surviving in the Company's archives.[2] It is signed by Stephen Peters, arms painter, who noted upon the document that it was made at the request of the Master and Wardens, " the original being lost in the fire of London ". The Company's ordinances, dated 28th May 1635, also bears in the margin a painting of the arms, but without supporters.[3]

A complete text of a certificate of the arms together with the grant of crest and supporters exists in the College of Arms.[4] This states that the Scriveners by virtue of their incorporation do keep a common seal and " doe beare for theire coat Armour Azure an Eagle volant Or holding in his mouth a Penner and Ink-horne Sable stringed Gules standing upon a Booke Gules garnished Or ". Clarenceux continues that he has granted for " a farther ornament to their said coat of arms . . . by way of addition these Supporters and Creast . . . A hand proper holding a Pen Argent the Sleeve Or turned up Argent, out of a Clowd proper, over all an Escrole with this motto Scribite Scientes and for their Supporters Two councelors standing upon an Escrole with the aforesaid Motto, mantled Gules doubled Argent."

[1] Guild. Lib. MS. 8720. [2] Guild Lib. MS. 8719. [3] Guild Lib. MS. 8718.
[4] Coll. Arms. MS. Misc. Gts. II/211.

Pl. 46   P.218

SHIPWRIGHTS, p. 220   SOLICITORS, p. 227

STATIONERS, p. 232

It is not common for mottoes to be specified in the texts of patents ; it is exceptionally rare to find, as in this patent, the motto designated in two positions. Mottoes are usually free to be chosen by the grantee, but when assigned in the patent they become an integral part of the armorial bearings. The substitution by the Scriveners of another motto beneath the arms, as is their current practice, is therefore improper. The practice seems to have begun with Stephen Peters' drawing which shows the adopted motto.

Arms were in use by the Scriveners at least one hundred years before they were granted in 1634. A coloured drawing of the coat is contained in a collection made about 1530,[1] and shows it substantially similar to the authorized version of the arms. The eagle, which in the earlier version has a glory about its head, is clearly intended to be the eagle of St. John, and its occurrence at so early a date undoubtedly indicates a pre-Reformation origin of the arms. The present use of the eagle as crest, and eagle with penner and ink-horn in association with their arms on an ancient seal of the Stationers' Company, provides some evidence in support of the theory that the two Companies had a common origin in the fourteenth century or before,[2] and it is possible that they had a yet earlier ancestry in a religious fraternity of St. John.

The counsellors which support the arms were counsellors-at-law ; the equivalent to the present-day barristers-at-law. As the writing of legal documents was the main activity of the working scrivener, the counsellors can aptly be said to be supporters of the Company.

[1] Ibid., MS. Vincent, " Two Ears of Wheat ", fo. K.
[2] *Bibliographical Society Transactions*, 2nd ser., vol. 18, p. 6.

Q

THE WORSHIPFUL COMPANY OF SHIPWRIGHTS

In an ordinance book among the Shipwrights' archives is an entry relating to 10th August 1483 which states that " it is not unknowne to all [that] the bretheren and sisters of the fraternitie of Saint Symon and Jude hath been holden in London by the crafte of Shipwrights of tyme out of minde ". This combination of religious devotions with trade functions was common among the pre-Reformation guilds whose aims included not only concern for their respective trades but also the spiritual welfare of members.

From the original centre of their trade near London Bridge the fraternity moved to Ratcliffe and Wapping. Here they came into conflict during the sixteenth century with a body of " foreign " shipwrights, so-called because they were not freemen of the City, who had established themselves across the river at Rotherhithe. The position of these foreign shipwrights was strengthened by the grant of a charter on 22nd April 1605 which incorporated them as the Art or Mistery of Shipwrights of England. This was followed by a second charter, dated 6th May 1612, in which the company is described as the Art or Mistery of Shipwrights of Redrith (i.e. Rotherhithe) in the county of Surrey. The chartered body strove for many years to bring the free shipwrights of the City under their control. In spite of an order in council of 1638 which declared that the latter were exempted from the rule of the " new corporation ", the quarrel continued. On 8th March 1684/5, however, the king accepted a recommendation of the attorney general that the free shipwrights be left under the rules of government " whereby they have for a long time been governed ". In an attempt to recover lost ground the foreign shipwrights decided to surrender their charter and to petition for a new one. This move was unsuccessful and a further attempt in 1705 also met with failure. Thereafter the foreign shipwrights disappear as an organized body, leaving the free shipwrights of the City in control of their trade.

The Company now exercises no supervision of the craft but it has endeavoured to promote technical education in the industry by organizing exhibitions and offering prizes and awards to apprentices and students.

THE ARMORIAL BEARINGS (Pl. 46)

Azure in a sea proper the hull of a ship or, and for difference in the dexter chief point a sword erect point upwards of the last, on a chief argent a cross gules charged with a lion passant guardant or.

Crest : Upon a wreath of the colours on an ark sable resting upon a mount vert a dove bearing an olive branch proper, and for difference in the prow of the ark a sword as in the arms.

Mantling : Gules doubled argent.

Motto : Within the ark safe for ever.

These arms, without the swords, were originally granted to a rival body of shipwrights by William Camden, Clarenceux, on 9th January 1606.[1] Known as the Foreign Shipwrights in distinction from the free shipwrights of the City, this community was incorporated in 1605

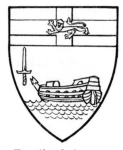

Crest   Detail of the arms

as the Art or Mystery of Shipwrights of England and later, in 1612, as the Shipwrights of Redrith, now Rotherhithe. When the foreign shipwrights surrendered their charter in 1685 and failed to secure another, their powers diminished and the company finally became extinct. Thereafter the free shipwrights assumed the arms of those they had successfully challenged and defeated.

When the arms were adopted is uncertain. Literary sources of the eighteenth century are unreliable due to their confusion of the two separate guilds. According to a petition by the free shipwrights in 1920, by which they sought to regularize the use of the appropriated arms, the company had assumed the arms " in or about 1784 ". No evidence is cited for this assertion but it is possible that the source

[1] The original letters patent of this 1606 grant are now in the custody of the Worshipful Company of Shipwrights.

was Thornton's History of London.[1] Thornton does not, however, clearly distinguish between the two companies and there are numerous earlier references which are at least of equal value, but they leave the question equally in doubt.

The petition of 1920 resulted in the issue of a royal warrant, dated 2nd March 1920, which required the Deputy Earl Marshal to accord to " the Ancient Brotherhood and Fraternity of Free Shipwrights the arms granted by letters patent of Clarenceux to the Art or Mystery of Shipwrights of England, 3 James I ", and instructed that they be exemplified according to the laws of arms and recorded in the College of Arms.[2] The warrant summarizes the development and conflict of the two companies as set out in the free shipwrights' petition, and allows the latter to " continue to bear " the arms, crest and motto in which the right of the foreign shipwrights had lapsed with their extinction. The Deputy Earl Marshal thereupon made an authorization to this effect on 6th April 1920,[3] and the armorial bearings,[4] incorporating the sword in the arms and crest for difference, were granted by Sir Henry Farnham Burke, Garter, Charles Harold Athill, Clarenceux, and William Alexander Lindsay, Norroy, on 24th June 1920.

[1] Thornton (W.), *New Complete . . . History . . . of London* (1784).
[2] A copy of the royal warrant is printed in Ridge (C. H.), *Records of the Worshipful Company of Shipwrights*, vol. 2 (1946), pp. xxxv–xxxviii ; the original is in possession of the Company.
[3] Ridge, op. cit., p. xxxix ; the original was lost by enemy action.
[4] Original patent in the possession of the Company.

Pl. 47

SKINNERS (p. 223)

THE WORSHIPFUL COMPANY OF SKINNERS

SKINNERS dealt in skins for fur garments. Their role was mainly that of the wholesaler and retailer of furs as well as manufacturer of apparel. Dressing of skins was performed by a separate craft of tawyers which later was absorbed by the Skinners' Company. In the Middle Ages the wearing of furs was rigidly controlled, being allowed only for the adornment of royalty, nobility and persons of wealth and importance. Vestiges of its use as a mark of distinction may still be seen in the fur trimming of mayoral and aldermanic robes and on other ceremonial gowns.

Owing to the importance attached to fur, the Company of Skinners attained a prominent place in civic life at an early date, and was among the first of the incorporated companies of the City, having received its first charter on 1st March 1327. It is now numbered among the Great Twelve companies, sharing with the Merchant Taylors the sixth place in order of precedence. One of the most notable of the Company's present-day activities is the governing of Tonbridge School, founded by a former Skinner in the sixteenth century.

THE ARMORIAL BEARINGS (Pl. 47)

Ermine on a chief gules three ermine caps tasselled and enfiled with crowns or.

Crest : On a wreath or and gules a lynx statant proper about the neck a wreath leaved vert purfled or.

Mantling : Azure doubled argent.

Supporters : Dexter a lynx proper, sinister a marten sable, about the neck of each a wreath leaved vert.

Confirmation of arms and grant of crest
and supporters by Thomas Hawley,
Clarenceux
1st October 1550

Mottoes : In Christo fratres ; To God only be all glory.

The original patent of Hawley's grant has not survived but a full copy exists in the College of Arms[1] and in the British Museum.[2]

---

[1] Misc. Gts. II/200.   [2] Harl. MS. 1470/154.

These copies have evidently been transcribed with care, and that in the British Museum bears a note that it was examined and agreed with the original in the possession of the Company by John and Augustine Withie in the year 1644.

In the text of his patent Hawley states that he was approached by the Master and Wardens of the Company

> to whom at there speciall sewte and instaunce, and shewing unto mee theire high authority of corporacion and the Armes therto belonging and they minding the further exaltacion and preferrement of the sayde crafte and corporacyon have desired me the sayd Clarencieulx to devise ordeine and sett forth to the sayd Armes, Helme and Creast and the Bestes therto belonging . . .

Hawley accordingly granted crest and supporters in the following terms :

> A lizarde in his proper couloure and a marterne sable about either necke a wreath levyd vert upon a helme on a torse golde and geules a Lyzarde standinge in his proper couler about his necke a wreath levyd vert purfled gold manteled asur dobled silver.

Although the " high authority of corporation " which the Skinners showed to Clarenceux was no doubt the Company's charter, there is no reason to assume that the " arms therto belonging " which were produced at the same time, indicate the existence of an earlier grant, now lost, for if such a grant had been exhibited, Hawley would in all probability have named the grantor thereof in his patent. No doubt what was shown to Hawley was a representation of arms then in use by the Company which proved acceptable to him as King of Arms, and which he therefore confirmed.

No blazon of these adopted arms is given by Hawley in his patent, but tricks are shown in the copies mentioned above which it is reasonable to suppose interpret the painting that had accompanied the original grant. A minor deviation in the mantling occurs in both these tricks which show the tinctures as azure and ermine instead of azure and argent as given in the blazon of the crest and supporters.

The arms are commonly found blazoned with the charges on the chief described as three ducal coronets (sometimes princes' crowns) or, capped ermine and tasselled or. Such blazoning obscures the origin of these charges, the prominent feature of which is the ermine caps

Decorated initials, A.D. 1487–1518/19, showing ermine caps with
and without crowns

and not the crowns or coronets which are mere developments of
successive elaborations of gold garnishing on the caps.

Ermine was among the most esteemed furs in which the skinner
dealt, being reserved by the sumptuary laws of the Middle Ages to
the use of royalty and nobility. Because of its importance ermine
was adopted by the Skinners' Company as a badge of the craft and in
a manuscript volume, known as the Book of the Fraternity of Our
Lady's Assumption, preserved among the records of the Company,
references are to be found to gifts of silver being " marked with a
powder of ermine " (1461), " marked with a powder of ermine tail "
(1475), and " marked with powdering " (1481).[1] That the ermine cap

Early form of arm, A.D. 1502/3, from the Book of the Assumption
(Skinners' Company MS.)

[1] Quoted in Lambert (J. J.), *Records of the Skinners of London* (1933), p. 102.

was an important emblem of the Company is also emphasized by its appearance in the hand of an angel in a fine illumination of the Assumption[1] in the same volume, while the yearly lists of members therein, beginning with that for the year 1487, include ermine caps in the decorative initials.[2] It is also to be noted that the gown of the Virgin in the painting of the Assumption is trimmed with ermine.

In their early versions the ermine caps are shown plain with no ornamentation, but in the list for the year 1491/2 a faint gold circlet appears, and this addition later becomes elaborated by subsequent artists into coronets of various shapes. An early example of the arms is shown in the Book of the Assumption at the foot of an entry of 1502/3, and here too the caps are without decoration ; the arms are otherwise in the same form as that given in Hawley's patent. But an entry for 1528/9, embellished with the arms, depicts fully developed crowns encircling the caps. Additional evidence for the evolution of the crowns may be found in a manuscript in the British Museum.[3] This manuscript, which has been attributed to the period 1480–1500,[4] shows the ermine caps encircled with invected bands of gold.

The lynx and the marten of crest and supporters both have reference to furs of the skinners' trade. In Hawley's patent the lynx is termed a lizard which was an alternative term for the lucern or, as it is now known, the lynx. Martens are a species of the weasel family whose skins produce fur of sable ; the sable tincture of this supporter is an obvious heraldic pun.

Furs made from the skins of both these animals were much prized. An act of Henry VIII's reign[5] prohibited the wearing of " furres of sables " by any man " under the state of an erle ", and similar, though rather wider provisions were made for " furres of blake jenettes or luserns ". Other regulations had been made from time to time in order to discourage the presumptuous from assuming the guise of nobility of which furs and other attire were the outward sign.

[1] Lambert (J. J.), *Records of the Skinners of London* (1933), pl. facing p. 108.
[2] ibid., p. 100.
[3] Harl. MS. 6163/111.
[4] See Wagner (A. R.), *Catalogue of English Medieval Rolls of Arms* (1950), p. 109.
[5] 24 Hen. VIII c. 13.

THE WORSHIPFUL COMPANY OF SOLICITORS

THIS is one of the few City guilds which have been formed in the twentieth century. On 17th March 1909 the City of London Solicitors' Company was constituted on the pattern of an ancient guild, and was registered as a limited company. Objects were to encourage professional intercourse and generally to further the status and practice of the legal profession and the administration of justice. Where appropriate it seeks the co-operation of other law associations and makes representations to authority on pending legislation and other matters touching the law. On 9th May 1944 the Company achieved a grant of livery from the Court of Aldermen whereby the former limited company, which was dissolved, was re-established as one of the livery companies of the City.

The Company is a strict craft guild in that it admits only those who practise or have practised within one mile radius of the Bank of England. At present it has no charter of incorporation.

THE ARMORIAL BEARINGS (Pl. 46)

·Quarterly argent and gules in sinister chief a deed with seals pendent proper, in dexter base a Roman lamp of the first, over all a sword point upwards in bend of the second.

Crest : On a wreath of the colours upon a fasces fessewise rods gules, axe and binding or an owl argent.

Mantling : Gules doubled argent.

Granted by Sir Henry Farnham Burke,
Garter
William Alexander Lindsay,
Clarenceux
Gordon Ambrose deLisle Lee,
Norroy
25th August 1926

Motto : Lex libertatis origo.

The above blazon is transcribed from the letters patent in the possession of the Company. In these arms is symbolized the debt that English law owes to ancient Rome, whose legal precepts still illumine the administration of justice.

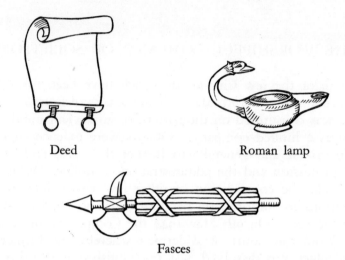

Deed   Roman lamp

Fasces

The fasces[1] were a symbol of the royal authority transferred to the higher magistrates of Rome before whom they were carried by the lictors; and represented the rods with which malefactors were scourged before execution.   Wisdom is exemplified by the owl.

[1] *Fascis lignorum*: a bundle of wood—tied with thongs.

THE WORSHIPFUL COMPANY OF SPECTACLE MAKERS

SPECTACLE making appears to have been first introduced into England during the sixteenth century and the London craftsmen had grown sufficiently important and numerous by 1629 to obtain a charter which was granted to them by Charles I on 16th May in that year. This incorporated them as the Master, Wardens and Fellowship of Spectacle Makers of London with power to control the trade " within our realm of England ".

Spectacles were sold not only by the maker at his shop but also retailed by other shopkeepers who appear to have been mainly haberdashers. In addition to the making and sale of spectacles, members of the craft were also concerned with the manufacture of mathematical and optical instruments. The relative importance of this additional activity is illustrated by the inclusion of charges symbolizing it in new, but unauthorized, arms adopted by the Company in 1810. Mathematical instruments were also claimed by the Clockmakers' Company as proper to their craft, and the rival claims were a cause of conflict between the two companies.

With the decay of the guild system during the eighteenth century, the Company's powers of supervision under its charter gradually declined and eventually fell into disuse. Connection with the craft was revived at the end of the nineteenth century by the institution of examinations and the award of certificates in optics. The Company's diplomas are accepted by the Government as entitling their holders to practise as qualified opticians under the National Health Service.

THE ARMORIAL BEARINGS (Pl. 45)

Vert a chevron or between three pairs of nose-spectacles proper framed of the second.

Crest : On a wreath or and vert two arms embowed vested vert cuffed or the hands proper holding a sun in splendour within an annulet gold.

Mantling : Vert doubled or.

Supporters : On either side a falcon proper belled or charged with a sword erect gules.

Granted[1] by Sir Algar Henry Stafford Howard,
Garter
Sir Arthur William Steuart Cochrane,
Clarenceux
Sir Gerald Woods Wollaston,
Norroy and Ulster
18th September 1950

No motto.

Apart from the absence of crest and supporters, and some variation in the tinctures, these arms had been used by the Company, without authority, at least since 1739.[2] Literary sources continue to record them until the end of the nineteenth century. A second coat was, however, adopted soon after 1810 and was subsequently recognized by the Company as the official arms. The reason for the change is to be found in the Court minute books of the Company : on 29th March 1810 the Upper Warden reported that " the stock could not be properly bought in as ordered at the last especial Court, by reason of his not having the seal of the Company ". It was therefore resolved that a Mr. Henry Lawson, a member of the Company, be requested to provide a seal of his own design ; this was duly produced and accepted on 28th June 1810.[3] The minutes of the meeting on that date give

Device of A.D. 1810

---

[1] Original patent deposited in the Guildhall Library, MS. 6573.

[2] Maitland (W.), *History of London* (1739).

[3] Guild. Lib. MS. 5213/4. I am indebted to Mr. Roland Champness, M.A., LL.M., F.S.A., Clerk to the Company, for directing me to these entries.

Ecce agnus Dei qui tollit peccata mundi

AMORE SITIS UNITI

Pl. 48

Q.230

TALLOW CHANDLERS, p. 236
TIN PLATE WORKERS, p. 240

Falcon supporter, belled and charged with a sword erect

the following description of the heraldic device invented by Mr. Lawson :

> Azure a pair of compasses (chevron-wise) between two pairs of spectacles in chief or, and a terrestrial globe in base proper, the frame and stand of the second ; in the centre chief point the achromatic prisms open proper.
>
> The crest : on a wreath of the colours two arms embowed vested azure each charged with three estoiles argent, cuff of the last, the hands supporting a serpent the tail in the mouth proper encircling the sun in splendour.
>
> Motto : A blessing to the aged.

The Kings of Arms, when making the formal grant in 1950, have reverted to the early and simpler insignia, and have expunged the additional emblems introduced to symbolize the ancillary interests of the Company. The motto, which has been associated with the Spectacle Makers' arms since their first known example in 1739, is not now generally used and no other has been adopted to replace it.

THE WORSHIPFUL COMPANY OF STATIONERS
AND NEWSPAPER MAKERS

THE term " stationer " derives from the medieval Latin word *stationarius*, a stall-holder as opposed to an itinerant seller of goods. The important role of the *stationarii* who produced, lent and sold books in the medieval universities no doubt played a part in eventually limiting the meaning of the word to one who dealt in books. In the Middle Ages the stationer combined the selling of books with the craft of producing them, and references to him in London in the fourteenth century, when the stationer as such first appears there, describe him indifferently as stationer, bookbinder, illuminator or textwriter. It is probable that the writers of court hand, who were mainly responsible for the preparation of legal documents, were at one time also included among the informal fraternity that comprised this group; these craftsmen, however, formed in 1373 a separate guild which was the forerunner of the Scriveners' Company. In 1403 the Text Writers and the Limners (illuminators) were formally united by civic ordinance into a single guild which was the direct ancestor of the present Company of Stationers. The similarity of the arms of the Scriveners and the Stationers is suggestive of a common origin. On 4th May 1557 the Stationers were incorporated by royal charter, and finally acquired the present title under a supplemental charter of 1937 which recognized the Stationers' amalgamation with the newly formed Company of Newspaper Makers.

During its operative guild life the Company had attained by ordinances, charters and Acts of Parliament, a wide measure of control over the printing and publishing trade of the realm. An embryo form of copyright was also obtained thereby and the first copyright act of 1709 confirmed the Company's register of publications as a record of title to copyright. This was largely effective until the passage of the copyright act of 1911. The Company still maintains a close interest in the trade and its members are confined to those connected with printing, publishing and allied professions.

THE ARMORIAL BEARINGS (Pl. 46)

Azure on a chevron between three books with clasps all or an eagle volant gules with a nimbus or between two roses gules leaved vert; in chief issuing out of a cloud proper radiated or a holy spirit wings displayed argent with a nimbus or.

Granted by Sir Gilbert Dethick,
Garter
6th September 1557

Crest : On a wreath or and azure an eagle wings expanded with a diadem above its head perched on a book fessewise all or.

Mantling : Azure doubled or.

Supporters : On either side an angel proper vested argent mantled azure winged and blowing a trumpet or.

Granted by Sir George Rothe Bellew,
Garter
Sir Arthur William Steuart Cochrane,
Clarenceux
Sir Gerald Woods Wollaston,
Norroy and Ulster
30th July 1951

Motto : Verbum Domini manet in aeternum.

Many of the early records of the Company were burned in the fire of 1666, and the patent of arms is believed to have perished with them. According to the enrolment of the grant in the College of Arms,[1] the original blazon was as follows :

> Asure on a cheveron an Eagle volant with a Diedem beetweene twoo roses gueles levid [vert] betweene iii bookes clasped gold : in cheife yssuinge out of a cloude ye sonne beames gold a holy Sperite the winges displayed silver with a diedem gold.

Crest and supporters had been adopted and used without authority at least from the eighteenth century. An examination of official publications of the Company has shown that the former was first used about 1789 and the latter about 1834, although angels appear, more as decorative accompaniments than heraldic supporters, as early as 1721.[2] In 1951 the use of crest and supporters was regularized. The

---

[1] Gts. I. 135 and Vincent 163, 158. A full transcript certified by George Harrison, Windsor Herald, 19th November 1874, appears in Arber (E.), ed. *Transcripts of the Stationers' Company's Registers*, vol. 1 (1875), pp. xxxvi–xxxvii.

[2] Nichols (J. G.), *Historical Notices of the Worshipful Company of Stationers* (1861), p. 24.

relevant grant recites that the Company being " desirous that the crest and supporters, which had long been used " might be " assigned with lawful authority ", the Kings of Arms accordingly granted them in the terms given in the blazon above.

In 1634 the arms were recorded at the visitation of London,[1] where the entry of the arms is accompanied by a trick of the Company's first seal. Depicted thereon is the figure of St. John the Evangelist and Apostle standing behind the Company's shield of arms with right hand raised and bearing in his left hand a cup from which emerges

Seal, September A.D. 1558

a serpent ; an eagle holding in its beak an ink-horn and penner stands to the dexter of the shield. Encircling the seal is the inscription *Sigillum artis Stationar : Anno Domini MDLVIII.*

The representation of St. John with the chalice and viper is a common occurrence in religious art. Its origin is the apocryphal " Acts of St. John " which narrate how the Apostle when challenged by the high priest of Diana at Ephesus to drink a cup of poison, does so without harm, thereby converting Aristodemus, the priest, to Christianity. The identification of St. John with the figure on the seal is confirmed by the presence of the eagle which, as one of the living beasts

[1] Coll. Arms 2nd C.24 fo. 9. An illustration of the seal is given in Arber, op. cit., vol. I, p. xxxvii.

Q.234

Pl. 49

LETTERS PATENT GRANTING ARMS TO THE WORSHIPFUL COMPANY OF PAINTERS, 1486
(no day and month given)

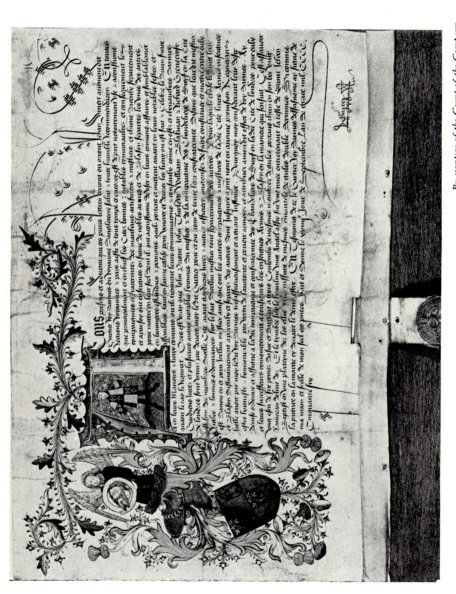

By courtesy of the Court of the Company

R.235

Pl. 50

LETTERS PATENT GRANTING ARMS TO THE WORSHIPFUL COMPANY OF
TALLOW CHANDLERS, 24TH SEPTEMBER 1456

of the vision of Ezekiel and of the Apocalypse, is a symbol of that saint. For with these beasts early Christian writers identified the four evangelists, St. John being represented by the eagle. Thus the eagle on the shield of arms and in the crest indicates the Company's devotion to that saint, whilst the Holy Spirit in the guise of a dove alludes to the source of wisdom and truth. Though this symbolism might imply the foundation of the Guild as a religious fraternity in honour of the Evangelist, there is no evidence which survives to support this possibility.[1]

A similar devotion to St. John as the patron saint of the writer's craft is to be noted in the case of the Scriveners' Company whose arms include the eagle holding ink-horn and penner.

Arms

---

[1] The early origins of the Company have been examined by Graham Pollard in *Bibliographical Society Transactions*, N.S., vol. 18, pp. 1–38.

R

THE WORSHIPFUL COMPANY OF TALLOW CHANDLERS

FROM evidence in its archives and from bequests made in wills, the Tallow Chandlers' Company appears to have been associated before the Reformation with two religious fraternities. One, in honour of Our Lady and St. John the Baptist, was founded by the Company as a whole, while the other, that of Our Lady and St. Elizabeth, seems to have been formed by the "yeomanry" of the guild. The symbolism of the fifteenth-century coat of arms provides further testimony of the Company's origin as a fraternity of St. John. As a craft guild the Tallow Chandlers are known to have been an organized community in the fourteenth century, and were granted a charter of incorporation on 8th March 1461/2.

Tallow Chandlers were primarily makers of candles, an activity which they shared with the wax chandlers. The latter, however, employed beeswax for their products which were mainly sold for church purposes, whereas the tallow chandlers used animal fats, supplied by butchers, to make a cheaper variety of candles for domestic use and for street lighting. Street lighting was from the fifteenth century, at least, the responsibility of each householder, and mayoral proclamations survive which required the inhabitants of the City to hang lanterns at night outside their houses. An act of Common Council of 1599 reinforced and extended these requirements, and no doubt contributed to the prosperity of the Company.

Although the guild was originally concerned with candle-making, it also acquired some control of the trade in other products. In 1576 letters patent were granted to the Company by the Queen for the maintenance of good standards in soap, vinegar, bitter hops and oils. This extension of trade was resisted by the City authorities but the Company continued to exercise a limited control.

The introduction of oil lighting and the granting of monopoly patents to street lighting contractors towards the end of the seventeenth century was a partial cause of the decline of the Company's prosperity and the use of its powers. In the succeeding century trade control and the right of search were discontinued.

THE ARMORIAL BEARINGS (Pl. 48)

On a field of six pieces azure and argent three doves argent membered gules, each holding in its beak an olive branch or.

Granted[1] by John Smert,
Garter
24th September 1456

Crest : On a wreath argent and azure the head of St. John the Baptist proper in a charger proper [i.e. argent] radiated or.

Mantling : Gules doubled ermine.

Supporters : On either side on a mount vert an angel vested, winged and crowned with stars or.

Confirmation[2] of arms and grant of crest
and supporters by William Camden,
Clarenceux
29th January 1602/3

Motto : *Ecce agnus Dei qui tollit peccata mundi.*

Celestial crown

Dove holding in its beak an olive branch

In his grant of 1603 Camden says

I have upon sight of their letteres pattentes, bearing the date the xxiiiith daye of September anno Domini 1456 . . . Confirmed their saide Coat of Armes, as it was first gyven ; corrected their Creast, and for furder ornament added two supporters, being Angelles, crowned with starres in token of light, wherof their mistery is a beautifull imitacion. All which . . . I . . . confirme, gyve, graunt, and allowe . . .

No blazon appears in the patent, and that given above is based on an

[1] Original patent at Tallow Chandlers' Hall. Reproduced in colour in the *Edinburgh Heraldic Exhibition Catalogue* (1891), pl. 5.

[2] Original at Tallow Chandlers' Hall. Monochrome reproduction in Edinburgh exhibition catalogue (1891), pl. 6. A full transcript of both patents is given in Monier-Williams (M. F.), *Records of the Tallow Chandlers* (1897), pp. 24-5, 31-2.

Arms after the painting in the margin of the 1456 grant of arms

interpretation of the painting depicted in the margin of the grant, and upon records in the College of Arms.[1]

Camden's alteration of the crest granted by Smert has no explanation, but it may be conjectured that he preferred a simpler device. Smert's crest was an angel seated on a cloud holding the head of St. John the Baptist in a platter. The conventional wreath about the helm is absent and the cloud itself forms the torse. In its original context the blazon is as follows :

Ay devise ordonne et assigne a la dite compaigne et confraternite des Chandeliers de Suyf en la dite Cite de Londres . . . les enseignes Armes et Blason en la maniere qui sensuit. C'est assavoir ung escu de six pointz dasur et dargent a trois coulombs de mesmes membrez de gules portans chacun en son bec ung ramceau dolive dor. Et le tymbre sur le heaulme ung Angel assis sur une nuee entretenant la teste de Saint Jehan Baptist en une plateyne dor les elles & garnissure de mesmes emantele de gules double dermines sicomme la picture en la marge cy devant le demonestre.

---

[1] Coll. Arms MS. EDN. 57/446.

In God is all our trust,
let us never be confounded

BY·FAITH·1·OBTEIGNE

LANA·SPES·NOSTRA

Pl. 51

R.239

TURNERS, p. 243
UPHOLDERS, p. 249

TYLERS AND BRICKLAYERS, p. 246
WOOLMEN, p. 267

Two other City guilds are known to have received grants from John Smert, namely the Girdlers and the Glovers ; a similar division of the field into six pieces with a single charge repeated three times was accorded to each.

Beneath the painting of the arms in the margin of the 1603 patent the motto appears as *Quae arguuntur a lumine manifestantur,* but this is no longer used by the Company. Another early motto which accompanies a trick of the 1456 arms reads " Delite in God & he shall give the [*sic*] thy desyre ".[1]

Both the crest and the doves in the arms have reference to the supposed origin of the Company as a religious fraternity of St. John the Baptist, the doves being in all probability inspired by John i. 32 : " and John bare record, saying I saw the Spirit descending from Heaven like a dove and it abode upon him ". The current motto also originates in the Gospel of St. John i. 29 : " Behold the Lamb of God, which taketh away the sin of the world."

[1] Coll. Arms Misc. Gts. I/49.

THE WORSHIPFUL COMPANY OF TIN PLATE WORKERS, *alias* WIRE WORKERS

THE Tin Plate Workers' Company was incorporated by a charter of 29th December 1670 as the Master, Wardens, Assistants and Commonalty of Tin Plate Workers, *alias* Wire Workers. The mistery of wire workers was the parent body from which the Tin Plate Workers stemmed. Its early life was complex and illustrates to an unusual degree the process of mergers, separations and reunions that is frequently to be noted in the lesser craft guilds which often found it difficult both to fulfil their communal obligations to the civic authority and to represent their trade with sufficient strength and authority.

Wire workers were originally " wire drawers ", or makers of iron wire. They were distinct from the craft of gold and silver wire drawers —an independent guild—although the process of manufacture was the same. The craft emerges in City records during the fourteenth century when, in 1386, masters of the misteries of " kardemakers " and " wyrdrawers " were elected to govern their crafts. Cardmakers were makers of coarse wire brushes for carding wool, and their use of wire brought them into close association with the wire drawers. In 1425 these two misteries are named as one when the mistery of pinners and the mistery of " irenwirdrawers and cardemakers " complained of interference in each other's trade. Their differences appear to have been composed, for in 1451 they jointly placed themselves by agreement under the protection of the Girdlers' Company which shared with them a common interest in bucklemaking. The chapemakers (makers of buckles and sword belt attachments) joined the wiredrawers to form a fellowship of wiremongers in 1479 on the grounds that " there is noon of sufficiaunt noumbre of iche of the said crafts to chose wardeyns ", and articles for its regulation were approved in 1481. When in 1497 the mistery of wiremongers was united with the pinners, it was ordained that this fellowship be called the wiresellers, and " the name of Pynners and Wyremongers annulled ". By a charter of 1568 the earlier union of the pinners and wireworkers with the Girdlers' Company, mentioned above, was confirmed and the resulting company was constituted as the Master, Wardens or Keepers of the Art or Mystery of Girdlers. In 1636 the pinners became an independent company and the Girdlers' union with the wireworkers was again confirmed by a charter of 1639. The present company, as now constituted, had its origins in 1669 when certain workers in tin plate and wire formed themselves into an independent society. In 1670 a charter of incorporation gave this body control of the trade in tinned iron plate and iron wire and all wares made therefrom. A list of such wares in 1686 includes mousetraps, bird cages, lattice work for windows, buckles, chains, clasps for garments, fish-hooks, pack needles, knitting needles, etc.

Powers of search and trade control are now no longer used, but members of the company include representatives of the tinplate and electrical industries, and scholarships are offered to students engaged in this work.

THE ARMORIAL BEARINGS (Pl. 48)

Sable a chevron or between three lamps, two in chief with one burner each the burners inwards, and one in base with two burners, argent garnished or.

Crest : On a wreath of the colours a spherical ship's lantern or ensigned with a royal crown of the seventeenth century all proper.

Mantling : Sable doubled or.

Supporters : On either side a tinplate worker of the eighteenth century vested proper.

Established by royal warrant
26th January 1956

Motto : Amore sitis uniti.

These arms have been used by the Company at least since 1680 but have been without authority until established by royal warrant on the Company's petition.

The earliest example of the pre-grant arms occurs in the *London Almanack* of 1680[1] in the margin of which is a crude engraving depicting them without crest or supporters. According to the Company's historian,[2] a copy of the bye-laws prepared in 1680 was illuminated with the arms but this document appears now to be missing, having presumably been lost by fire during the late war. The same source states

---

[1] Morden (R.) and Lee (P.), *London Almanack for XXX years,* (1680).
[2] Ebblewhite (E. A.), *Chronological History of the Worshipful Company of Tinplate Workers* (1896), p. 6.

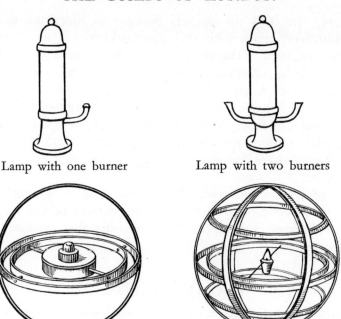

Lamp with one burner   Lamp with two burners

Spherical ship's lantern

that the crest was adopted sometime before 1748, in which year it was " ordered that a new copper plate with the Company's arms be engraved for printing Court Day Summons . . . and that such addition be made thereto as Master Gigner shall think proper ".[1]   This copper plate was used to print the frontispiece to the Company's history and depicts the supporters.

Products of the tinplate workers' craft are represented by the charges in the arms and by the crest.   The spouted lamps are examples of a type of oil lamp, in use during the seventeenth and eighteenth centuries, the wick protruding from the spout.   The " spherical ship's lantern " was a form of lamp, termed a rolling lamp,[2] in which the light was swung on gimbals to maintain it on an even plane.

[1] Ebblewhite, op. cit. p. 36.
[2] *Encyclopedia Londinensis*, vol. 12 (1814), s.v. Lamps, and plate ; Rees (A.), *Cyclopedia* (1820), s.v. Lamps, and plate.

THE WORSHIPFUL COMPANY OF TURNERS

In 1310 six turners were sworn before the mayor not to make any other measures than gallons, pottles and quarts, and were enjoined to seize any false measures found in the hands of others whether free of the City or not. In 1347, because "falsities and deceits" were found in wooden measures for wine and ale, all the makers of such measures, called "turnours", were summoned before the mayor and ordered to make only measures which conformed to the standard. Each turner was moreover required to adopt a mark of his own with which to stamp his products, and all marks were to be registered in the Chamber of London. Again in the ordinances of 1435, which gave the mistery of Turners powers to regulate the craft, reference is made to various types of wooden measures, and it is clear that these were an important product of the turner's lathe. Other articles made by the turner included various items of wooden domestic wares which were cheap and durable for common usage. A list of such articles is set out in the 1608 ordinances, drawn up by the Company after its incorporation by royal charter on 12th June 1604. It includes shovels, scoops, washing bowls, chairs, wheels, pails and trays, in addition to wooden measures.

The 1604 charter, at the petition of the freemen of the society of turners of London, constituted them as a body corporate by the name of the Master, Wardens and Commonalty of the Mystery or Art of the Turners of London. The usual provisions were made for the government of the trade, involving search by the wardens for imperfect goods within the City and five miles of the same, and rules were made for the internal government of the Company. After its powers of trade control ceased to be exercised, the Company has diverted its influence to the encouragement of good craftsmanship. Exhibitions have been held for the display of turnery in materials of all kinds, and prizes awarded to craftsmen and students.

THE ARMORIAL BEARINGS (Pl. 51)

Azure a Catherine wheel between two columns or, in chief an imperial crown or and in base a hatchet fessewise to the sinister head downwards argent handled or.

Crest: On a wreath or and azure the figure of St. Catherine crowned or wearing a mantle azure furred ermine, holding in the dexter hand a Catherine wheel or and in the sinister a sword argent hilted or, the point downwards.

Mantling: Gules doubled argent.

Granted[1] by Sir Richard St. George,
Clarenceux
17th December 1634

Motto: By faith I obteigne.

Until the grant of 1634 the Turners had used the armorial device of *Gules a Catherine wheel or*; a narrative blazon of this occurs in a manuscript of 1587[2] and a rough sketch, without tinctures, is shown in William Smith's *Breffe description* of 1575.[3] The latter example is replaced, however, in Smith's fair copy of 1588[4] by a different coat, again without tinctures, which shows; On a chevron between three planes three compasses extended, on a chief an escallop enclosed on either side by a hatchet and staff in saltire. No reason can be offered for this change and from the evidence of other examples of the pre-grant arms, there is little doubt that the simple Catherine wheel was the device generally in use by the Turners.

This spiked wheel was the instrument of torture from which St. Catherine miraculously escaped unharmed; it has consequently become the emblem of that saint. Because of her eloquence and learning St. Catherine is generally regarded as the patroness of students and philosophers, but she has also, as a result of her emblem, been adopted as the tutelary saint of wheelwrights and mechanics. Whether the emblem was used by the Turners on account of its traditional use by other similar crafts, or whether the Company was originally founded as a fraternity with vows to St. Catherine has not been determined. Many of the medieval guilds began their lives as religious brotherhoods, and there are records of the saints to whom they owed

---

[1] Original deposited in Guildhall Library, MS. 3309. A full transcript appears in Stone (A. C. Stanley-), *The Worshipful Company of Turners* (1925), pp. 288–9.
[2] Brit. Mus. Harl. MS. 839.
[3] Guild. Lib. MS. 2463.
[4] Harl. MS. 6363.

Arms and crest

their respective devotions,[1] but no such evidence has been found in the case of the Turners.

The other charges of the arms, the hatchet and the columns, represent an implement of the craft and one of the products of the turner's art.

The original patent of arms blazons the achievement as follows:

Azure a Katherine wheele between two collumbs or in chiefe an imperiall crowne or and in base a hatchett argent wth the handle or and for their creast upon a wreath of theire coulers or and azier the picture of St. Katherine wth a crowne upon her head or having upon her a mantle of azure furred wth ermin holding in her right hand a Katherine wheele or and in her other hand a sword argent hilt or the point dounewards.

Although not so described in the original blazon, St. Catherine is depicted in the painting in the margin of the grant dressed in a pink gown beneath her azure mantle, with a gold girdle about the waist and a nimbus around her crowned head.

[1] St. Catherine is the patron saint of the Carmen's Company which can prove descent from a fraternity under the protection of that saint.

THE WORSHIPFUL COMPANY OF TYLERS
AND BRICKLAYERS

TILERS do not appear in civic records as an organized body until the beginning of the fifteenth century when a master of the Mistery of Tilers is found appointed in 1416. Before this time ordinances were made concerning building, notably on the use of tiles for roofing as a fire precaution, but it seems that control of the tilers' trade was directly under the rule of the City. Such organization as the fellowship subsequently achieved was abrogated in 1461 by a Civic ordinance which enacted that thenceforth the tilers of the City be regarded as labourers and not incorporated, nor be deemed to constitute an art or society. In 1468 their privileges were restored on the grounds that the trade was corrupt through the lack of adequate control. One hundred years later, on 3rd August 1568, the Fellowship acquired its first charter which incorporated it as the Mistery and Art of Tilers and Bricklayers of London. The addition of " Bricklayers " to the title indicates a later degree of specialization in the trade, for tilers originally were indiscriminately employed on the tiling of roofs, floors and walls ; the wall tile, as it was known, being merely a form of brick.

The decline of the Company as a functional guild was precipitated by an event that ironically brought the trade its greatest prosperity. After the Great Fire of 1666, it was decreed that only brick or stone houses were to be built. The limited force of freemen tilers was incapable of the task, and provision was made for a flood of non-freemen to enjoy all the privileges in the City previously confined to members of the Company.

VINUM ANIMUM EXHILARAT

Pl. 52

R.246

VINTNERS, p. 253

THE ARMORIAL BEARINGS (Pl. 51)

Azure a chevron or, in chief a fleur-de-lis argent between two brick-axes palewise or, in base a "brush" also or.

Crest : On a wreath or and azure a dexter arm embowed vested party per pale or and gules, cuffed argent, holding in the hand proper a brick-axe or.

Mantling : Gules doubled argent.

Motto : In God is all our trust, let us never be confounded.

Granted by Sir Gilbert Dethick,
Garter
Robert Cooke,
Clarenceux
William Flower,
Norroy and Ulster
3rd February 1569

The original patent has not survived and the above blazon is based upon records in the College of Arms. In what appears to be an abstract[1] of the patent, the blazon is given as " Azure a chevron betweene two brickaxes and a brush gold to their Creast upon a heaulme a Torse silver An Arme Coupy party per pale or and gules holding in his hand proper a brickaxe gould mantelled gules doubled Argent ". To this is added a note in the same handwriting that " the brushe in base the two brickaxes in cheife and a flower de luce between them in the tricke though none mentioned in the blazon ".

A trick annexed to a full copy[2] of the grant shows the fleur-de-lis as argent, and this is confirmed in the trick and certificate of the arms and crest as recorded at the 1634 visitation of London.[3] In this copy the wreath is described as or and azure, and this has been preferred to the incomplete rendering of a " torse silver " given in the abstract referred to above.

These arms, which followed upon the incorporation of the Company in the year preceding the grant, display the double-headed bricklayer's axe as an obvious symbol of the craft. Since the guild was incorporated as the Company of Tylers and Bricklayers, it might be expected that the " brush " would be a tool of the tiler, but it does not appear, as such, to have any direct relevance to the trade. Except for the entry in the record of the patent in the College of Arms, the " brush " is generally described elsewhere as a bundle of laths, and this seems a

---

[1] Misc. Gts. 5/152.   [2] Vinc. 162/116.   [3] 2nd C.24/5.

Brick-axe   "Brush", based on Coll.
                          Arms 2nd C.24/5

probable explanation of the object; laths are indispensable in the tiling of roofs. In the trick in the College of Arms the "brush" is drawn so that its outline resembles that of the brick-axe. This may have been due to the artist's desire for symmetrical composition and it is possible that such drawing was the cause of its misdescription.

The fleur-de-lis as a symbol of the Blessed Virgin Mary may point to the Tilers' early association as a fraternity with vows to that saint.

THE WORSHIPFUL COMPANY OF UPHOLDERS

An upholder, or upholster, was originally one who dealt in soft furnishings which involved the use of stuffing to " uphold " them. The ordinances of the Company, which were endorsed by the mayor and aldermen in 1474, specify among the merchandise of the craft such items as feather-beds, pillows, mattresses, cushions, quilts, curtains and " sparvers ", or bed-canopies. It was the function of the Company to safeguard the quality of these goods which, as the ordinances say, the buyer " seeth without but knoweth not the stuff within ". Because of " corrupt stuff " used for filling by the unscrupulous, an Act of 1495 (11 Hen. VII c. 19) enlarged the Company's powers of inspection and control throughout the kingdom. It was a natural extension of the upholder's trade to include clothing, and he is called by Stow a " fripperer or upholder ". Mourning apparel appears also to have come within his ambit ; John Gay in his *Trivia* speaks of

> Th'upholder, rueful harbinger of death,
> Waits with impatience for the dying breath.

Thus he assumed also the role of undertaker, furnishing either house or funeral.

The upholder appears very early in the City's records, and the grant of arms testifies to the Company's importance in the fifteenth century, but it was not until 14th June 1626 that its corporate life was endorsed by royal charter.

THE ARMORIAL BEARINGS (Pl. 51)

Sable three spervers ermine garnished azure and gules, beneath the sperver in base a lamb couchant argent on a cushion or, above the lamb a cross formy fitchy gules.

Granted by William Hawkeslowe,
Clarenceux
11th December 1465

The original patent or arms has not survived and the above blazon is based on what purports to be a verbatim transcript of the grant in *The Sphere of Gentry*, 1661, by Sylvanus Morgan.[1] Hawkeslowe's blazon

[1] *lib.* 2, p. 94.

according to Morgan is: " I have avised, graunted and given . . . a field sable, three spervers ermin, a lamb silver, couchand upon a pillow of gold." In a marginal gloss Morgan adds : " In the original though it be not expressed in blazon, the tents are trimed with blew, and red : the lamb must have a cross forme fitche over the head gules." Such minor elaborations in the illumination are a not unusual feature of patents in the fifteenth century when blazons tended to a bare simplicity.

Morgan's reputation as a heraldic writer has suffered from his over-industrious and misguided determination to find a mystical symbolism

Arms

in coats of arms. Nevertheless there seems to be no reason to doubt the accuracy of this transcript, and his gloss on the painting suggests a careful observation. Belief in Morgan's reliability in this instance is supported by a manuscript[1] in the handwriting of Edward Hasted (1732–1812), wherein the writer gives the Upholders' blazon as : " Sable three spervers ermine a lamb silver couchant upon a pillow of gold." He adds that the grant was " approved and entered in the visitation of London 1634 by Henry St. George, Richmond", and continues " I copied this by the original patent and the sparvers must be with Blew and Red according to the form triced [i.e. tricked] underneath & the Lamb must have a Cross Potent Fitchee over it Gules ". The " form tricked underneath " is an incomplete trick, obviously only intended

[1] Brit. Mus. Add. MSS. 5533 fo. 113.

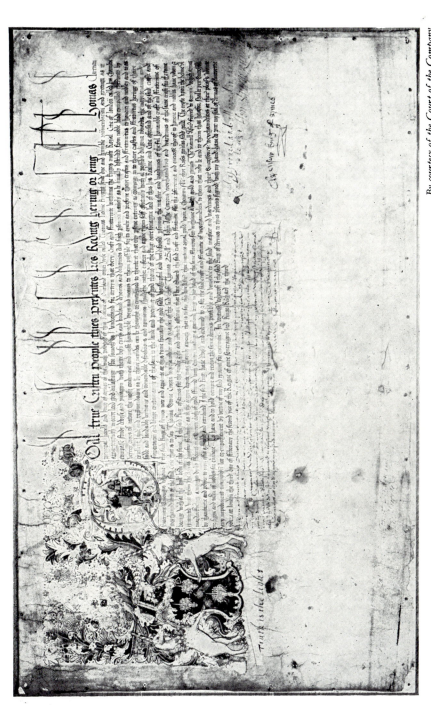

Truth is the Light +

By courtesy of the Court of the Company

R.250

Pl. 53

LETTERS PATENT GRANTING ARMS TO THE WORSHIPFUL COMPANY OF WAX CHANDLERS,
3RD FEBRUARY 1484–5

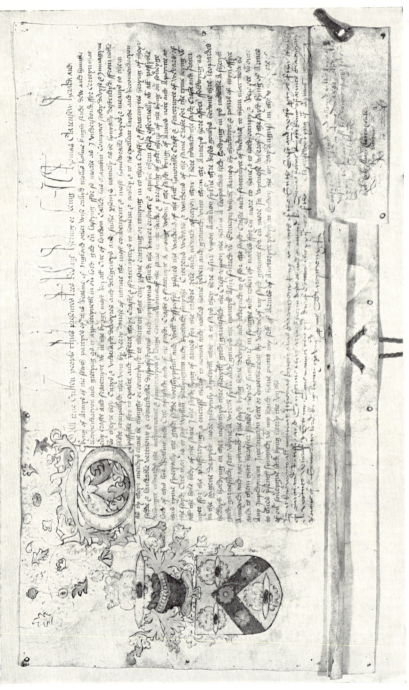

Pl. 54

LETTERS PATENT GRANTING ARMS TO THE WORSHIPFUL COMPANY OF WEAVERS,
4TH AUGUST 1490

By courtesy of the Court of the Company

S.251

to exemplify the writer's comments. This independent testimony conforms so exactly to Morgan's rendering as to carry conviction.

Yet another transcript of the patent exists.[1] Its source is not stated, but it is clearly not based on either Morgan's or Hasted's manuscript, since it gives the endorsement on the patent of arms which the other two omit. No comment is here given on the tinctures of the blazon, but the text agrees in all relevant particulars with both Morgan and Hasted.

Confirmation of Morgan's transcript from official sources is impossible since there is no text of Hawkeslowe's patent in the College of Arms. The only official record that exists there is a trick of the arms in the 1634 visitation[2] which, translated into blazon, gives : sable three spervers [no tincture shown] lined ermine the upper panels argent edged azure, in front of that in base upon a cushion or a lamb couchant argent, over its back a cross formy fitchy gules. This differs from Morgan's account in three particulars : the tinctures of the spervers; the relationship of the lamb to the sperver in base; and the position of the cross. The last two points are not of great significance. A crude perspective of the lamb in relation to the sperver might well cause different observers to give varying interpretations. Reason, however, suggests that the lamb on the pillow would be within, or beneath, the sperver, which is clearly meant for a canopy of royal dignity. There is a close similarity in this device to the old fifteenth century crest of the Merchant Taylors' Company which included a pavilion, *alias* sperver, " within the same our Blessed Lady St. Mary the Virgin . . . sitting upon a cushion azure." The position of the cross above the lamb is similarly not material, for the *Agnus Dei*, which is here intended, is variously depicted in art, and the symbolism is not impaired whether the cross be above the back of the lamb or over its head.

The tincture of the spervers is, however, of cardinal importance to an accurate blazon. The 1634 visitation should be authoritative on this point but is, in fact, unhelpful. Although tinctures are indicated in the trick for the lining and for incidental features of the spervers, no colour is given for their exteriors. It is, therefore, not possible to accept this trick as a guide, and, indeed, the appearance of haste in the execution of the drawing tends to discredit its general reliability.

[1] Crisp (F. A.), *Fragmenta Genealogica*, XIII (1905), p. 20.
[2] 2nd C.24/381.

s

Nevertheless the 1634 visitation is an official record to which great importance must necessarily be attached, and, although there are good grounds for accepting Morgan's version of the arms, the conflict therein with an official document is irreconcilable. In these circumstances only a ruling by the Kings of Arms can eliminate doubt as to the correct arms of the Company.

A crest is found attributed to the Upholders at an early date. This occurs in a manuscript collection compiled about 1530 by Thomas Wall, Windsor Herald and subsequently Garter King of Arms. Wall gives therein : " Upholdesters of London to their crest a pavylyon asur lynyd ermyns the pole and pomels gold in a wreth blue [and] or ma[ntled] blue [and] argent." [1] The fact that the pavilion, or sperver, is here blazoned azure can throw no light on the tinctures of the spervers in the arms since a sable field with azure charges would be an impossible combination. Wall's note appears to be the only reference to a crest for the Company and, in spite of Wall's official status, it has no authority.

Hawkeslowe's incorporation of the *Agnus Dei* in the arms suggests a possible origin of the Company as a fraternity dedicated to St. John the Baptist, whose symbol of the lamb and cross, a frequent occurrence in Christian art, derives as an emblem from John i. 29, 36 : " Behold the Lamb of God . . ." In placing the lamb beneath a sperver, the designer of the arms not only gave to this religious symbol the dignity of a canopy as is common in representations of holy or royal personages, but contrived at the same time to employ an article in which the upholder was wont to deal; the cushion has a similar reference to the trade. Evidence that spervers were part of the stock-in-trade of the upholder is provided by the Company's ordinances of 1474[2] referred to above.

The Company uses no motto.

[1] Item 295 in the original MS. in the possession of the Society of Antiquaries. Published in *The Ancestor*, vol. 11, p. 178 ff., and vol. 12, p. 63 ff.

[2] See *Corporation of London. Calendar of letter book, L* ; ed. R. R. Sharpe (1912), p. 121.

THE WORSHIPFUL COMPANY OF VINTNERS

THE Vintners Company had its origins in the efforts of the native vintners to control the wine trade carried on in London by the Gascony wine merchants. These merchants had, at the beginning of the fourteenth century, acquired special privileges contrary to the interests of the London merchants. To strengthen their position, the vintners of London obtained royal letters patent on 15th July 1364 which forbade anyone to trade in wine unless free of their mistery. Powers under this charter included the election of four persons to see that wine sold in taverns was reasonably priced and to correct and amend all defaults among tavern keepers. The mistery became a perpetual corporation by a charter of 23rd August 1437 under the name of the Master and Wardens of the commonalty and mistery of Vintners.

Few powers are now exercised by the Company, but it still employs " tackle porters " who are available to those engaged in the wine trade in London ; and free vintners, that is those who are free of the Company by patrimony or by apprenticeship, enjoy the right of selling wines in certain towns without a justice's licence or excise licence.

By ancient privilege, the Vintners' Company shares with the Dyers' Company permission from the sovereign to own a game of swans on the Thames. Each year swan-uppers perform the ceremony of rounding up cygnets for the purpose of marking their bills with the marks of ownership.

THE ARMORIAL BEARINGS (Pl. 52)

Sable a chevron between three wine tuns argent.

> Granted by Roger Legh,
> Clarenceux
> 17th September 1447

Crest : On a wreath argent and sable a caravel or laden with tuns proper the sails gules the mainsail charged with a cartwheel or and from the masthead a pennon argent.

Mantling : Sable doubled argent.

Supporters : On either side a swan the dexter a cob the sinister a pen both nicked in the beak with the mark of the Company all proper about the neck of each a riband azure pendant therefrom a bunch of grapes also proper.

Granted by Sir George Rothe Bellew,
Garter
Sir John Dunamace Heaton-Armstrong,
Clarenceux
20th June 1957

Motto :   *Vinum exhilarat animum.*

The original patent of the 1447 grant has not survived and the authority of the arms rests upon a number of tricks which appear in

Crest

the records of the College of Arms.   Although these tricks agree as to the form of the arms, there are discrepancies of dating.   Two entries give the regnal year as 6 Henry VI (1427/8),[1] while a third[2] records that the arms were granted " by Clarenceux King of Arms of the South . . . 17th Sept. 1447 the 20 Hen. 6 [i.e. 1441/2]."   Official opinion has determined the date as 17th September 1447.

The arms were confirmed at the 1590 and 1634 visitations of London.

Before 1957 the Company had no supporters or crest, but a coloured trick in the College of Arms[3] sketches an incomplete outline of a crest and sinister supporter showing the former as a hand grasping a vine-branch bearing grapes, with what appears to be a fox for supporter. These are obviously tentative additions to the arms and are not authori-

[1] Coll. Arms G.10/121 ; and 1st H.7/61.   [2] Coll. Arms. 2nd C.24/221.
[3] Coll. Arms. G.10/121.

Pl. 55

WATERMEN AND LIGHTERMEN, p. 256
WAX CHANDLERS, p. 258

tative. The fox and grapes suggest an allusion either to the Song of Solomon (" Take us the foxes, the little foxes that spoil the vines "),[1] or perhaps to Aesop's fable of the fox and the grapes.

The caravel in the authorized crest represents a type of boat which was used to carry wine tuns and its mainsail reproduces the arms—gules a cartwheel or—attributed to St. Martin of Tours in a late fifteenth-century English roll of arms in the British Museum.[2] St. Martin is the patron saint of the Company and his pre-Reformation association with the Vintners is clear from the fifteenth-century common seal of the Company which depicts St. Martin on horseback sharing his cloak with a beggar. The adoption of this saint as patron is no doubt explained by the origin of many of the medieval guilds as religious fraternities centred around a local church for the purpose of worship. The church of St. Martin Vintry, which was burnt in the fire of 1666, was in the area where the medieval wine merchants conducted their trade, and it was this activity which gave to the ward and district its name of Vintry.

The male and female swan supporters refer, of course, to the ancient right of the Vinters' Company to maintain a game of swans on the Thames.

---

[1] Song of Solomon ii. 15.   [2] Harl. MS. 6163/20.

THE WORSHIPFUL COMPANY OF WATERMEN
AND LIGHTERMEN

UNTIL the middle of the eighteenth century, London had no bridge other than London Bridge, its streets were ill-conditioned and often unsafe. The boat was therefore not only essential for crossing the river but also a convenient and pleasant means of travel from place to place. Boatmen plied for hire in great numbers, the lightermen supplying a cargo service and the watermen providing passenger transport. Although the City authorities made attempts from time to time to protect citizens from extortionate charges and incompetent boatmen, no effective organization of the watermen existed until an Act of 1555 introduced a form of licensing of able boatmen who might ply between Gravesend and Windsor, and settled the rates of fares. The mayor and aldermen were required to appoint each year eight watermen to ensure that the provisions of the Act were enforced. Other legislation followed, and in 1700 an Act amalgamated the lightermen with the watermen. In 1827 the Company was incorporated as the Master, Wardens and Commonalty of Watermen and Lightermen of the river Thames. This act was superseded by the Watermen's and Lightermen's Act of 1859, which reduced the western limit of the Company's licensing control to Teddington lock. In 1908, with the constitution of the Port of London Authority, the Company's licensing powers were transferred to that body. The Company retains its powers of binding apprentices to learn the trade, and the admission of freemen.

THE ARMORIAL BEARINGS (Pl. 55)

Argent, in base barry wavy of six azure and argent a boat proper, on a chief azure two oars in saltire or between two cushions argent fretted gules trimmed argent tasselled or.

Crest : On a wreath argent and gules a dexter arm embowed vested argent holding in the hand proper an oar erect or.

Mantling : Gules doubled argent.

Supporters : On either side a dolphin haurient argent finned, eyed and tusked or.

Motto : At commaundement of owre superiors.

Granted by Robert Cooke,
Clarenceux
18th September 1585

The original patent has not survived nor does any record of the blazon exist in the College of Arms. A trick of the arms is, however, given in the record of the visitation of 1634,[1] and an earlier and more complete one occurs among the collections of the College of Arms.[2] The latter appears to have been copied from the original patent and may be considered the more reliable. It has therefore been adopted as the basis of the blazon given above.

Minor differences of tincture only are found in these two tricks, the chief of which is that in the 1634 visitation the boat is shown on waves of the sea proper. But as barry wavy azure and argent is no more than a conventionalized rendering of the sea, this is without great significance. Moreover the latter convention is better design than a naturalistic sea which is more suitable for pictorial composition than for heraldic art.

[1] Coll. Arms 2nd C.24/223.   [2] Vincent 154/41b.

THE WORSHIPFUL COMPANY OF WAX CHANDLERS

ORDINANCES of 1358 for the government of the craft of wax chandlers stipulate that all who make " cierges " (i.e. wax tapers), torches,
" priketz " (candles for placing on a spike of metal), great candles and
all other things pertaining to the trade, should do so of good wax un-
mixed with fat or other adulterants. Prickets, torches and tapers for
use at " mortuaries " are specified therein. Ordinances of 1371 also
refer to the use of the wax chandler's wares for funerals and at Candle-
mas, when tapers were hallowed and borne by women in remembrance
of the purification of the Virgin Mary. The " mortuary " candles were
those used at rites for the dead, and the word no doubt explains the term
" morter " which is used for the resplendent candlesticks depicted in the
Company's arms. Apart from the use of wax candles in great house-
holds and in other secular buildings, the wax chandler's wares were sold
mainly for religious ceremonies, whereas the tallow chandler, who be-
longed to a distinct company, produced cheap candles from animal fat
for domestic and street lighting. The wax chandler's raw material was
beeswax which was purified and bleached. This was often supplied by
the customer for making into candles, and it appears to have been in
the Middle Ages a negotiable commodity, numerous references being
found to the payment of fines in wax. Innumerable bequests in medieval
wills for the provision of candles or tapers at ritual observances are an
indication of the demand for the wax chandler's wares. To meet the
demand, wax was imported as well as produced at home, entries occurring in the City records of the fourteenth and fifteenth centuries which
relate to Spanish, Portuguese, Moorish and Polish waxes.

The mistery of wax chandlers was first incorporated as a perpetual
community on 16th February 1483/4, and this was followed by a number
of further charters giving the Company control of the trade in the City
and within ten miles thereof.

Although the trade had been a flourishing one, the general tendency
towards simplification of religious ceremony after the Reformation,
and the introduction of other forms of lighting, diminished it. The
Company now uses none of its chartered powers over the trade.

THE ARMORIAL BEARINGS (Pl. 55)

Azure on a chevron argent between three morters royal or, three roses gules seeded or.

Creſt : On a wreath or and gules a maiden veſted in a surcoat of cloth of gold furred with ermine, kneeling amongſt divers flowers proper and making thereof a garland.

Mantling : Azure doubled ermine.

Granted[1] by Sir Thomas Holme,
Clarenceux
3rd February 1484/5

Supporters : On either side a unicorn argent gorged with a garland of various flowers proper, the horn wreathed or and gules.

Granted by Thomas Benolt,
Clarenceux
11th Oĉober 1530

Motto : Truth is the light.

On 12th Oĉober 1536 Thomas Hawley, Clarenceux, issued a new patent of arms[2] to the Wax Chandlers which modified the arms given above. But at the 1634 visitation of London, only the 1485 patent, with its 1530 confirmation and grant of supporters by Thomas Benolt, was produced to eſtablish the Company's right to bear arms. Evidence of this appears on the 1485 patent which bears an inscription that the arms were viewed, approved and allowed by Henry St. George, Richmond Herald at the visitation of 1634 ; no mention is made of Hawley's patent of 1536, either here or in the records of the visitation in the College of Arms.[3] The effeĉ of this suppression of the later patent is to resuscitate the earlier version of the arms and make it the authoritative coat. Since Hawley's grant was made only six years after Benolt's confirmation of the 1485 patent, it can well be assumed that the suppression of Hawley's patent was a conscious aĉ of the Company, probably with the concurrence of the King of Arms. Hawley's grant had, in fact, made only minor changes and had been sought by the Company solely to elucidate the earlier grant. His role in this respeĉ is made clear by the wording of the patent which says that the wardens of the

---

[1] Original in Guildhall Library, MS. 9521. A coloured facsimile is also in Guildhall Library, large prints L.37.

[2] Original in Guildhall Library, MS. 9522. A transcript appears in *Soc. Ant. Proc.*, 2nd ser., I, p. 206.

[3] 2nd C.24/378. The summons to attend the 1634 visitation is among the Wax Chandlers archives : Guildhall Library, MS. 9523.

Company brought before him a grant of arms by Sir Thomas Holme, Clarenceux, dated 3rd February 1484/5, saying that therein were " dyverce wordis so obscure and darkely wrettyn deffuse to be understande and also ther armes ther beśts with ther creśt not planly nor ryght sett forthe in pyċtur "; they therefore desired Clarenceux " to over se peruse and corek the sayd wordys and the armes ".

The blazon which Hawley was desired to correct reads as follows :

asur thre morteres royal gold upon a cheveron silver thre Roses goules seded golde. The creśte upon the helme a mayden kneling a monges dyvers Floures in a Surcote cloth of gold Furred with ermyn making a garlond being in hir hand of the same Floures sett withinne a wreth gold and goules. The mantell Asur furred with ermyn.

A confirmation of this coat, dated 11th Oċtober 1530, is appended to the patent by Thomas Benolt, Clarenceux, who adds : " Also I have devyssed and grauntyd to the same worshipfull company the unycornes to uphold theyre armes as they do apyere in the sayd margyn." These supporters, for which no blazon is given, have been added to the 1485 exemplification, being partly painted over the mantling ; they are argent, each gorged with a garland of various flowers proper, the horn wreathed or and gules. Beneath the painting of the arms has been written the Company's motto, probably contemporary with the 1634 visitation.

These arms were revised by Hawley in the following terms :

Asure on a cheveron argent thre Rosses gullys seded betwen thre morterres Royall golde apon the helme on a wrethe argent and gullys a Mayden in her here knelynge in a Rossyare, the rossis gulles, having on here a syrcott of clothe of golde furred wythe armens makyng a garlande of dyverse flowres, mantellyd gulles dowbled argent, supportynge the armes tow unicornes gulles droped argent unglet horned and pisselled [or].[1] About ther neckes at thend of a flatt cheyne thre Rynges golde.

Hawley's revision can hardly be said to have simplified Holme's original blazon, and it may be that his failure to improve it in any significant way decided the Company to reśt their claim to arms at the 1634 visitation upon the fifteenth century patent which at leaśt had the merit of greater antiquity.

The Wax Chandlers are not alone in having been granted roses upon a chevron by Sir Thomas Holme. The Weavers and the Grey Tawyers,

---

[1] This tinċture is supplied from the painting of the arms in the margin of the patent.

which later was merged with the Skinners, both received from him
these charges, and it is a legitimate speculation whether a like device
in the apparently unauthorized arms of the Brasiers' Company may not
indicate a lost patent by Holme. Holme bore a chaplet of roses in his
own arms and, being of Lancashire origin, had additional cause for a
predilection for the rose.

The morters on the shield represent a form of candlestick probably
used at funeral obsequies or during rites in remembrance of the dead.

After the arms depicted in the margin of Hawley's grant, A.D. 1536

The epithet " royal " in this context would seem to imply a morter of
more than common splendour; a similar use survives today in the
familiar phrase " battle royal ".

That the design of Holme's crest may involve some symbolism of
purity is suggested by its later development by Hawley. Holme's
blazon describes the maiden as kneeling among divers flowers; Hawley
says kneeling in a " rossyare ". The word " rossyare " is undoubtedly
a phonetic rendering of the French *rosière*, and there may here be a

reference to the custom of *la couronnement de la rosière*, an event of great antiquity in some French villages ; *la rosière* being the maiden to whom is awarded a wreath of roses for virtuous conduct.

The maiden crest probably induced Benolt to choose the unicorns for supporters. Legend asserts that this fabulous beast could only be trapped by setting a virtuous maiden in its haunts, whereupon it would approach her, lay its head in her lap and sleep. It may not be too fanciful to see in Benolt's colouring of the beast's horn a different colour from the rest of the animal, his recognition of its resemblance to the candles made by the wax chandler ; heraldry's language is frequently that of the pun and obscure association. It is also tentatively suggested that, for the same reason, the penis of the unicorn was later similarly emphasized by Hawley—" pisseled or "—a crude example of that allusiveness which plays so prominent a part in heraldry. An alternative explanation of Hawley's deliberate elaboration of the supporters may be that he chose to illustrate the phallic background of the unicorn legend in the most obvious way.

Pl. 56

S.262

WEAVERS, p. 263
WHEELWRIGHTS, p. 266

THE WORSHIPFUL COMPANY OF WEAVERS

WEAVERS in London were concerned with the weaving of linen and woollen cloth ; and later of silks, an art taught by the weavers of the Low Countries whose influx into England during the fourteenth century was encouraged by Edward III. Members of the guild were primarily producers of cloth, its sale being the prerogative of such misteries a the mercers and the drapers.

The Company of Weavers has the distinction of possessing the longest pedigree substantiated by records of all the City guilds and it is a tribute to its members' piety that the Weavers' first charter of Henry II (*c.* 1155) is still preserved among the Company's archives. This charter confirms to the guild all the liberties and customs granted to it in the reign of Henry I and, by forbidding all except members from engaging in the craft, includes the first direct reference to that monopolistic character which was an essential feature of the guilds. Exclusive control of their trade was broken by the formation of fraternities of Flemish and Brabant immigrant weavers in the fourteenth century. Although differences were formally composed by an agreement of 1497, friction continued and the history of the Company is chequered with attempts to maintain its monopoly against alien encroachment, as well as against the development of specialist crafts such as the burellers and the linen weavers. Further disturbance to the autonomy of the Company was caused by refugee Huguenot weavers who settled mainly in the Spitalfields area of London in the sixteenth century. These immigrants eventually proved too numerous for the Company to control and it was their invasion of the trade which contributed to the gradual cessation of the Company's enforcement of its powers during the eighteenth and early nineteenth centuries. The Company's resources are, however, still disposed for the advancement of the industry and craft of weaving.

THE ARMORIAL BEARINGS (Pl. 56)

Azure on a chevron argent between three leopards' heads each holding in the mouth a shuttle or, three roses gules.

Crest : On a wreath argent and gules a leopard's head crowned holding in the mouth a shuttle or.

Mantling : Azure doubled ermine.

Granted[1] by Thomas Holme,
Clarenceux
4th August 1490

Supporters : On either side a wyvern ermine, langued and membered gules, on the wing displayed garnished or a rose gules.

Motto : Weave truth with trust.

Granted[2] by Sir William Segar,
Garter
10th August 1616

Thomas Holme's original blazon reads as follows:

I . . . have yeven and granted . . . asure uppon a cheveron sylvere thre roses goulys betwne thre leopardes heddys holdyng in ther mowthys thre shetylles gold garneshed the crest uppon the helme a leopardes hed holdyng in ys mowthe a shetyll gold garneshed sett withyne a wreth sylver and goulys the mantyll asure furred with ermeyn which armys by thactoryte and poure of myn offyce . . . I, the said kyng have devysed and ordeyned . . .

Confirmations of these arms in 1530 and 1590, by Thomas Benolt, Clarenceux, and Robert Cooke, Clarenceux, respectively, have been added to the patent.

Although not so blazoned in the grant the leopard's head of the crest is shown with a gold crown in the painting of the arms which appears in the margin of the original patent.

The supporters are blazoned in Segar's grant in the following terms:

Two Wyvers Ermyn on their Winges displayed Garnished Gold two Roses gules Langued and membered of the same.

" Wyver " is an older variant of " wyvern " which is a species of heraldic dragon endowed with two legs only. The form " wyvers " also occurs in two dockets of Segar's confirmation in the College of Arms.[3] These fabulous beasts have a prominent place in bestiaries which attribute to them numerous mythical qualities, but none is applicable to their choice as supporters of the Weavers' Company. Their use seems to have been determined solely by the phonetic resemblance

---

[1, 2] Original patents deposited in the Guildhall Library, MSS. 4643 and 4644. A complete transcript, with photographic reproduction, of the 1490 grant appears in Consitt (F.), *The London Weavers' Company,* vol. 1 (1933), p. 216. *Note :* vol. 2 of Consitt's work has not appeared.

[3] Misc. Gts. II/16 and VI/87.

Crest, leopard's head, crowned, holding in the mouth a shuttle

Wyvern supporter after the grant of A.D. 1616 (Guild. Lib. MS. 4644)

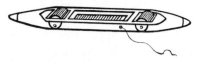

Shuttle

of the word "wyvers" to the name of the Company; the original pronunciation of this word is, incidentally, disclosed.

Segar's original patent is very worn and much of the writing is now illegible without photographic aids. The text is, however, given at length in the two dockets mentioned above.

THE WORSHIPFUL COMPANY OF WHEELWRIGHTS

THE Wheelwrights' Company is one of the younger City guilds. The first indication of aspiring unity is seen in a petition of 1631, which the wheelwrights in conjunction with the coach-makers of the City addressed

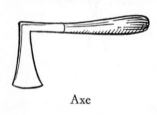

Axe

to the Court of Aldermen. This document drew attention to the increasing dangers of faulty workmanship, and set out the advantages to the trade of incorporation by royal charter, with its powers to control the craft. Subsequent independent action by the wheelwrights achieved for them a charter on 3rd February 1669/70, and secured control of all wheelwrights within the City and five miles compass. A system applicable to medieval economy was not, however, suitable at so late a date, and the powers granted appear never to have been fully effective.

THE ARMORIAL BEARINGS (Pl. 56)

Gules a chevron between three wheels or, on a chief argent an axe fessewise proper the handle to the sinister.

Crest: On a wreath of the colours a dexter arm embowed, vested gules cuffed argent, holding in the hand proper a mallet or.

Mantling: Gules doubled argent.

Supporters: On either side a horse rampant argent.

Motto: God grant unity.

These arms are without authority and the earliest example seen occurs in 1739.[1]

[1] Maitland (W.), *History of London* (1739), p. 614.

THE WORSHIPFUL COMPANY OF WOOLMEN

THE continuator of Stow's *Survey of London* was compelled to observe in 1633 : " The Company of Wooll-packers, I know not what to say of them." Of the part played in the trading life of London by the Woolmen and of their organization, the present writer can only echo such an honeſt admission of ignorance. Woolmen in the Middle Ages were among the wealthieſt of English merchants and the source of their riches is witnessed by the frequency of the woolpack symbol which occurs in a number of memorial brasses throughout the country. Nevertheless the hiſtory of this company is the moſt obscure of all the London guilds. No serious attempt has been made to trace its origin, and little appears to be readily available in the City's records. It is possible that its obscurity is due to its having been overshadowed by the trading Company of Merchant Staplers which controlled the export of wool during the whole of the formative period of guild life.

A miſtery of woolmongers exiſted in the fourteenth century, for in 1328 overseers were eleƈted to rule the craft. No doubt it was of much earlier origin in view of the importance of wool in the medieval economy. Ordinances agreed by the mayor and aldermen in 1488 for the better rule of the " craft of woolmen and woolpackers " are not illuminating, apart from their requiring the appointment of a maſter and two wardens and the usual provision for the control of apprentices. Stow, cited above, attributes to his woolpackers the present arms of the Company of Woolmen, and the wording of the 1488 ordinances suggeſts that these were one miſtery. It is probable that they were joined in one guild but their aƈtivities were separate. A woolman appears to have been a merchant engaged in the role of middleman between the grower and the exporter, or Merchant Stapler, and there seems little reason to doubt that woolmonger was an alternative name for him. The woolpacker was concerned with packing wool in sacks for transport and was usually employed by woolmen rather than growers.

Another employee of the woolman was the woolwinder who made up wool into bundles for packing. An Aƈt of 1532 " for the true winding of wools " lays down that no person may wind any fleece insufficiently washed and no foreign matter should be permitted to remain therein.

Crest

Among the duties of the Company of Woolmen was said to have been the licensing of woolwinders, and this, according to a report of the Company in 1884, was carried out until 1779. The Company has no charter that is known, and its former functions of trade control are no longer exercised.

THE ARMORIAL BEARINGS (Pl. 51)

Gules a woolpack argent.

Crest : On a wreath of the colours in front of two distaffs in saltire gules flaxed or the wheel of a spinning wheel or.

Mantling : Gules doubled argent.

Motto : Lana spes nostra.

Granted[1] by Sir George Rothe Bellew,
Garter
Archibald George Blomefield Russell,
Clarenceux
Sir Gerald Woods Wollaston,
Norroy and Ulster
19th November 1954

Although these arms were authorized only in recent times, they were in use by the Company, without crest, at least as early as 1575.[2] Their symbolism is so evident that it requires no comment.

The crest was first introduced with the 1954 grant.

[1] Original patent in the possession of the Company.
[2] Guild. Lib. MS. 2463.

GLOSSARY OF HERALDIC TERMS IN THE TEXT

This glossary is not intended to give comprehensive definitions of heraldic terms, but only to explain those that occur in this work in relation to their context.

Addorsed—back to back; also endorsed
Annulet—a ring
Appaumé—a hand with the palm displayed
Argent—silver; often represented by white
Armed—in relation to beasts and birds refers to teeth and claws; in man it means clad in armour
Attired—refers to the antlers of deer
Azure—blue

Barry wavy—composed of undulating bands of specified colours horizontally disposed
Base—lower part of the shield
Bend—a band enclosed by two parallel lines crossing the shield diagonally from the dexter chief to the sinister base
Besantee—powdered with besants, i.e. gold roundels
Blazon—verbal description of heraldic insignia
Bordure—a border surrounding the shield

Carnation (carnat)—flesh-coloured
Celestiaulx (celestials)—representations of the sun emerging from a cloud; sunbursts
Chevron—inverted V-shaped band
Chief—the upper third of the shield demarcated by a horizontal line. In chief: refers to the part of the shield occupied by a chief but not so demarcated
Clayed (cleyed, clewed, clowed)—refers to the hoofs or claws
Colomb (coulomb)—a dove
Couchant—of a beast recumbent on its legs with its head up
Counterchanged—an interchange of colour and metal between charge and field
Couped—cut short by a straight line
Coward—of a beast with tail between its legs
Crined—refers to the hair of the head
Cubit arm—the forearm couped below the elbow

Debruised—refers to a charge overlaid by another
Dexter—the right side of the shield or coat of arms from the viewpoint of the person wearing it, i.e. the left side of the observer

269

Displayed—with wings expanded or spread out

Doubled—refers to the lining of the mantling

Embowed—bent or bowed

Endorsed—*see* Addorsed

Enfiled—encircled or collared

Engrailed—an edge composed of a series of concave indentations; the opposite to invected, q.v.

Environed—wreathed or entwined

Erased—torn off and leaving a jagged edge, cp. couped

Erect—upright, perpendicular

Ermine—conventional representations of ermine fur by black spots on a white ground

Fesse—broad horizontal band across the middle of the shield.

> In fesse: refers to charges horizontally placed across the shield
> Per fesse: division of the shield by a central horizontal line
> Fessewise: synonymous with per fesse; or refers to the horizontal position of a single charge (e.g. a sword) upon the shield

Fimbriated—said of a charge having a narrow border of a different tincture

Fitchy—describes the lower limb of a cross when ending in a tapering point

Flanche—the flank of a shield cut off by a convex line

Flashed—flecked

Fleam—a razor-like surgical instrument; a lancet

Flory counter-flory—decorated with fleurs-de-lis alternately displaying heads and tails

Formy—refers to the ends of a cross splayed and flattened as in the Maltese cross

Fretty—narrow interlaced bands forming a pattern of lozenges

Garb—a sheaf of corn

Garnet—garnished

Garnished—minor decoration of a charge with another tincture

Gorged—encircled about the neck

Griffin—heraldic beast with head, forepart and wings of an eagle and the hind-quarters and tail of a lion; the head has prominent ears

Guardant—with the head full-face towards the observer

Gules—red

Gutté de sang—spotted with drops of blood

Gyronny—having the field divided into triangular pieces formed by straight lines radiating from the middle point

Haurient—refers to fish in a vertical position, head upwards as though breathing

Housed—refers to the saddle-cloth and trappings of a horse

Hurt—an azure roundel

Impaled—two coats of arms displayed side by side on one shield

Incensed—with fire issuing from mouth and ears

Invected—an edge composed of a series of convex segments of a circle ; the opposite to engrailed, q.v.

Issuant—issuing out of

Jacent—lying down

Langued—tongued

Leamed—radiated ; shining with rays of light

Lozenge—a diamond-shaped figure

Mantling—conventional representation of a small mantle depending from the junction of the crest wreath and the helm

Membered—refers to the legs and beak of a bird

Mullet (Molet)—star-shaped figure ; conventional representation of a spur rowel.

Mural crown—a crown composed of an embattled wall

Naiant—swimming

Nimbus—a halo

Nowed—knotted

Opinicus—heraldic beast having head, neck and wings of a griffin and the body of a lion but with a bear's tail

Or—gold

Ounce—heraldic beast of the cat tribe

Pale—a broad vertical band on the centre of the shield.
> Per pale (or palewise) : division of the shield by a central vertical line
> In pale : similar charges placed one above the other

Paly—describes a shield with a number of pales upon it

Party—indicates the division of the shield by various lines as specified, e.g. party per fesse

Passant—walking

Pellet—black roundel

Pellety—powdered with black roundels

Phoenix—fabulous bird with the capacity of consuming itself in fire and rising again from its ashes

Porfled—minor decoration of a charge with an additional colour ; garnished

Proper—natural colour

Purfled—see Porfled

Purpure—purple

Quarterly—division into four parts by a vertical and horizontal line

Radiant, radiated—with rays of light emanating

Rampant—of a lion erect with three paws raised, and tail erect, in an attitude of attack

Regardant—formerly synonymous with guardant, but now meaning looking to the rear

Roundel—circular disc

Royne—an implement of the Cooper's craft

Sable—black

St. Julian's cross—a cross in the form of a saltire with a short crosspiece near the end of each arm

Salient—of an animal about to spring, two paws raised and two on the ground

Saltire—a diagonal cross

      In saltire : of two charges crossed in the form of a saltire

Semee—strewn or powdered with

Sinister—the left side of the shield or coat of arms from the point of view of the person wearing it, i.e. the right side to the observer

Slipped—with stalk attached

Statant—of a beast standing with all four paws on the ground

Supplanting—overcoming

Timbre—the crest

Torse—crest wreath

Tressure—narrow band running parallel with the edge of the shield

Undy (Onde, Ondy)—wavy lines across the shield ; conventional representation of the waves of the sea

Unguled—refers to the hoofs of an animal

Vert—green

Volant—flying

Vulning—wounding

Wreath—twisted wreath of colours around the helm

Wyvern—heraldic dragon with only two legs

INDEX OF MOTTOES

A Deo et caelo symphonia (former motto of the Musicians' Company) : Harmony from God and from Heaven.

Al worship be to God only (Fishmongers).

Amicitiam trahit amor (Gold and Silver Wyre Drawers) : Love draws friendship.

Amor et obedientia (former motto of the Painter Stainers) : Love and obedience.

Amor queat obedientiam (Painter Stainers). This obscure motto is discussed in the chapter on the Company.

Amore sitis uniti (Tin Plate Workers) : Be ye united in love.

Arbor vitae Christus, fructus per fidem gustamus (former motto of the Fruiterers) : Christ is the tree of life, the fruit thereof we eat through faith.

Arts and trade united (Fanmakers).

As God will so be it (former motto of the Blacksmiths).

Assher dure (Ironmongers) : *Acier dur*, i.e. hard steel.

At commaundement of owre superiors (Watermen).

Blessing to the aged (Spectacle Makers).

By faith I obteigne (Turners).

By hammer and hand all arts do stand (Blacksmiths).

Cave Deus videt (former motto of the Fruiterers) : Beware for God sees all.

Come ye blessed, when I was harborless ye lodged me (former motto of the Innholders).

Concordia parvae res crescunt (Merchant Taylors) : With harmony small things become great.

Corde recto elati omnes (Makers of Playing Cards) : All are exalted by a good heart.

Corio et arte (Cordwainers) : With leather and skill.

Crecy, Poiters, Agincourt (Bowyers).

Da gloriam Deo (Dyers) : Give glory to God.

De praescientia Dei (Barbers) : From the foresight of God.

Decus et tutamen (Feltmakers) : Ornament and protection.

Delight in God and He shall give thee thy desire (former motto of the Tallow Chandlers).

Deus dat incrementum (Fruiterers) : God giveth increase.

Discordia frangimur (Glass-sellers) : By discord are we broken.

Drop as rain, distil as dew (Distillers).

Ecce agnus Dei qui tollit peccata mundi (Tallow Chandlers) : Behold the lamb of God that taketh away the sins of the world.

273

Gaude Maria Virgo (former motto of the Coopers): Rejoice, O Blessed Mary.
Give thanks to God (Girdlers).
Give us our daily bread (Farmers).
God can raise to Abraham children of stones (Paviors).
God grant grace (Grocers).
God grant unity (Wheelwrights).
God grant us to use justice with mercy (former motto of the Joiners).
God is our guide (Masons).
God is our strength (Ironmongers).
God the only founder (Founders).

Harmony (former motto of the Musicians).
Hinc spes affulget (Innholders): Hope shines from here.
Hold fast, sit sure (Saddlers).
Honor Deo (Mercers): Honour to God.
Honor God (Carpenters).

In Christo fratres (Skinners): Brothers in Christ.
In God is all my trust (Pewterers).
In God is all our hope (Plumbers).
In God is all our trust (Brewers).
In God is all our trust, Let us never be confounded (Tylers and Bricklayers).
In the Lord is all our trust (former motto of the Masons).
In the sweat of thy brows shalt thow eate thy bread (Gardeners).

Join loyalty and liberty (Joiners).
Join truth with trust (former motto of the Joiners).
Justicia et pax (Plumbers): Justice and peace.
Justitia virtutum regina (Goldsmiths): Justice is the queen of virtues.

Lana spes nostra (Woolmen): Wool is our hope.
Let brotherly love continue (Plaisterers).
Let us love one another (Basketmakers).
Lex libertatis origo (Solicitors): Law is the foundation of liberty.
Littera scripta manet (Scriveners): The written word abides.
Love as brethren (Coopers).
Loyalty and service (Master Mariners).
Lucem Tuam da nobis Deus (Glaziers); O Lord grant us thy Light.

Make all sure (Armourers and Brasiers).
My trust is in God alone (Clothworkers).

Omnia desuper (Broderers): All things come from above.
Omnia subiecisti sub pedibus, oves et boves (Butchers); Thou has put all things beneath
his feet, all sheep and oxen.

Opiferque per orbem dicor (Apothecaries) : I am called throughout the world the bringer of aid.

Our trust is in God (Saddlers).

Pour parvenir a bonne foy (Cutlers) : To attain good faith.

Praise God for all (Bakers).

Quae arguuntur a lumine manifestantur (former motto of the Tallow Chandlers) : What things are clear are made manifest by light.

Recipiunt foeminae sustentacula nobis (Pattenmakers) : Women receive support from us.

Remember your oath (Poulters).

Sal sapit omnia (Salters) : Salt savours all.

Scribite scientes (Scriveners) : Write, ye learned men.

Scite, cito, certe (Carmen) : Skilfully, quickly and surely.

Serve and obey (Haberdashers).

Soli Deo honor et gloria (Leathersellers, and a former motto of the Goldsmiths) : Honour and glory to God alone.

Speed, strength and truth united (Framework Knitters).

Spes nostra Deus (Curriers) : God is our hope.

Surgit post nubila Phoebus (Coachmakers) : After clouds comes the sunshine.

Tempus rerum imperator (Clockmakers) : Time is the ruler of all things.

They sewed fig-leaves together and made themselves aprons (Needlemakers).

To God only be all glory (Skinners).

True and sure (Fletchers).

True hearts and warm hands (Glovers).

Truth is the light (Wax Chandlers).

Unitas societatis stabilitas (Parish Clerks) : The stability of a society rests upon unity.

Unto God only be honor and glory (Drapers).

Verbum Domini manet in aeternum (Stationers) : The word of God endureth for ever.

Vi et virtute (Farriers) : By strength and courage.

Vinum exhilarat animum (Vintners) : Wine maketh glad the heart.

Vulnerati non victi (Cooks) : Wounded but not conquered.

We are one (Armourers and Brasiers).

Weave truth with trust (Weavers).

Within the ark safe for ever (Shipwrights).

INDEX

References to illustrations are given in italic type.

Printed in Great Britain by Butler & Tanner Ltd., Frome and London
Code Number 524.259